AVID
READER
PRESS

ALSO BY JOE McGINNISS JR.

Carousel Court

The Delivery Man

DAMAGED PEOPLE

A MEMOIR OF FATHERS AND SONS

JOE McGINNISS JR.

AVID READER PRESS

NEW YORK AMSTERDAM/ANTWERP LONDON TORONTO SYDNEY/MELBOURNE NEW DELHI

AVID READER PRESS
An Imprint of Simon & Schuster, LLC
1230 Avenue of the Americas
New York, NY 10020

For more than 100 years, Simon & Schuster has championed authors and the stories they create. By respecting the copyright of an author's intellectual property, you enable Simon & Schuster and the author to continue publishing exceptional books for years to come. We thank you for supporting the author's copyright by purchasing an authorized edition of this book.

No amount of this book may be reproduced or stored in any format, nor may it be uploaded to any website, database, language-learning model, or other repository, retrieval, or artificial intelligence system without express permission. All rights reserved. Inquiries may be directed to Simon & Schuster, 1230 Avenue of the Americas, New York, NY 10020 or permissions@simonandschuster.com.

Copyright © 2025 by Joe McGinniss, Jr.

All rights reserved, including the right to reproduce this book or portions thereof in any form whatsoever. For information, address Avid Reader Press Subsidiary Rights Department, 1230 Avenue of the Americas, New York, NY 10020.

First Avid Reader Press hardcover edition October 2025

AVID READER PRESS and colophon are trademarks of Simon & Schuster, LLC

Simon & Schuster strongly believes in freedom of expression and stands against censorship in all its forms. For more information, visit BooksBelong.com.

For information about special discounts for bulk purchases, please contact Simon & Schuster Special Sales at 1-866-506-1949 or business@simonandschuster.com.

The Simon & Schuster Speakers Bureau can bring authors to your live event. For more information or to book an event contact the Simon & Schuster Speakers Bureau at 1-866-248-3049 or visit our website at www.simonspeakers.com.

Interior design by Ruth Lee-Mui

Manufactured in the United States of America

1 3 5 7 9 10 8 6 4 2

Library of Congress Control Number (LCCN): 2025944470

ISBN 978-1-6680-0485-2
ISBN 978-1-6680-0487-6 (ebook)

For my son, who I treasure.

And for my father, who I miss.

"DECEMBER [1970]: *My birthday. I was twenty-eight. The year-end edition of* Playboy *was published, containing interviews with nine authors 'who have scored with the bitch goddess of fame.' Mario Puzzo, James Dickey, Kurt Vonnegut, Studs Terkel, Michael Crichton, Sam Houston Johnson, Dan Wakefield, Gay Talese, and myself. Great to be young and a Yankee. Except I lay awake, trembling, every night.*

"OCTOBER: *The baby was born. I went to the delivery room and held my wife's hand as she gave birth. It was a boy. My wife cried, 'Thank God!' For five days I visited her and the baby in the hospital and slept in the house with my daughters. Then I brought my wife and baby home. The next morning, I went away again.*"

—Joe McGinniss, *Heroes*, 1976

"*All writers are, to one extent or another, damaged people. Writing is our way of repairing ourselves.*"

—J. Anthony Lukas

AUTHOR'S NOTE

In the pages that follow is the truth as I experienced it—as a son and brother and husband and father—for better and worse.

For the sake of privacy, certain names have been changed.

PROLOGUE

NOVEMBER 2001

"Welp," my father said, his first word to me in months. The man whose demons were winning looked up at me plaintively, exhausted. Withdrawal was kicking in. His eyes were sunken and jaundiced, his unshaven face ashen. His thinning hair looked whiter than I'd remembered. That's when I noticed his sneakers had no laces.

There's no preparing for it. I've been to conventional hospitals before, and I've given my name and the name of the patient I was there for and printed my name and the date and the time on a sign-in sheet. And I've sat in the pale light of sterile waiting rooms hoping for the best. But that afternoon, unlike any other hospital visit, I avoided eye contact with the other visitors because we all carried the same secret shame and acknowledging one another may just kill the last thread of hope I had carried into the redbrick building with the bars on the windows: this wasn't happening. My father wasn't really being detained in a North Adams psychiatric ward.

The antiseptic smell of the fluorescent-lit hallway hit as soon as the orderly pressed the large red button wired into the wall and serious-sounding locks clicked and the heavy door was pulled open.

Two keys were required to open his holding cell door. There was a head-level, small thick-glass square for staff to check on patients, but it was smudged and oily, like someone had been leaning or rubbing or banging their sweaty forehead against it. Maybe Dad?

He was sitting on a metal chair, elbows on his knees, pitched forward and looking up at me almost wistfully. He hardly seemed a threat.

I didn't know the protocol for this kind of thing. We'd normally embrace in a muscular hug. That didn't feel appropriate. I waited for him to take the lead, unsure even where or how to stand.

There was faint bruising around his neck and forearms. Somewhere within the sunken face, the loose excess skin I hadn't noticed before, as though everything required to keep it in place just gave out, along with everything else. He was the same man who had once delighted in hoisting me up onto his broad shoulders, who pitched Wiffle balls to me and threw the Nerf football again and again, and then sat in television studios, poised, tall and lean, warm and likable as he discussed the murderers and politicians and places about which he authored bestselling books for which he'd earned millions of dollars.

That version of my father was there that cold gray afternoon. He had to be, or I wouldn't have driven nine hours from Washington, DC, to the old mill town of North Adams, Massachusetts, to make sure he was getting the care he desperately needed.

My sisters couldn't be there. Cynthia lived in Paris, and Sarah had reached her breaking point long before anyone else. Dad's unwinding was taking a toll, her weight loss and insomnia and persistent abdominal pain were proof. Both of my older sisters had young children, who needed their mothers to be emotionally and physically healthy. Dad was draining and had been for years.

And yet, this hospitalization wasn't for a car accident or a fall. He'd committed crimes and terrified everyone who cared about him. *Dad*, I thought. *That is my father sitting there. That's Dad, detained in this dank space.*

My new fiancée, Jeanine, would have stood close to me, and I'd have felt the urge to grab her hand, turn and leave, just to get outside and then maybe into the car and then maybe even drive away, and fast. But she was back at Dad's house, after making the six-hour drive north from Philadelphia with me, because she shouldn't have to see my father like this.

How would Dad have reacted at thirty, visiting his own father in the psychiatric ward? Would he have stuck around? Tried to figure out a long-term fix? Would he have shown up at all? Or maybe took one look at his stricken father and left because, really, what the hell was he supposed to do? The man refused help and that wasn't changing and Dad had his own life to live.

He was impulsive like that. And compulsive and rash. He was all appetite, a gambler, drinker, and eater. He was large, about six three, but hardly a fighter. He had the big soft hands of a man who hadn't changed a tire or thrown a punch in decades, if ever.

He was unchecked passion and ego, yet loving, warm, and so exceedingly intelligent and cynical. I planned my words before I dared open my mouth around him. And I'd have time to choose my words around him because even with flushed red cheeks stuffed with whatever exotic meats he grilled or pasta or both, he was still going, somewhere near the end of a tale about Italians I'd never met but felt like I knew because he knew how to tell a story.

Writing came first for him, always and ahead of everything—family, money, and stability. First, he wrote about sports, then a column about anything that moved him, then he followed his instincts and wrote a bestselling book at twenty-seven; it was 1969 and the world was his. But he had a wife who was a nurse, not a reader, and three young children who needed their father as much as he needed to write. Something had to give. He couldn't do it all.

Unlike Dad in this moment, what should have been his lowest, I was young and healthy, felt grounded and confident. I'd tracked him down in Italy after his first of two suicide attempts and arrest and subsequent escape from the Italian police. And months prior, that summer, I'd proposed to my girlfriend on the rooftop deck of a tiny oceanfront studio in Hermosa Beach. I was thirty and there was nothing I couldn't do.

I stood while he sat. He was out of answers. I had ideas about rehab and sobriety. I could see the first rung of a ladder he could grab. I found myself talking, addressing him calmly, trying to reassure him: it was up from here.

What did I know? I knew he was lucky to be alive and no one, even him, wanted him dead. I knew that he was there, in the psychiatric facility in North Adams in November of 2001, because he was arrested and dragged from his house in Williamstown the night prior. And that before that, he'd been arrested in Italy for assaulting the police officers who'd been summoned to his apartment after he'd sent suicide emails to all his children and consumed a handful of pills and a bottle of grappa. I knew he tried to kill himself a second time upon returning to Williamstown.

I knew Jeanine could have run screaming when I'd asked her to drive up from DC to get my father sprung from the psychiatric ward. She had more reasons to than I could bear to consider. I knew that Gavin, the second son of my dad and stepmother, Nina, was fourteen and kept looking to me for reassurance that he deserved and I couldn't give.

Years later, Gavin would compare Dad, at his worst, to a puppy pissing on the rug. What good was yelling at him? He didn't know any better. Jeanine had a father like that. But anyone could see her father struggled from physical maladies. Stricken with multiple sclerosis, he could barely walk.

I'd told her: you don't have to come. But she insisted and I knew she would, and that was one more reason I was marrying her.

At one point, I pulled a second metal chair over so I could sit next to him. I held his hand. There were no signs of punches landed or defensive wounds. The fact that I was checking my father's hands only added to the surrealness of it all. As did the act itself, holding his hand, something I hadn't done since I was a child.

"It really does get better from here, Dad." I said this like I meant it. I was ascendent and choosing resilience and guarded optimism over despair. We were diverging in real time.

I was there with my fiancée and our lives lay ahead of us and Dad was detained without a belt or shoelaces with his exhausted second ex-wife and traumatized youngest son looking on, wondering how much more they could take.

I wasn't just like him. That was never clearer. I had his height and some of his intelligence and sense of humor and even cynicism. Determination, too. He was dogged to a fault. He'd get the story, go wherever it took him, the battlefield in Vietnam or the shared house with a murderer. He'd run one more mile, then five, then the marathon. And another until his knees gave out.

The tricky thing about determination—its origin story is rarely a pleasant one. And for all the achievements of the manically obsessed, whether writing a bestselling book or scoring forty-eight points in a high school basketball game, the same fire that fueled the result was rarely a controlled burn. Determination to achieve, to right a wrong, to prevent heartbreak or loss or avoid facing the most painful parts of our past. Determination in both Dad and me was primal and unwieldy.

Ten more makes, in a row, I'd insist to myself before leaving a basketball court in high school. Hang the net, swish the shot so perfectly that the net caught on the rim and hung there. I wouldn't leave until I'd done it. No matter how late, dark, or cold it was outside, how blazing the fire of broken blisters on my toes. I could picture the bloodstained sock I'd peel off later at home.

At fourteen, I could channel Dad's rejection of pretention and artifice and the worst of the Manhattan publishing types into my own disdain for the white suburban monoculture of beer drinking, lacrosse, soccer, and rock music. There was no falling in line, going along with the crowd, fitting in. He thrived on idiosyncrasy. We both did.

But our similarities ended there. *They'd better*, I told myself, sitting across from him, still disbelieving. The damage he'd done to himself, and to his children, was profound and nothing I would repeat.

Dad launched into marriage and parenting so young and too soon. It didn't suit him, so he left my mom and my two sisters and me, before I was born.

I'd end up patient to a fault, determined to learn from his mistakes with my own relationships. Marriage could and should wait. I pushed it to the limit. My longtime girlfriend verged on giving up. But I had good reason for delaying: I'd fuck it up, doom our marriage to failure, just like Dad, if I wasn't careful. I couldn't do that. I had to do better. That's what I told myself.

He drank. So much drinking. Always drinking. It both scared and scarred me. He was a boisterous or melancholy drunk. Never mean, never violent. But always, every night I spent with him, a drink. And never just one. It defined his life, as it had his parents. So I never dared. Not a sip.

He worshipped Bob Dylan and Bruce Springsteen and Italian opera and soccer; I was all hip-hop and alt-rock and basketball. His appetite was voracious. At a meal, he sucked down a plate of oysters and three beers and reached for more before I had buttered my bread.

I spent a lifetime in his orbit, held close by the same unseen forces that kept me from getting closer. Or was it less complicated than that? Distance between us was a choice, his, and he made it from the start. He saw the tears and heard the pleas and kept going. Could I possibly do the same? Or even worse, to a child of my own?

It was years later, nighttime, warm and rainy, a summer storm blowing through, with the two of us, my son and me, in the car. I was doing eighty on 495, heading home, windows down and fourteen-year-old Jayson's smartphone in my free hand because I'd ripped it from his grasp and held it out the window, threatening to toss it if he didn't find the words, the answer to my impossibly unfair question: "What is *wrong* with you?"

His tears mixed with the rain that blew in.

"What is your malfunction?" I asked, gaslighting my child. A more urgent question: What was mine? I was behaving with my son in ways Dad never had with me. And yet, like him, I was dogged to a fault. All appetite and demands from my teenage son. It was clear that night that I'd gotten it wrong. The situation was urgent, careening out of control like a Volvo speeding down a dark and winding, icy mountain road with an alcoholic father alone at the wheel years ago, or another Volvo, years later, speeding along a windswept highway with the windows down and that father's son, now a father himself, with his scared child riding shotgun. Disaster was imminent in both cases. Only in one would it be averted.

I'd been convinced for years: I was in the clear. I never did drink, and I didn't just stick around when my child was born. Dad would do that, too, later, during his second marriage. But I wasn't just present, I was loving it. Fatherhood came first, ahead of everything, and none of it felt like sacrifice. It was a high, an addiction, even.

I was behaving in ways dangerously similar to my father at his worst. And because of it, my son was at risk.

Though we both wrote, I started late. Dad was prolific and wildly successful at the youngest of ages. I was neither and, unlike him, never put writing books first. While obsessive, I was never willing or able to leave my son, even for short spells, to do it. And like Jayson, I was a ballplayer, though not as gifted.

So I was, it seemed, something of a bridge between them. Maybe that was my role. Maybe it was a decision I'd made, even subconsciously, the moment Jayson arrived. Maybe even months or years before. Maybe it was during those three dreadful days in Massachusetts when it was my father looking up at me for comfort, even answers, that something shifted and I knew that, at the very least, I would never fall so far, inflict so much pain, force my son to visit me in a psychiatric ward. That was a low bar I could certainly clear.

Yet there I was, almost two decades later, losing my mind with my young son, scaring him to tears. And I couldn't explain or begin to understand that awful stormy, summer night with Jayson riding shotgun in the car.

I was somehow convinced I was doing what a father of an adolescent boy should. I was following impulses and instincts, providing what he needed, ugly as it sometimes needed to be.

I trusted myself with what I believed was an earned arrogance about fathering my son. It was easy to swaddle him and tickle him and absorb the gentle weight of his tiny body as he slept on my chest, rising and falling with each meditative breath. And turn the page of his colorful bedtime stories and watch him select another, knowing what he'll reach for, even if I occasionally buried the overly long Richard Scarry volume he inevitably found, knowing it would prolong the routine; or seeing if his sleepy eyes would catch the pages I'd sometimes skip on the third or fourth book. But he'd need more and different and better from me later.

Motivation and structure and discipline emerged as priorities for the boy verging on adolescence. It was a new age and stage for us both. A more sophisticated approach was required—a skill set I didn't inherit, possess, or acquire.

What did my sensitive, gentle adolescent son need from me when playground and bedtime story dad wasn't enough? When he struggled in ways I'd never anticipated, why did I struggle more?

Unlike my dad, I was there every morning when my child woke up, and every night when he slept, and every hour of every day in between. It came easily, almost naturally, as though my new role, father to Jayson, was my true calling. So much so that my stumbles, and ugliness, and demons that emerged in all the wrong places were just part of the process. That's what I told myself for years until it was almost too late.

But this true calling found me hurtling down a highway, losing my mind, like my father before me. I'd stood in a psychiatric ward with him years earlier, wondering how he'd let it get so bad.

And even then, he still had time. He had advantages his own parents didn't. We knew more than ever about the mind and addiction. He could get better care, get healthy, make amends. He'd already done more for his own children than his father ever did for him. He had reason for optimism, if not shoelaces, a belt, or permission to leave that airless room.

"Progress is being made!" I could have been screaming on that summer night in the car when I lost my mind. And I'd have meant it. There were years of proof, I'd have insisted. I'd been more present and attentive and nurturing in fourteen years than my father had ever been. I was raising the fatherhood bar, giving my son everything he deserved, every hour of every day. But that's the danger with blind spots; you don't see the crash coming until it's too late. Pull me over that night, detain me, too. Just like Dad. Any intergenerational parenting progress I'd made was suddenly and terrifyingly at risk because my son was reeling. And I was the cause.

ONE

1976

BEFORE

The photoshoot was on Saturday. A big magazine was doing a story about Dad's new book.

He picked the three of us up from school. He was easy to spot: over six feet tall with dark hair that always needed trimming, and to be sure, he was always waving and calling out to us with his smile of crooked teeth. Of the three of us, I was the youngest at six and the one who ran to him, and he scooped me up in his powerful arms and hugged me so tight, and I let him hoist me off the ground and carry me to his metallic-blue Suburban, where we piled in and buckled up and were off.

I did the math in my head: half of Friday; all morning, afternoon, and night on Saturday; and more than half of Sunday with Dad. He lived close enough to pick us up once a month and drive to whatever house he and Nina were renting in New Jersey.

The Philadelphia rock station crackled through the speakers as he tuned the radio and Cynthia and Sarah sprawled out in the back seat and I'd climbed into the back-back as the mood shifted only slightly when we left Swarthmore and cut through the dreary suburbs of

Rutledge and Ridley Park and strip malls and gas stations and cookie-cutter redbrick houses because I knew the route by heart and what was to come. The one inevitable stop before the highway.

A small, dimly lit bar and liquor store set back from the main road. He signaled and slowed, and I deflated as he pulled in and parked and left the radio on and we waited. I stared at the glowing neon red OPEN sign and watched the front door, hoping for some reason he'd emerge empty-handed.

Minutes later the door would push open, and he'd clutch two heavy-looking paper bags that clinked when he placed them in the front seat, and it was all the regular stuff: beer and wine and gin and vodka. Nina wasn't a drinker, maybe an occasional beer, a glass of wine at dinner. Dad shopped for himself. He knew what he liked and bought it all.

From the liquor store it was a quick hop to the turnpike and some combination of back roads and secret shortcuts and the long, winding rural road and under the covered bridge and a few more turns past the sledding hill, and right there, down the little gravel driveway and past the garage and carport, sat the four-room, two-hundred-year-old Sergeantsville, New Jersey, farmhouse.

He'd moved far enough away so that there would be no confusion about whose responsibility it was to get us ready for school, to pick us up, to take us to the dentist or piano lesson or basketball game. To get us fed and make sure homework was done and that we didn't spend too much time in front of the television or on the phone. To rebound my missed shots.

He didn't have to worry about pop-ins or surprise visits, one of us kids barging in after school unannounced. Ninety minutes away meant life as he wanted it; drinking without restraint and parties when he felt like it and getting high and sleeping it off and writing and editing and jogging and listening to records and reading newspapers and magazines and taking long phone calls with old high school friends and planning trips to horse races and mountain ranges and more writing and drinking.

The follow-up to his record-setting, fame-making debut, *The Selling of the President*, was a spare, thinly veiled autobiographical novel about a young famous author crashing and burning on his book tour. Few people read it. The reviews written were unkind.

His new book wasn't going to sell, either. But we didn't know the difference and didn't care. Time with him was the point. He'd recently decided he wanted to write about Alaska. He'd been there and back. He was going again. There was no telling for how long. Our feelings were irrelevant. He did what he felt.

We dropped our things on the carpeted living room floor and scrambled down to the brick-floor basement kitchen for potato chips and root beer. The weekends were all Bob Dylan and Bruce Springsteen and Hank Williams records on the stereo and barbecues lit and Pachinko and Othello played and Polaroid pictures taken and walks in the woods and skipping rocks across the nearby creek and throwing the Nerf football to me until I nailed the perfect leaping touchdown catch.

Cynthia and Sarah would dress up in Nina's funky seventies clothes, colorful scarves and bell-bottoms and floral dresses that didn't fit. And we'd finish mint chocolate chip ice cream and feed the fire in the massive stone fireplace with rolled up sheets of old *New York Times* and line up bottle caps from the beers Dad drank; the Heineken red star and the Löwenbräu lion and the Guinness harp and all the others I'd ask him about, holding them up, and he'd call out the name and I'd repeat it quietly to myself and, finally, after I'd divided and tallied them, I'd call out the winner, second place, and third.

Dad read to my sisters, then to me, his big arm wrapped around my six-year-old frame, my hand and head resting on his chest, tucked into him, a perfect fit. He sang songs to me at night when he tucked me in. He never raised his voice with me. As a child, I found only his absence and his drinking unsettling.

Someone from the magazine would be there the next morning to take pictures. He'd set it up that way, having the kids he left, who featured prominently in the new book, at the house for the photo shoot. Readers would see he was a loving dad, and that would make him sympathetic. And that was important. No one wanted to read about an asshole child-deserter.

The new book was *Heroes*. It was an examination of his life and personal failings interspersed with vignettes about the search for American heroes. It would go largely unnoticed, his second consecutive flop in the seven years since his debut.

Aside from having us present, front and center, he didn't care how he appeared in the pictures, whether his hair was tangled or what readers of the piece might think about his Olympia Beer windbreaker, whether there was a small tear in the sleeve from romping through the woods with his children. He was thirty-three and had already achieved more success in his chosen career than most could dare dream.

Creativity was in his genes. His grandfather was a renowned architect of churches and other majestic buildings that stand today throughout New England. His own father was an MIT graduate and an architect and ultimately a failed travel agent. And Dad was architect of his own life, creating something from nothing, words on a page that readers and publishers valued enough to allow him to earn a living writing.

He started as a sports reporter for the *Bulletin* in Philadelphia. He covered the 76ers, and following a tough home loss, he pestered Wilt Chamberlain about his missed free throws, would things have turned out better if he'd spent more time practicing his foul shooting? Wilt tossed the gallon of milk he'd been guzzling and charged my skinny father and only his teammates who held him back prevented a beatdown.

Not long after, he was given a column with the *Philadelphia Inquirer*. Three times a week his words became the "must read" column in Philadelphia. Corrupt city politics and gritty Philadelphia color and the war in Vietnam were subjects about which he had something to say. He knew how to string words together to make the point, to get to the heart of matters, to articulate what readers were feeling and pull it all together. And so off he went to Vietnam, and before he left he found his way into Robert Kennedy's Senate office in Washington, DC. He wanted to ask about the war and Bobby's campaign, should he decide to challenge LBJ. Kennedy had a new book of essays about the issues of the day. From a box of them he pulled one out and signed it for the twenty-four-year-old columnist as he left.

Kennedy verged on his run for the presidency, a campaign that would end with his assassination seven months from that autumn afternoon in Washington. My father was on his way to Vietnam, not to fight, but to report.

For Joe McGinniss

With best wishes for the future—and when you find the answers please let me know.

Bobby Kennedy
November 7, 1967
Washington, DC

He gave me the book. It rests on a small table next to my desk. I open it sometimes and study Bobby Kennedy's penmanship, lightly run my index finger over the black ink, imagine Dad sitting across from him as Kennedy inscribed it, feeling full, important, seen by his hero. The book cost $4.95. It was published by Doubleday, and Kennedy dedicated the volume to "my children, and yours."

A few months later Dad flew with Kennedy into Philadelphia and rode with him in the open-top convertible as he campaigned in the blue-collar, white Republican suburbs of Philadelphia. His column about the event described thousands of screaming kids climbing all over themselves to be close to something special. Like ants over a sugar cube.

Kennedy said to his wife and Dad and the few others in the car after they left that it didn't matter what he said that day. And then he turned to Dad: "Looks like you had quite a trip through the Delta." He'd not only remembered him, but he'd also read his column. Dad, merely twenty-four-years-old, swelled. A hero of his not only knew him but read his work. That was the last time he saw Kennedy.

The call came in the middle of the night. It was his mother and she told Dad that Kennedy had been shot. He asked where. He thought she said "the leg." He flew to Los Angeles and paced the Hospital of the Good Samaritan waiting area with Jimmy Breslin and George Plimpton and the Kennedy children and Jacqueline arrived from Paris and the hours stretched on until Kennedy's press secretary came in to wake Jerry Bruno, the advance man who was with JFK's motorcade in Dallas, to tell him: "It's over."

Dad left the hospital floor where Bobby Kennedy died and flew from Los Angeles to Philadelphia, where he took a taxi home to my mother and sisters, ages two and three months.

It was the summer of 1968. Martin Luther King and Bobby Kennedy were murdered. The country was teetering, his hero was dead. The center wasn't holding and beautiful baby girls and an adoring wife at home didn't placate. In fact, their needs were as burdensome as they were justified. They needed a present and loving father. An engaged and accessible husband. A breadwinner and caretaker; a reliable steady presence. He needed something else altogether. There was no middle ground. Not with Dad.

His own father never threw a ball with him or hugged him tightly or took him to playgrounds or baseball games. Joseph Aloisius McGinniss, his father, the orphaned boy who had no idea how to parent, was socially awkward and a heavy drinker.

Had it been discovered in his lifetime, a diagnosis may have placed Dad's father on the autism spectrum. He'd disappear for weeks at a time to drink and do whatever else he needed to do. Maybe try to work through and make sense of his experiences as an orphaned boy raised in the house of a Catholic monsignor.

• • •

In *Heroes*, Dad described his childhood as lonely and bleak. He was tall and skinny and lacked coordination. His mother, a telephone operator from Queens, New York, had miscarried three times. In 1942 at the age of thirty-nine she gave birth to her only child. My father.

She was an alcoholic and would hide bottles around their cold, quiet, mid-century modern house on Green Acres Court. She would sit for hours staring out the living room window and tell my father she "had the blues." She went away to a hospital "to get happy," Dad was told by his father. When she returned, his father promised him, she'd smile and laugh, and everything would be wonderful. But that didn't happen. So, she went back to the hospital again. And then again.

He spent hours alone in his bedroom. He prayed for friends. I slept in his childhood bedroom when we visited my grandparents. It was always cold and there were stuffed animals on the shelves and bed, their fur coarse and old smelling, so that cuddling with them was impossible. Still, I kept them close.

He was sent to Catholic high school and then to Holy Cross because the dream school of his parents, Notre Dame, rejected him. And then finally, at last, he launched himself out into the world. He was free.

Much later, he'd dutifully return when his father suffered a stroke. Dad walked the hospital hallway with him, holding on to his arm to keep him from falling, and then the tumor was found, and the prognosis rendered, and those were his father's last days alive.

Despite the cold, quiet dysfunction of his childhood, Dad had learned and memorized the words to lullabies, which he gladly sang to us at night. He had a barely passable falsetto singing voice. I do wonder where he learned to hug so tight that I *felt* how much he loved me. He crawled on the carpeted floor with any one of us on his back, falling together in laughter, time and again. Maybe that was him doing all the things he'd wanted to do with his own father.

And then he'd drive us home and drive away.

Maybe, like height, cynicism, depression, and drinking, that was inherent, too, the walking away.

Only a few months had passed since Bobby Kennedy was struck down in June of 1968 when Dad overheard a conversation on a train that would plant the seed for the idea that would become his first book. Two men were discussing landing the "Humphrey account."

In the wake of President Lyndon Johnson declining to run for re-election and Bobby's assassination, Hubert Humphrey solidified his position as the presumptive Democratic Party nominee for president. An advertising firm was hired to package him like a product and sell him like toothpaste or cigarettes to the nation in time for the 1968 election.

Dad inquired with Humphrey's campaign: Could he come aboard and write about the process? The answer was no. In response, he called the Nixon campaign and asked them the same question. Roger Ailes, with whom he'd maintain a lifelong relationship despite their political differences, said yes.

A local Philadelphia paper ran a prelaunch profile. There was my "tall and angular" dad with his three-year-old daughter, Cynthia, on his lap. His other daughter, Sarah, was eighteen months and unusually calm. She had his dark hair.

"She likes anyone with a drink in his hand," he quipped. My mother, the "pretty, blond wife," was trying to corral Cynthia, who had bounded in and latched on to his leg. He finally extricated himself and headed back to the kitchen to make more drinks.

Before the launch, the impossibly young family of four, Dad, twenty-six, and Mom, twenty-four, spent five weeks in the Berkshires seeing B.B. King and the Who and my mother's parents. Before their return home, Dad made sure to visit the Saratoga and Green Mountain racetracks to place his bets.

He always craved action. He was the drinker and the gambler with no compulsion checked, every want indulged. Traits only domesticity, the needs of his young children and wife and the life they were building together, could tame. That was the long-shot bet he placed.

The young family returned home to Swarthmore for one last time. The book launch was set. The stratosphere awaited.

What was next? He was asked in the newspaper profile.

He mentioned a novel. "After six drinks, I'm convinced I can do it."

The Selling of the President spent thirty-one weeks on the *New York Times* bestsellers list. He was the youngest person since Anne Frank to have a book top the list.

He'd impressed young literary assistants and publicists at parties held in his name and started with a martini and then another and a third and the wine and champagne and Irish coffee and then again the next night and this was New York City and Chicago and Boston and San Francisco and Los Angeles and London and it was the highest of highs and he was no longer the skinny, lonely boy from Rye. He was a star and there was no coming down from the high.

The garbage? Two nights prior he was doing *The Tonight Show* and getting drunk with Norman Mailer at the Beverly Hills Hotel, and he was expected to take out the trash on Magill Road? The world (that mattered) wanted a piece of McGinniss. What did McGinniss think? What did he see? What did he know?

And at home? Different questions. Two little girls who wondered when he was going away again. And a wife wondering who he was seeing when he did.

Cynthia was the first child, conceived when the marriage seemed sound. They owned a redbrick house in the Philadelphia suburb of Drexel Hill. Though avoiding the Vietnam draft motivated the start of a family so young, the birth of my sister was a joyous occasion.

Sarah followed two years later, in 1968, as the marriage began to fail.

He'd met Nina at a publishing party. She was young and pretty and worked for his publisher. He'd flown home to Philadelphia hungover and took a taxi to the house on Magill Road and slept until midafternoon the next day. When he woke, my mother asked if he'd been with another woman. He said yes.

Cynthia was old enough to notice Dad was home less frequently. Then not at all. He'd been there every night tucking her in, and every morning feeding her breakfast. Then he wasn't. Where did he go? Why did he leave her behind?

He and Nina secretly rented a little house in a secluded patch of New Jersey where he could indulge his impulses to read, write, drink, and fuck. It was the kind of life that allowed one, if he felt like it, to carry long mirrors outside and lean them against trees and snap Polaroids of girlfriends blowing him. That wasn't something he could manage on Magill Road in Swarthmore with his two little girls and newborn son in the crib. It was the early seventies, and he was more rock star writer than the father I'd soon be missing.

A year after Dad left, Sarah got sick. She was three and her nose wouldn't stop bleeding. It was her platelets—she had none. She was hospitalized for weeks. She was stuck with needles many times a day and had bruises all over her little arms from the injections. She dreamed of angels, she said. Dad was sure it meant she would die. He read and sang to her and held her little hand when the doctor stuck a long needle into the bone, extracting marrow from the hip. When she returned home from the hospital, healed, he left again. That was no longer his home.

He was three years shy of thirty and adored and envied, needed, resented, and missed. And he was celebrating. And his life was his job, and his job was a celebration and life was a party and he was the toast of every town that mattered, everywhere but 628 Magill Road.

He was leaving for London for the British publication of his book. He told my mother he'd be leaving the family for good when he returned.

She said she was going with him, to London. She was soon to be a single mother working full-time as a registered nurse. She chose nursing school because she wanted to help people. She was the daughter of a GE plant worker from Pittsfield, Massachusetts. She had no family money and had never left the East Coast, much less the country. The marriage was over. She wasn't going to miss out on seeing London. So she went, to see what she could, while she could. The parties were grand, and Dad was the star, pulled in all directions.

My mother couldn't compete. She wasn't a writer or creator or editor or even much of a reader. On original pages of *The Selling of the President*, watermarked Trojan Onion Skin typing paper, my father's ballpoint pen scrawl atop the first impossibly thin paper: "Chapter 1—revised." In faded pencil, my mother's all-caps handwriting I knew so well: "BEAUTIFUL!!"

That was the extent of her written reaction to his work. What more could she offer? She wasn't Nina. She was a twenty-four-year-old graduate of St. Luke's Nursing School in Pittsfield. She was a mother of two daughters who was losing her husband, everything she'd planned and hoped and worked for and had every reason to expect.

They returned from London. My mom told him she was pregnant. I was an accident or a last attempt by my mother to keep Dad from leaving for good. My conception didn't change his mind. Mom's doctor suggested she might want to consider termination.

While my mother finished another nine-hour shift at the hospital and raced home to pay the babysitter and get dinner ready for her three children, Dad was clearing his head on a hike through the Rockies in 1974 and deciding he wanted to write about heroes.

There were sections of the book about his own less-than-heroic life. He didn't hold back. He laid it bare. He described the life he lived with Nina. The music and drinking and getting high and skinny-dipping with her and her sisters and sleeping it off. And he'd write and she'd read and edit, and he'd take calls from his agent in New York and his new friends in Los Angeles and old friends from high school and talked big and thought big and made big plans and signed a new contract and celebrated some more.

He detailed less-glamorous elements. There were admissions and confessions and so much heartache and depression and alcoholism, his institutionalized parents, their bankruptcy and debt and death. And of course Cynthia and Sarah and me left behind.

Heroes was too painful for his mother, a woman crippled with so much self-loathing she would cut herself out of pictures. She'd go into bookstores and remove copies of the book from the shelves.

His father gave him a list of reasons he should stay with my mother. My sisters and I were near the top.

Dad wrote about Cynthia calling bullshit on his bluster about loving her more than all the blue in the sky. "You say that then you go away again." He wrote about his excruciating loneliness praying for friends and with passing reference to the priests and monsignor who looked after him as an altar boy in Rye, New York. The same monsignor who had helped raise his orphaned father. He wrote about fear and escape and fame and girlfriends and guilt.

I was eleven when I first read the book. I only read the parts about him and my sisters. It didn't make me cry, but did give me a headache that seemed to last for weeks and seemed to return every time I thought about those passages. I couldn't sleep well before I'd read it and struggled even more after.

My bedroom had been his office. So for me, he was at once inescapable and elusive. My days were filled with my sisters and mother and neighborhood and school friends and childhood distractions. The nights left me alone in the darkness, haunted by his absence. I'd push the window open no matter how cold and let the hum of passing traffic quiet my mind.

He referenced therapy with my mother in *Heroes*, but he was barely thirty and a literary star with an adoring, awestruck girlfriend. The arduous and unglamorous work of self-examination and sobriety and taming compulsions held no appeal. He'd done the hardest part: he'd left his two daughters and unborn son and wife. He had the rest of his life to recover.

Saturday, the day of the photo shoot at his house, was cool and bright and breezy. He toasted Eggos and fried bacon for us and ate yogurt with wheat germ. The photographer arrived and was kind and patient and had no trouble arranging Cynthia and Sarah and me, ten, eight, and six, around my father. We orbited him like little planets. We clung to his strong arms and perched atop his broad shoulders.

In the words of the author of the profile: "The children are beautiful and open children, obviously at ease with their father—and he with them."

Dad was asked about his next book, the one about Alaska. "I picked the subject. I really like mountains and camping. [After *Heroes*] I was so tired of the inside of my own head I wanted to do something concrete."

I wouldn't be going with him, though he'd fly my sisters and me four thousand miles on our own in 1977 for three weeks in the summer. Maybe it was hard for him being so far from us for so long, especially at that stage in our lives, all the moments he missed. But I didn't get that sense. I had the feeling he was content with things just as they were.

As always, Sunday landed hard. There was a stark melancholy routine to the day. The morning passed quickly, and records may have played but the music only reminded me of the day before or Friday night when I had the whole weekend ahead of me.

The clock would read noon and then one and lunch would be offered, but we had no appetite because it was almost time to leave. By two, the Eagles or Giants game had been flicked on but went unwatched and my sisters were packed and ready. And it was time. The long, quiet drive home in darkness.

He dropped low to meet my hot, tear-streaked face with his. Words like "soon" and "before you know it" drifted past me. And then the horn tapping as his blue Suburban rolled away, the red taillights never flashing white, no braking, stopping, reversing to come back for me.

It was hard to see in the glint of red taillights on those Sunday nights, but that was him doing better. More obvious examples filled the two days I'd just spent with him. That's where the tears came from. Children know when they're loved.

He was going where he wanted, to live how and with whom he chose. I was part of that, but barely. I was a fraction of his month, two full days, and a week here or there. He had that kind of power. He could slice and dice me into pieces of the whole person I was meant to be.

TWO

2007

AFTER

Maybe it was his head. It was this perfectly round thing and when I put him in his little blue onesie and swaddled and lay him gently down on his back and his tiny fingers wrapped around my index finger and squeezed I couldn't understand how I existed before that moment. Maybe I didn't. I barely did, I sometimes thought. Though less and less those days. My wife was proof of something. Though I had no money in the bank, I had two degrees I wasn't using and $80,000 in student loan debt and my first novel would be published soon, finally.

And there he lay, looking like Harold from the children's story about the baby and the purple crayon, his grip confirming that I was both present and necessary. That grip and his open eyes finding mine, and there's a picture to prove it and I look at it sometimes and feel it again, that rush that stands alone, that brings it all back and reminds me just what I'm here for. Not to write, like my father. But to be a father who writes.

. . .

The first few nights at Sibley Hospital in Washington, DC, when the nurse came in to check his vitals and then his bedtime, when she returned to wheel the swaddled little thing in his baby bin to his baby sleeping lounge for his second and third and fourth nights on the planet. And the morning of departure on the day of the Breast Cancer Awareness run through springtime blossoms of leafy green Washington and the sea of pink shirts as I drove, hands wrapped around the steering wheel, the two of them in the back seat, a short steady super-smooth ride home: this beautiful little family was mine.

Other than emails, the SIM card on my smartphone was an endless stream of pictures and video clips because this wasn't all really happening, was it? My son couldn't be as glorious as he was, could he? I wasn't taking any chances, documenting everything.

Similac six-packs and bottles of breast milk and pacifiers and flushable wipes and Cheerios and Baby Mum-Mums and laughter and fatigue and soothing bedtime Johnson & Johnson baby lotion and *African Playground* CDs and lullabies in the padded rocking chair next to the white crib the drawers beneath which Sarah came down and neatly filled with folded and organized onesies and socks and shirts and shorts. And the acquired skill, more art than science, of laying baby Jayson, swaddled and sleeping, just so and shifting pressure from hands to chest, then slowly rising, gaining bodily separation and standing upright and slowly pulling the zipper closed on his crib netting (lest he ascend the railing and tumble over the side) and tiptoeing across the creaky loft floor without waking him.

Some nights I'd stay. There was a colorful blanket and throw pillows and an array of books in a nook we labeled "the super cave" between the crib and small shelves we had installed for his first years of life, this small space for him and bedtime stories and lullabies like my father used to sing to me. And I'd lie on my back and listen to him breathing and the intermittent suckling sounds he made with his pacifier and try to hold it together. Tears were inappropriate for the moment. They came, though, and didn't really want to stop. It was all too good. It couldn't last. I didn't deserve to feel that way, that in love with my child, my life.

The last time I felt anything similar was every weekend at my father's as a child and every afternoon and brunch with Jeanine my first year in college. There is an obvious throughline. It wasn't complicated. The torrent of endorphins unleashed by the love of a father or a girl overwhelmed me. Like a weekend with Dad, nothing good ended well.

And then, suddenly, this perfect creation, Jayson, simultaneously vulnerable and all-powerful, holding my emotional life in his tiny little hands. I rode the high. I was duty bound and invested. I packed his little bag with wipes and diapers and backup pacifiers and Baby Mum-Mums and his sippy cup and strapped him into his excersaucer and lifted him in the air, descended three flights of stairs and carried him to the French nanny next door, pausing along the way to let him study the pollinating bumblebees in the lustrous pink azaleas.

This was three mornings a week. Then I'd walk Vegas, our gentle yellow Labrador, through quiet tree-lined streets past the playgrounds we'd frequented, and then back home to read emails from my publisher with good and better news about my first novel until it was time to retrieve Jayson. There was a reason why Jeanine labeled this stretch of life a "Golden Age." And when I ventured out on my own, to the gym or to hoop on Sunday nights, my phone was checked reflexively between sets or games in the event something was wrong with Jayson. This perfect little life was indeed delicate. Only a certain level of manic, obsessive investment of time and energy offered any hope against the worst.

Then the Summer Olympics aired. The opening ceremonies in Beijing. A stadium filled with one hundred thousand people. A man suspended by a single cable atop the arena running on air. It was magical. And then seven-foot Yao Ming and a three-year-old boy on the track, walking together. Jayson asleep on my chest, his fingers wrapped around my thumb. I was sobbing like a child.

I lost fifteen pounds in two months. I could only pick at scrambled eggs and skipped dinners. I couldn't look at my two-year-old son without tears forming. I was unbearable. It was unsustainable. I was like my father when he drank, present but unreachable.

Dad sent me a stack of books about meditation and depression. He emailed me about our genetic predispositions and reassured me from afar, a skill he'd fostered over decades. Depression was a black pit, he'd said. He waged a lonely lifelong battle trying to emerge from it. He referenced therapists and antidepressants, but wasn't specific about his own protocols. I'd learn later he didn't have many, other than to consume increasingly more prescription pills.

The home office of the in-network provider was located on a tree-lined street. A large white midcentury modern three-level home had an entrance for patients under a carport.

I was there for drugs. He could prescribe them. He was in his seventies and tall and lean with thinning white curls. He had a cast on his right hand, his writing hand. Fishing accident, a hook through the thumb, then infection and surgery. He may never get movement back.

His scrawl was loopy and slow. So, I spoke slower, and took long pauses between complaints. Yes, my father was the writer. He'd read a few of his books. His energy picked up. I suddenly became slightly more interesting. I said I was sure anything I was going through was chemical because it was genetic, my father and mother and their parents were all a mess, chemically. They were depressed and alcoholic. My father's depressed and an alcoholic, too. And addicted to benzos. "So of course I'm fucked, right?"

I told him I was like Adam Sandler in *Punch-Drunk Love* with my crying problem. He hadn't seen it. He can't stop crying, I explained. Out of nowhere he's suddenly sobbing.

He wrote some more. And then a prescription. I got what I went for and the pills helped.

I returned for a few weeks and always felt bad talking too much.

He was old, tired, and it looked like it hurt for him to walk and it was hard for him to write. He was hanging on, I thought. Retirement meant something he wasn't ready to face. He reminded me of my father, only healthier.

He slouched in his leather chair. I leaned forward in mine only to keep the energy up. I talked about my dad. I told him what I believed: it was fine to complain and deconstruct and blame a parent for my inadequacies until I had a child of my own. Then reasons don't matter. My child deserves the best version of myself. The reasons for my failure aren't the point. He suffers either way, whether I'm inadequate because of my father or because of genetics or both.

"That's something my father never did," I said, self-satisfied. I was the hero of this story, the good father doing the right thing for his child. I was the upright *Homo sapiens* on the evolutionary chart and Dad the lesser version trailing behind. "So maybe I'm not fucked."

Another lifetime ago, I was twenty-eight and couldn't breathe, cornered and suffocated by a loving girlfriend who thought more highly of me than she should have. I wasn't ready to give her a tenth of what she deserved. There was no therapist for me then or chemical interventions, because if you asked me I'd have insisted: medication was for the weak-minded. I was a strong, young man and would figure it out.

I sat there years later, in the home office of a psychiatrist, gazing at the framed abstract piece on the wall: three circles intersecting, red and orange and blue. I was there, trying to feel better because it wasn't just about me. Jayson needed me to feel better or else he'd be fucked, too.

The doctor was quiet. He'd stopped writing. His head was pitched slightly forward, eyelids low, and he exhaled and his breathing slowed and I stared at him and watched him dozing and wondered how long I should let him sleep.

The version of myself who held it together barely long enough to find an in-network psychiatrist and drive himself to an appointment because my wife and son deserved a fully present partner and parent was years in the making. The man who would finally relent and accept chemical intervention as long as it meant he wouldn't piss away another moment with his son was driving a Volvo with a car seat in the back and Richard Scarry books scattered on the seat and sippy cups of warm apple juice on the floor. A few years prior I had been the petulant jackass convinced I was living the way I needed to, alone and broke but free. I was averting relationship disaster and future parenting malpractice. Idling in the leafy affluent corner of Washington, DC, in a crappy studio apartment working a part-time tutoring gig for the American University basketball team, flirting and making out with women I didn't know very well, writing what I thought was a novel, barely paying the rent, deferring mountains of student loan debt because soon, I was sure, I'd land a six-figure book deal and launch my career and adult life.

I was nearing thirty, evolving in real time: from a needy and insecure boy convinced anyone he loved would surely reject and desert him, into the man suffocating in a hotel suite on his birthday with the love of his life. An overwhelming impulse to run had me breaking down because freedom was everything. If I forged ahead into commitment and marriage and parenting, I'd do what my father did or worse.

Jeanine took the train down from Manhattan to DC. The Marriott downtown was a surprise. She opened the door and led us inside. A bouquet of gold and blue balloons and floral arrangement and glistening confetti and a cake and cards that told me in her sweet trademark handwriting with some colored-in bubble letters: "I Love You!" and "Happy 28th Birthday!!"

I was moody and ornery. My chest felt tight. Despite my moods and neuroses and her high-achieving Manhattan life she'd made for herself, Jeanine was trying to make it work with me.

And who was I to deserve that? I had no car and no real income and ate tuna from cans and converted loose change into bills at the grocery store so I could buy coffee and bagels and more tuna.

I stewed in the hotel suite she'd paid for, brooding on the edge of the king-size bed staring at the display of love and sweetness before me. Somehow all I saw was a hole, black and cold and bottomless, one more step and down I'd fall.

"Tell me what's wrong," she asked again, just as gently as she did the first two times. The rest of my life was sitting right there: I could finish school and move to Manhattan. I could drop out and move there sooner.

I said nothing. There weren't words for it. A cold sensation, tightness in the throat, shortness of breath, something bordering on panic.

And brilliant, gorgeous Jeanine, all generosity and love and sweetness and maturity and vulnerability and laughter, offering herself to me. I had Arizona on my mind. A convertible and desert highway and some little adobe in the Sonoran foothills where I'd write and drink coffee and meet desert women and drive and marvel at the openness of everything. All the wanderlust of my father, but without the courage to take the leap.

So the notion of commitment became a sensation—constriction. Immediate pressure to plan for an engagement, then a wedding, then children, and all of it felt like walls and ceilings and floors converging.

I flipped the table over. I tossed a chair. The flowers and cake were ruined. When it was over, I was sweating and in the hallway, and down the stairs, and on the busy downtown street walking nowhere fast. I was just like my father, only worse. I'd achieved nothing, was going nowhere and was stubbornly, wholly alone.

The street I walked that gray afternoon, if you followed it in the opposite direction, past my tiny box of an apartment and kept going until you weren't just out of DC but north to Swarthmore, Pennsylvania, where a decade earlier I was the thin, earnest, overly serious eighteen-year-old moving into Mertz Hall for my first year at Swarthmore.

I was the basketball recruit refusing to sweat it out in the hot early weeks who lugged my air conditioner from my mom's house to the dorm. My roommate loved me. I played Earth, Wind & Fire and Public

Enemy CDs on my sister's old stereo system and decided hundreds of pages of reading a week for a single class had to be a joke. I was invited to pledge one of the two fraternities on campus and got into a heated debate with a basketball teammate about the socially corrosive effects of the Greek system. "Meatheads drinking beer" wasn't my thing. By November I was in love.

Jeanine was a sophomore gymnast and cheerleader from Philadelphia, the daughter of public school teachers. She was pretty and introspective and a struggling engineering student whose ambition impressed me.

She was empathetic and thoughtful and made me laugh. Her house was a twin in the Germantown section of Philadelphia, in the shadow of housing projects, the sidewalk in front filled with empty crack vials. Her mother chased strawberry-stealing prostitutes from their garden.

Jeanine was the bright-light daughter of educators and niece of renowned novelist William Gardner Smith, peer to Richard Wright and James Baldwin, who escaped America's racist choke hold for a life in Paris. She was perpetually clad in mustard tops that complimented her chestnut-brown eyes; she teased me when the snowballs I threw missed her badly and she stood there in the falling snow with hands on her hips and head to the side daring me; she was the quiet girl with the confidence to call and invite me to a party and to kiss me back.

We'd only been together for a couple of months when I decided I couldn't live without her. She had almond-shaped eyes that made some of the women in parking garage booths speak Amharic to her before I knew what Amharic was. Her fingernails were sporadically manicured, and we watched *Cheers* and *The Simpsons* and laughed at all the same punch lines and her skin was dark and smooth and she had tiny feet I loved to massage.

I was in love. Any hope for me was in the hands of the sophomore gymnast who made me laugh.

It was November. It had been two months. My feelings weren't rational. I'd drop everything for another half hour watching *Cheers* with her in my single bed.

I was the child of divorce. Insecurity was baked in. Time was precious and limited. It was a simple equation. Basketball would require loads of time and energy, which meant less Jeanine and a greater risk of losing her. It wasn't complicated.

And college ball was hard. "You're not in high school anymore!" Coach bellowed from the sideline during brutal preseason drills. Everyone was good or better. I needed more strength and to shoot better. I had to run a mile under six minutes and couldn't. I had to be able to jump rope and failed. I could have been doing that all summer in preparation and hadn't.

I had to put in more work, more hours, more, more, and more. Then, maybe, I'd catch up to the rest of the team. That's how it was or felt and it was only October. And the five hundred pages of reading would still be there. And the three twenty-page papers and midterms and finals and it was a mountain of work, and I was hiking it alone, wholly ill-equipped and no one cared.

I didn't ask Dad for advice. He'd likely tell me what I didn't want to hear: give it a season. I'd put so much into the game; basketball was such a huge part of my life for so long, it would be a shame to drop it so soon.

His words may have landed differently had he been a part of my basketball journey, training and rebounding for me as a child and teenager, a constant fixture at games, one of those parents who left work early to see their child play. *Don't play to please me*, he'd have told me. *The desire has to come from within or you'll be miserable* is exactly what he would have said.

There is a middle ground. A parent playing a role in helping his child learn an evolving definition of desire and joy. Pain and difficulty weren't the end, but a test: How much do you really want something? Maybe had it been part of a lifelong conversation and commitment, ideas like that would have landed.

It was a long, cold walk across campus to inform the coach, who was smoking in his small field-house office, that I was done. I'd earned a coveted spot on his recruiting list and after weeks of deliberation and losing sleep and appetite and flirting with depression, before the first game was played, I quit.

I knew what I felt and did that. I was all impulse. I met and fell in love with a girl, so if it was her birthday I'd walk to the florist in town and then carry the bouquet to her engineering class and wait outside the door. I'd panic if I didn't know where she was at nine o'clock on a Thursday night because there were other guys before me and what if she was with one of them again? Where would that leave me? Left again and clearly not worth sticking around for. So I walked around campus and circled library stacks looking for her. A freshman in college in emotional free fall because the girl might not love me back. I felt it, so I did it. There was no impulse to figure out why. All I had in life was what I wanted to do.

If I'm being charitable, maybe some emotional survival instinct was triggered those first months when Jeanine entered my life. *That sweet soul might just be my salvation, save me from myself, those genetic dirty bombs gifted me by my father.*

But I was too young and ill-formed to get it right that year and the many that followed. And I was still adrift at twenty-eight but healthy and educated and would surely find my way.

I had "a keeper" in Jeanine, Dad told me. Better not screw around too long and lose her, he warned. I didn't mention my hotel suite outburst, the relationship I was destroying and the reasons why. What the hell could he have told me anyway?

Backed up on Chain Bridge Road in McLean heading home from day care at his mother's job, daddy and son. It was a sunny and warm late afternoon in June. Jayson had been five for a month.

He'd been riffing for a while. Like most children his age, he had a lot to say—observations, questions, theories, wants: "I want my birthday to be on every day," he decided.

The glow of late-afternoon sunlight found him, gentle shadows brushing his impossibly soft cheeks, sitting there in his red, long-sleeve Spider-Man shirt with plastic Star Wars rings on most of his little fingers, counting out loud: "Two hundred and seven, two hundred and eight, two hundred and nine, three hundred! Three hundred and one, three hundred and two . . . three hundred and nine, four hundred! Four hundred and one, four hundred and two . . . four hundred and nine, fifty hundred! I mean, um, five hundred! Five hundred and one, five hundred and two—"

"What are you counting to?"

"I'm showing you some of the numbers that count to infinity!"

He'd been staring out the window, an unusually long stretch of silence. I could feel him thinking. He was a thinker. Ponderous. Silly to be sure, but serious and sensitive.

He offered a list of foods that would make him stronger, "like carrots, broccoli, cauliflower, and I'll never forget, I'll never forget, chicken." He paused. And swallowed and caught his breath and reset.

"What's a good thing to do and a bad thing to not do?" he asked.

"You tell me."

"You cannot say Daddy's stupid or Mommy's stupid. That's a bad thing. That's an unkind thing. So, I'll never say that. I never said that. I never even said that."

Brushing teeth when Daddy tells him to was a good thing to do. "Just go and do it," he chirped.

"I'll do good listening for the rest of my life. I promise, I won't do any bad listening. I promise. I will not. I'll try to not." He hedged at the end of it, which made me smile. But his need to please was striking, and later, watching the video of him again, it gave me pause: even then, he felt pressure to please.

He stopped and thought. I could see him working it out, searching for the words.

"My brain is fighting against the bad things that are in my mind. And the bad things are fighting the good things in my mind."

"Who's winning?" I asked.

"The good guys. Because one of the bad parts of my mind is out."

"Which part?"

"The brown part is the bad and the pink part is the good. So the pink part is winning." I don't know why he chose the colors he did. Maybe there was some image of a brain in a book or cartoon he'd watched that used pink and brown in the depiction. Google "cartoon brain" and every image is pink. I was white and pink and Jeanine and he were brown. "Now there's only one brown left," and his gaze, distant, inward maybe, and his head pitched forward slightly, and he brought a thumb to his forehead, deep in thought, a breakthrough occurring: "Now the good guys won! They really did! So now I'm going to do good listening for the rest of my life!"

It made sense. The picture he painted, the brain at war with itself. A battle waged and won during a stop-and-start commute home from preschool. If only it were that easy.

He was spared abandonment, illness, Asperger's. Unlike Sarah, he had no bleeding disorders or brushes with death and seeing angels in his dreams that convinced his parents he would die. No parental indifference or addiction. He had two present and loving adults in his home who would always be there. We'd provide for and protect him as best we could from the cruelties and threats of the outside world. Bees were still going to sting, friends were going to kick him in the shins, and accidents would happen, but he knew that at the very least his mother and father would never do him harm.

As for me, there was arrogance in my conviction that I'd be exceptional, not merely good enough. That's what I knew from the start, when his impossibly small fingers wrapped themselves around my index finger. My purpose suddenly and magnificently conceived like some kind of singularity. I was his father.

THREE

THE SEVENTIES

BEFORE

At a certain point, maybe by age nine or ten, the naive little-kid questions I'd asked for years were answered. No, Dad wouldn't marry our mother again even though he'd said he still loved her. I'd finally realized love meant something different for adults. Or for him.

It never occurred to me to ask if I could live with him, nor was it offered. He lived with Nina in their cozy house for two. She was warm and kind. My sisters and I liked her. She was especially tolerant of Dad's bad habits, like the drinking, extreme mood swings, and his harsh tone with her, like when he'd call out to her from another room and we'd watch her rush to him, avoiding eye contact with us because it had to feel demeaning for her, and still she went.

"Nina!"

"Coming! Sheesh."

Always simmering near his surface was rage I'd never glimpsed or felt myself.

They married in 1976 in Manhattan with two friends as witnesses in the carpeted office of someone with proper authority. He wore a dark suit with a red flower on his lapel. Nina looked gorgeous, wore her long, straight brown hair parted in the middle and a scoop-neck white dress and strappy white shoes.

He knew how he had to live. There was no room for a child.

From that 1976 profile for which my sisters and I posed with him during the weekend visit:

> Joe McGinniss is a nice guy and his friends adore him and speak of him with something like reverence. They mention his interest in horse racing and his enthusiasm for country and western music—and his parties. McGinniss shrugs off the parties. "The best party was the final celebration of *Selling of the President*," he said. "It was a legendary party and lasted three days. It took ten days to clean up the house."

The house he's referring to must have been my mother's, on Magill Road, in 1969, a year before my birth.

Where were my sisters during that party? Was my mom at that final celebration, that legendary three-day party? Or was Dad somewhere else, leaving that detail off the page? Was he at the secret house he and Nina rented not long after meeting? Had he lied to Mom and said he had to be in Manhattan for something book-related?

The reality for Dad was the writer-as-rock-star life suited him. A wife and two little girls with another baby on the way did not. His was a project-based life and his name was his brand. He craved action and adulation and the adventure and the unknown, the new horizon. Waking up at seven to change diapers and feed two little girls and push baby carriages to the playground was something he'd never craved.

The adulation of his children and his wife wasn't enough. He needed more, achieved it, and was hooked. Pursuit of that high would always come first. Tempering impulses wasn't a challenge he was willing to engage.

Years later, Gavin and Mason, his sons with Nina, would discover that grim reality for themselves. As would Jayson, my son, not from his grandfather but from me.

The meeting of my parents was a coin toss from never happening at all. St. Luke's nursing school required one month of work at a psychiatric hospital in Hartford. My mother was attending, after an unfulfilling stint as a nineteen-year-old telephone operator.

Her friend set up a blind date for her and a friend, three nursing students and three nineteen-year-olds from Holy Cross College who were visiting Hartford. The first nursing student to descend met her date and headed outside. Then came my mother and her friend, both the same height, who eyed the two boys—a guy named Pee Wee and my father, who was, unsurprisingly, the taller of the two. It was, as she explained, up to the boys to choose. My father won a coin toss and chose Mom.

He spent a year in Worcester writing for the newspaper there. She finished nursing school. It was 1965 and the war in Vietnam escalated. There would be a draft. All single men eighteen years and older were eligible. My parents were twenty-two and twenty-one and in love enough, so they married. They bought Dad time.

They were hardly alone in their reaction to the draft. Wedding mills had popped up all over the country as couples rushed to beat an August 25, 1965, deadline set by President Johnson. There are famous photos of young couples cramming themselves into small chapels in Las Vegas.

The ceremony was traditional Catholic. A white dress and a suit and vows and rings and guests at the church in Pittsfield and they were off. As he described it in *Heroes*: "I loved her so much I thought I would burst. I had always been lonely, and so had she, and now we would not be lonely anymore."

When more men were needed and the rules were changed—married men without children were being drafted—Cynthia was conceived. It wasn't a coincidence.

Five years later Dad was famous and gone. Left behind was my shattered mother with her nursing degree and three young children and a brown station wagon and the house she'd need to pay off.

Unlike his own father, though, Dad craved some amount of bonding with his young children. It was a healthy impulse, but hardly overpowering. I was nine and alone with him, awake in the middle of the night somewhere in Canada.

It was dark and the room shook, bells sounded, steel on steel as the train cut through the darkness on its way to Montreal. I was strapped into the top bunk. Dad slept beneath me. There was nowhere else in the world I'd have rather been. The overnight train in a room of our own, the only two people in the world.

And suddenly I was walking the streets of the gray city: "Look at that!" he exclaimed. "Can you believe it?!"

A huge banner atop the marble steps of a Montreal museum announced: a Tintin comic book exhibition. He insisted it was a happy accident. I'd been obsessed with the comic book boy reporter and his dog, Snowy, and their myriad global adventures since a second-grade book fair. He fed my habit with one brilliantly colorful book after the next until I had them all.

Purely by chance? There was a Tintin exhibit when he and I happened to be in Montreal? Reasons didn't matter. We shared that overnight train and every hour of those few days. Dad and me and no one else. He made it seem so easy. In short bursts, for him, maybe it was.

One hot Saturday afternoon in 1978 he drove from New Jersey and then another hour into Philadelphia and stood with Cynthia hoisted on his shoulders in a sweltering auditorium for hours waiting in line so she could glimpse and finally, sweaty and exhausted, get a signature on a glossy picture of her childhood heartthrob John Travolta.

But he didn't want Cynthia on his shoulders *every day*. He didn't want to drift off to sleep with Sarah or me or both of us next to him *every night*. And none of us understood brain chemistry or genetics or addictions. We knew what children knew: how it felt.

• • •

It would be a Tuesday or Thursday and Mom would be home for less than an hour after ten hours at the hospital and she would smoke a cigarette or two and pour three cans of Campbell's soup over white rice and then Cynthia would follow her to the metallic-green Pontiac and they'd drive to the Main Line for fifty-minute sessions with the same therapist who couldn't keep Dad from leaving. Some nights instead of Cynthia it would be Sarah or me.

I sat in the dimly lit carpeted room of the bushy-haired doctor whose teeth clicked when he spoke. I did some strange puzzles that were kept in olive-green boxes while he watched.

Sometimes I stared at his mouth and tried to figure out how his teeth made that clicking sound when he spoke. Most of the time I effortlessly answered questions that I don't remember.

After a year of sporadic sessions, the appointments stopped. Maybe it was the time commitment or the money or both. Dad never made the trip from New Jersey to make it easier for Mom. He never did put aside even one Thursday a month to stay in the house and take us to therapy.

Maybe he stopped sending money for appointments because he knew my mother always struggled to ask him for help. They spoke cordially every time he dropped us off after weekend visits. He'd stand in the kitchen, drink a beer or politely decline if he wanted to get back. I'd sit on the carpeted stairs out of sight and listen to them talk, not to glean anything but just to figure out when the conversation was wrapping up so I could reappear and hug him once more. When he'd call, my mother spoke in the same humorless tone. His big stories were for Nina now. And Mom didn't want to hear them anymore anyway. He understood.

Alimony was all that was legally agreed to. There was no extra for the house or to let her get off her feet, maybe work fewer middle shifts and weekends.

He wasn't seeing a therapist then, either, as far as I knew. He jogged and drank and had Nina, which was apparently enough. Though he wrote in *Heroes* about his belief in genetic predispositions and the benefits of cognitive therapy and Freud and Jung and psychiatry, he had his own life under control. Or knew well enough how to respond when he lost control.

He knew firsthand from his parents what addiction and depression looked like. He knew the damage they could do to a child. His mother made efforts and they were extreme and traumatized him. Her hospitalizations to get happy. How helpless he felt watching his mother driven away, time and again. Then those weeks alone with his quiet, aloof father.

And later, when she remained depressed, morose, fatalistic, and drunk, all those years later, how could he not wonder: What was the point? She spent most of her adult life in and out of therapy and hospitals and to what end? She tried, though. Effort was made. Clearly not enough, but it was something. She had a husband who insisted she try.

He wrote about it in one book, but rarely talked about his mother's affliction. Was she on antidepressants? When and how did she stop drinking? Did he talk to her about his own addictions? He may have shared this with someone, but never me.

But he also knew, as I did, some amount of therapy and self-reflection and even tinkering with our brain chemistry was required of anyone in our gene pool if something better than what came before was going to be achieved. He knew that the work of overcoming addiction and depression, or managing them, wasn't just something you did when things were bad.

He knew the effort needed to be ongoing, in good times, too. But in his thirties, famous and newly married to someone who understood what had to come first for him, he was convinced he could manage on his own. Was drinking a problem? Only if it interfered with his work or parenting. He was convinced it didn't. Was he depressed? About leaving his children and wife behind, yes. About his own lonely, painful childhood, likely so. But when the demons were quiet, life was grand. He was free and high, writing and drinking and fucking, sleeping it off, starting slow, revving up and repeating. He was sure he had it all figured out. Or at least achieved an equilibrium that left him in charge, living the life he deserved.

Though Dad chose distance from us, his mother wanted to be close by. She adored her grandchildren. And Dad appreciated the lack of immediate responsibility for his aging, alcoholic mother. As much as she was close by, she was still alone and lonely. There was a long red sofa in the lobby of the Wildman Arms apartments in Swarthmore that could seat a few people comfortably, or one adult woman if she chose to lay down, drift off after a few afternoon cocktails, as my grandmother tended to do.

The building stood twelve stories high with units overlooking Crum Creek. My grandmother moved down from Rye when the house on Green Acres Drive became too much for her to manage alone. A choice was made, with some encouragement likely from Dad, to live close to her grandchildren. It was best for everyone, but mostly him.

My sisters and mother and I would visit her on Sundays and sometimes have dinner or just spend a few quiet afternoon hours. We'd check all the usual porcelain dishes and bowls for candy. Cynthia and Sarah played with her makeup, and she'd sometimes have newspaper or magazine stories she'd clipped for Dad, but would give to Mom in his absence.

She'd slip us five- or ten-dollar bills on our way out and always held our faces in her soft, warm hands when she kissed us goodbye. I hated looking back at her alone on the sofa as we left because she couldn't mask her loneliness and would sigh and deflate as we closed the door behind us. She missed her son, Dad, most of all.

One afternoon a boy I knew from school was with a friend of his when he asked, suppressing laughter: "Does your grandmother live in Wildman Arms?"

I told them she did.

They looked at each other and laughed.

"She loves you, man! I mean a lot!"

When I asked they told me about a shoeless old woman, my grandmother, lying on the lobby couch in the middle of the afternoon asking them if they knew me.

She'd been dropped off by the van that took residents to lunch at the Towne House restaurant in Media, where she'd drink martinis and need help getting back in the same van that took her home and she'd stop at that red couch and sit, slouch, then finally lie there alone for hours.

When it was clear she could no longer safely live alone, Dad moved her to a Vermont nursing home forty-five minutes away from his new Williamstown, Massachusetts, home instead of the one down the street.

He'd moved again, too. And I don't recall conversations about it. I don't remember feeling sad or wondering why. Dad wasn't there, so what difference did it make if he was ninety minutes or six hours away? We weren't consulted. He didn't ask, he explained. We were older and the flight was direct and under an hour from Philadelphia to Albany, then a one-hour drive to the house in Williamstown. We could visit as often as we wanted. Stay for weeks in the summer. He was excited. I was indifferent, numbed to his explanations. Rather than move closer for our teenage years, he bought a house in a town to which he had no prior connection. He was happy. He was living the life he'd wanted. Farther from us than ever. But did we really want him back in town? To hear tired excuses from him about why he couldn't have us over or watch us play a basketball game or rebound missed shots? To see him drink every night? To snap or explode at Nina? Or argue with our mother about why he couldn't do more?

Too many nights like that and there'd be no telling who I'd become.

FOUR

2014

AFTER

The best part of every day: weekday afternoons. Grab a juice box, a snack, Goldfish crackers, a couple of apple sauce pouches, scramble for some cash in case the ice cream truck comes, his basketball if he forgot it.

Jayson was eight and a hybrid point guard in the mold of Steph Curry, his basketball idol, whom he resembled to the point that his nickname among the older kids at school became "Little Curry." In the mornings, when he got dressed for school, he'd announce that he was going "full Warriors" and don the jersey and shorts and socks and backpack that, yes, were all my doing. How could I resist?

When he took a shot on the nine-foot hoop outside after school, he held the follow-through, like I showed him, and make or miss, his brown eyes darted to find mine every time. "You don't need to look at me, Jayson," I wanted to tell him. But not really, not yet. "You're doing great," I'd say instead, or give a thumbs-up, a smile I couldn't contain.

· · ·

"Can you stay?" his small voice asked from the top bunk in his cozy, blue-walled bedroom in the Spring Valley house we rented in Washington, DC. I placed the worn copy of Where the Sidewalk Ends ("Hungry Mungry and The Worst" and "Sarah Cynthia Sylvia Stout Would Not Take the Garbage Out") on the shelf near the head of his bed and turned on a CD of Senegalese lullabies Cynthia had given me and lowered the volume and turned on his moonlight that hung on the wall.

"Of course," I answered, always. The best part of every night.

And I'd listen to him whisper to himself, lines from stories we'd read and he'd sigh, content, and his breathing slowed as he drifted off and I'd exhale, too, on the bottom bunk as Jayson slept. I could have lain there forever, six inches off the carpeted floor of a rented house, my son dreaming, floating three feet above me.

Leave this boy and see what happens, I'd tell myself some nights. I'd let myself imagine telling him why I wasn't there when he woke up. Why I left. Why I wouldn't be there to read him stories every night. I would tell him I still loved his mom. I'd tell him I loved him more than anything in the world. I'd see the tears streaming down his little brown cheeks and hug him so tight and then let go, get into the car and drive away. I'd glimpse him in the rearview mirror, standing helpless, crying and confused. And then again, and again. Visit after visit, over and over.

What would that do to him? I wondered. Who would he become? That was a power I possessed, and it made me uneasy. All he knew from me was nurturing and safety and laughter and comfort. I could bring it all crashing down tomorrow.

How broken would I have to be to inflict that kind of pain, to see him in the rearview and not circle back? To adjust and with his mother find a middle ground? I could move out, but only a few blocks or minutes away. I could spend nearly as much time with him because it was important.

I'd never found an answer to the same question about Dad, why he didn't find it essential to be close, to cause less pain.

But most nights I wouldn't think like that. Instead, I'd fall asleep peacefully and wake up not long after sunrise and watch him start his day, his little bare feet descending the ladder from the top bunk or sometimes an eager leap to the carpeted floor. Thump! The expanse of a single day, an open-ended adventure in this golden age of our charmed life and I was there for it.

I was testing myself and passing with flying colors. I was not just like my father. I was in charge. I could make it what I wanted. Jayson and me. All I had in life was what I wanted to do. Lying on the bottom bunk, Jayson dreaming his little-boy dreams. That was it. That was everything.

Another parent asked me on the playground after school one day if I had any interest in coaching a basketball team. They'd had one in prior years and were looking to resurrect it. I asked Jayson if he'd want to play on a team if I coached it. He didn't hesitate.

None of the kids really knew the game. Some kept their hands in their pockets; some wandered to the bleachers to eat sandwiches between quarters and others threw hook passes to themselves or fell to the ground after every shot.

But a picture snapped by Jeanine during one of our first practices: a handful of second-grade Lobos gathered around me, the coach, down on one knee. Jayson with his little arm resting across my shoulders, laying claim.

We lost every game, badly. Which didn't matter. They voted on a team name, the Lobos beating out the Mutant Space Dragons. We were just getting started. We were building something. I wasn't going anywhere.

The easiest part about coaching second graders was that they were supposed to be terrible. And they were. And it was beautiful. And we laughed about the sandwich breaks and the opposing team from a Catholic school whose parents were barking at the teenage referees about missed calls or double dribbles. And billionaire Capital One founder Rich Fairbank coaching opposite, bellowing defensive schemes and play calls through a plastic bullhorn, the bag of brand-new composite leather basketballs behind him. The echoes of whistles and shrieking kids and terrible acoustics and Jayson dribbling through defenders had me more juiced than I thought I'd be or should have been. We lost badly to the Catholics and the billionaire boys and everyone else.

We improved a little bit each week. We stopped wearing pants and passing to ourselves. And my mind raced. Third grade would be different. We'd figure out how to practice more between games. We'd learn how to pass, defend, and make a layup. I brainstormed basic offensive sets that a third grader might understand. And Jayson was too good to lose this badly. If he were a little better, they wouldn't lose so much. I saw a path forward: the Lobos would march on, and Jayson would lead them.

FIVE

1983

BEFORE

He hadn't invited me. But I'd spent three fun weeks in Williamstown that summer walking across the street from Dad's house to the private K–9 school for day camp and made some friends when it occurred to me that I could stay. I asked and without a whole lot of hesitation that I can recall, he'd said yes.

He was thriving then. He had a big new book and a two-year-old son with Nina, and my sisters and I were progressing as adolescents did, three teenagers sharing one bathroom and one full-time working parent and one car.

Only real emergencies required Dad to change his routine. If I got thrown into the sharp corner of wall during some hallway horseplay and suffered a bloody concussion at school? Mom could call a neighbor from work to pick me up and keep an eye on me. Sarah wiped out on her bike and was a bloody mess? Her sister and brother could get her home and grab a neighbor and clean her wounds while we waited for Mom to get home from work. Dad would be briefed on the phone later, when the worst was behind us, when Mom had gotten everything under control. It was an ideal arrangement for him.

When I came to stay, he was nearing forty and verging again on publishing stardom and giving parenting another try. He'd be present for his new son with Nina and wouldn't just do better than his father had with him, but better than he had for my sisters and me. I wanted a piece of that, to see what that felt like—Dad trying harder for me.

Mom was crying when she put me on a one-way US Airways flight from Philadelphia to Albany, New York, the last week of August. They let her board the plane and say goodbye. I wore a red-and-white US Air button to signify my status as a child traveling alone.

I remember arriving and seeing the familiar small collection of upstate New York locals and mopes gathered at gate 2A of the Albany airport waiting for their people. Among them stood Dad: taller than the rest. His dark hair and tight lips, beaming at the sight of his soon-to-be thirteen-year-old son. He wore loose khakis and running shoes and a faded polo shirt and hugged me tight, like always. It felt different, though. I was there to stay. And he was there to parent me as best he could.

Maybe he saw my arrival as predictable and overdue; of course I'd sought him out. A son needed a father, or at least to know him, what kind of man he was. Not the weekend version, but the Tuesday-afternoon-in-February man, when the winter was punishing, the words weren't flowing, the reviews sucked, and the publishers weren't happy and the twelve-year-old boy was suddenly there every day, needing guidance and support and reassurance and structure. A parent who was an example. A stable, dependable adult who would always put the needs of his child ahead of his own.

It's hard not to wonder now, all these years later: Did I have him at his best? Did I somehow corral him at the pinnacle of his parenting potential? He was arguably at the peak of his adult life. He was waking early, seven or seven thirty, and filling the woodstove and maybe grabbing a quick run and writing all day and talking and laughing and singing to his new son, Mason, and teaching and seemingly sleeping soundly at night.

On its face, his life was idyllic when I arrived. His neighbors were professors from the college who lived steps away and there was Sunday morning volleyball on a makeshift grass court and long summer afternoons reading the *Times* and the *Globe* and listening to Springsteen and Dylan records and barbecues and playdates for Mason.

He taught a class thirty minutes north up Route 7 in Bennington, Vermont, where he was dissecting Didion and Wolfe and Capote for his students, among them Bret Easton Ellis and Donna Tartt and Jonathan Lethem and Jill Eisenstadt.

He'd spend office hours showing them what he saw in their work, taking Jill's vignettes about her Rockaway life and arranging the pages on the carpeted floor: "If you put this first and move this and lose that and add this. See . . . then it builds and there's narrative structure and you have a novel!"

At one point, a letter arrived in the mail from one of his students. Donna Tartt wrote to thank him for being the first reader of her debut novel. It was set at a small New England college. He was blown away by the work. She was calling it *The Secret History* and he was pretty sure it would be huge. He'd pored over her manuscript and offered myriad notes and a ringing endorsement.

Bret's bloated, meandering, coke-fueled winter-break project originally titled *Beyond Belief* (copies of which I found among piles of loose papers in my father's basement decades later) was transformed with my dad's help into *Less Than Zero*. Dad showed it to his agent, and it was published not long after. Bret, in turn, dedicated the book to him.

But even Dad at his best needed that drink. I lay awake during my first months there having conversations with him in my mind, the ones where I'd persuade him to drink less, then not at all.

• • •

I read in *Heroes* about his parents and their drinking and sadness and his lonely childhood and his doomed fate—he'd be just like them. Unless, maybe, he could outrun it. I was there in his house, finally, trying to keep up.

I'd deflate as he drank. I'd eat fast and ask to be excused because the alternative, watching him drink, made me sad. Some nights I couldn't control myself and would exhale or say something under my breath.

"Pardon me?"

"Enough," I said.

"Enough?"

"You've already had a whole bottle of wine," I managed.

"Nina's had some."

"A glass."

"Two," she said.

"And before the wine? Do you have to drink so much every night?"

"No," he said. "I don't need to drink. I enjoy it." He was rational and reasonable in his explanation.

His drinking wasn't an impediment to living a happy life. It didn't prevent him from being a loving father every day to Mason, and to me since I'd arrived. If his drinking ever interfered with his life, he promised he'd take a hard look at it.

"So," he reminded me, "emptying bottles of gin down the kitchen sink is neither helpful nor necessary."

His house at 42 South Street was built in 1820 and used to be an inn. It had five upstairs bedrooms connected by closets in the rear of each room so maids could pass through unseen by guests. The only hints at his rock star life in New Jersey was the single rolled joint I'd found snooping through his dresser and the racy Polaroids of Nina in the bottom of a carry-on bag deep in the closet. The 4,200 square feet of the new house nearly tripled the space of my mom's house. Three and a half bathrooms, one for Dad and Nina and one each for Mason and me.

There was room at the inn for more, but it was only Dad and

Nina and Mason—who was displaying unusual, if not unsettling, intelligence—and Lucy, the golden retriever rescue, and some cats and then, suddenly, me.

Through my upstairs bedroom window, instead of dark shadows and would-be home intruders coming to rob Mom's house for the third time, and the turnpike and bright white glow of the Mobil gas station sign, I gazed out over the expansive backyard with the English garden and a carriage house that was occasionally rented out to a student or vising professor from the college. If I stayed long enough, maybe I'd transition there, have a house to myself.

Lucy slept in my room and followed me everywhere, even across the street to school, where sometimes she'd wander the halls looking for me. If she wasn't with me, she'd walk a mile or so across the Williams College campus to the main street in town and hang out with students and strangers all day and eat sandwich scraps, steal tummy rubs, and wander back home around three or four when she knew I'd be home or out on the field after school playing ultimate frisbee and she'd hang out there and we'd walk home together. This was a picture that surely brought my father peace, me and my dog in this idyllic setting, making new friends, turning thirteen. He never had so many friends. He never had a dog.

It didn't occur to me then that letting Lucy roam the town all day was both irresponsible and dangerous. She could have strayed too far, eaten something toxic, been hit by a car or dognapped (as she eventually was, just after I left, by an actor named Kiefer Sutherland). But we had a lot on our minds. Dad was preparing for his career relaunch, and I was a seventh grader in a new school with a new life.

Lucy's free-range existence was one more indicator of Dad's approach to life and those closest to him. For him, everything he did seemed an extended reaction to his emotionally suffocating childhood. When his mother was lying on the couch with "the blues," or naked and drunk on her bed with the door open, or being hospitalized to "get happy," she was convinced the worst would happen to him if he left her sight.

He'd been forced to endure his childhood, face intractable dysfunction every lonely day for eighteen years. As a child, he couldn't begin to solve his parents' problems. No child could. Who could blame him for craving new horizons? There were no passed-out mothers on couches or aloof disappearing fathers on the open road or the racetracks.

Running and freedom and action became his priority and an instinct he would embrace and a skill he would master. Hitchhiking to the Kentucky Derby in high school, or later, across the country in college during a competition with classmates to see who could get the farthest west from the Worcester, Massachusetts, campus of Holy Cross before the end of spring break. When Dad heard Vin Scully calling a Dodgers game on the radio, he knew he'd won.

And when the instinct to run returns later, when he's older and not a child? And it isn't a parent's mental illness pushing him away but a loving wife's desire to have him home, with his beautiful little girls who naturally adore him? Four years of marriage and three years of parenting was the limit. Perseverance, domestically at least, was a finite skill for Dad, and he'd used most of his surviving his childhood.

Later, with Nina and their two sons, distance and freedom, both geographic and emotional, remained a priority. There was, in retrospect, a striking similarity between the way Dad tended to Lucy and the way he parented Mason and Gavin.

The family had money and time. There were no challenges they couldn't spend their way out of. Lucy could be let out in the morning to roam, and she'd return when she chose, usually by dinnertime.

His sons, like Lucy, could do as they wished. Mason wouldn't poop. They didn't make him. Mason wouldn't call them Mom and Dad. They didn't correct him. Mason wouldn't speak. "He'll talk to us when he wants to."

Maybe Nina asked for more. Or maybe she felt like she was getting all she needed. Though I never heard her demand more or different from Dad. They'd figured out what worked for them, and most importantly, for Dad.

A magazine cover story heralded my dad's return to publishing prominence: "Rising from the Ashes of Fame."

Fatal Vision was the book, and it was going to be big.

It told a story that began on the frigid, rainy night of February 17, 1970. Twenty-six-year-old Princeton-educated US Army Special Forces Green Beret surgeon Jeffrey MacDonald murdered his pregnant wife and two daughters, ages five and two. His wife, Colette, had been bludgeoned, both forearms fractured and stabbed twenty-one times in the chest with an ice pick and sixteen times in the neck with a knife. His daughter Kimberly was bludgeoned around the head and stabbed multiple times with a knife. His two-year-old daughter, Kristen, was stabbed thirty-three times with a knife and sixteen times with an ice pick. MacDonald only suffered multiple superficial stab wounds from a knife in his chest.

The word "PIG" was scrawled in blood on the headboard of MacDonald's bed. Found near the living room couch where MacDonald had fallen asleep: a copy of *Esquire* magazine with a story about the recent Manson murders in which drug-fueled hippies committed gruesome murders and had scrawled the word "Pig" on the front door of victim Sharon Tate's home. MacDonald told investigators that a group of drugged-out hippies stormed into his home and murdered his wife and little girls using knives and rubber gloves, not that they brought with them but found under the sink in his kitchen. The knife and ice pick that belonged to MacDonald and were used to kill his family were found in the backyard the next morning, somehow all wiped clean of fingerprints by the drugged-out hippies.

An army investigation of the crimes committed in MacDonald's Fort Bragg residence cleared him of the charges. He moved to Southern California and started a new life. He'd gained notoriety and appeared on *The Dick Cavett Show* during which he exaggerated the wounds he'd received. Colette's father was so disgusted by MacDonald's demeanor that he pursued the case. He learned that MacDonald, prior to the murders, had been having multiple affairs as well as consuming copious amounts of a dangerous, since recalled, amphetamine called Eskatrol.

Over the course of nine years, Colette's father doggedly sought to reopen the case. As a result, MacDonald faced another trial, this time in a civilian court, for the murders.

Dad learned about the story not long after he and Nina made a temporary move to Los Angeles, where he would write a column for the *Los Angeles Herald Examiner* in the summer of 1979, the same summer he'd flown my sisters and me out from Swarthmore to spend a few weeks in his Woodland Hills rental. While there, he'd come across a newspaper piece about a disco party that local police association friends of a man called Jeffrey MacDonald were throwing to raise money for his legal fee for an impending criminal trial.

He called MacDonald and they met the next day. MacDonald was living in an oceanside condo in Huntington Beach and had bought a yacht and convertible and was petitioning big-name authors to write about his impending case. He'd wanted Robert Redford to portray him in the movie. He'd had a deal with the writer Joseph Wambaugh, but that fell apart when MacDonald insisted on a share of the book profits. My father, however, agreed to the arrangement and after three consecutive commercial flops, my dad had his next book.

I'd spent so many sleepless nights at my mother's house, peering into the darkness of the backyard, sure I'd spot someone lurking, approaching. At Dad's there was nothing to fear. There were no break-ins or robberies in Williamstown. There was only calm and routine and quiet. Crisp September nights and I'd lie on my bed and exhale in the stillness of the house.

Dad kept the doors to the house unlocked and the keys to the car in the ignition. I'd open my bedroom window at night before the winter cold set in and drift off to the sounds of crickets and the breeze and slept as soundly as I had in years, Lucy at my feet. His house was a refuge from a certain kind of fear.

But a familiar feeling emerged, subtle but unsettling: the sense that my presence was welcome and accepted, but not essential. I felt like, as I had with Mom and my sisters, something other than central. I was two people, yet not whole. With mom and my sisters, I was the teenage boy, a stand-in for the man who'd devastated them. How could they not see him when they looked at me? And treat me accordingly, even subconsciously? And with Dad, I was the son who sought the father, not the other way around. Wanting versus being wanted. That distinction is everything when you're a child. Formative even.

At Dad's there were no high school stoners or choppers tearing down the backyard turnpike. I didn't have to wrap my pillow around my head to drown out the sounds of Cynthia in the upstairs bathroom. There was no tiptoeing around my mom after work because she needed a minute, just walked in the door, was on her feet all day, could she have a cigarette or two and some time to breathe, get out of her uniform, sit down for a bit? Maybe she'd glance at the newspaper, then figure out dinner. She was alone in it, the three of us and her, every responsibility her own.

My homework had to get done and the dinner table had to be set and the meal had to be prepared and dentist appointments had to be kept and after-school tennis and baseball and basketball and chorus and therapy on Thursday nights forty minutes each way in rush hour traffic and the lawn needed mowing and there was no gas so walk across the turnpike to fill the gallon can at the Mobil station and the leaves needed raking and the car needed new tires and the house needed a new roof. And all of that cost money she didn't have and required one more uncomfortable conversation with my dad because he waited to be asked rather than make it easier for Mom. And Mom made the calls and detailed the costs of us: Cynthia's braces and Sarah's class trip to Williamsburg and my basketball camp. That was as hard as it got for him: listening to the list of expenses for which he'd painlessly send a check.

And finally, to bed for all of us after the teeth brushing and baths or showers and the next morning were we all awake and dressed? And breakfast eaten? And cats fed? And who was taking which bus? And who was getting a ride? And who was doing what after school and my mom was working middle that night so I'd have a babysitter and could order pizza and she'd call if she could before I went to bed.

Dad might or might not call. And if the phone rang and I picked up, I'd know after a sentence or two whether I'd listen to him any longer or hold the phone away from my ear, because what was the point when he'd been drinking? It was all so slow and exaggerated and depressing.

I left all that behind for a seat at his dinner table.

He knew something about everything. I was scared of nuclear war and Reagan sucked and politics mattered and I asked him about candidates at the dinner table and he could tell me who was good, who was a fraud, who could win. I liked Hart and Jackson. He liked Cranston, but thought Hart had a shot. I timed my queries between updates to Nina about MacDonald and the attorneys and motions and appeals and Putnam and Dell and agents and next books. I also knew I had to ask my questions before the second bottle of wine.

Once he'd opened and worked halfway through it, I'd stare at his glassy eyes and distant gaze and watch him sigh and exhale and he'd slouch and sound like his mother and I wondered how he seemed more exhausted than my mom ever had.

The next morning, though, every morning, I'd come out of my bedroom and stop in my tracks in the upstairs hallway when I heard it: the typing. Dad. Rapid-fire, almost manic. A machine-gun discharge of clicks and dings and zips, a finished page, a blank one rolled and locked in, more clicks and dings. A mid-page or mid-sentence pause. Silence. The torrent of thoughts and ideas and arguments and facts and questions and conclusions suddenly stopped. The wooden floor creaked beneath my feet. Not another step or he'd hear me, maybe get up and open the door and find me standing there like a fool. Like I was eavesdropping. Because I was.

But he never heard me. He sat at his wooden desk shifting in his chair, exhaling through his nose, reading, considering, deciding, then another shift and a few clicks and clacks and another short pause, then some more typing, and then the rush of words and the hum of my father's vocation, his calling, his creation of something from nothing resumed, his reason for living and leaving.

This was the first sound I heard nearly every day with him, a force of nature he could barely tame, even at his peak. What I heard was the decision he'd made long ago, the priority he'd set above all.

My new classmates rode buses down from Vermont or over from North Adams because their parents had decided the public schools where they lived weren't good enough and they could afford better. Everyone skied or played soccer or field hockey or lacrosse and wore the same sweaters and jackets and hats and boots and gloves. And they all liked the Police and Duran Duran and some liked Prince and Michael Jackson. They were all white and friendly and fun and I fit in until the first snow and everyone got excited because it meant five months of downhill and ice-skating. I had no interest. I only wanted three things: an indoor basketball court, something the school didn't have; a girlfriend; and for Dad to drink less.

On weekend mornings he'd pace the kitchen in thick wool socks and khakis and a flannel shirt. He'd announce for anyone within earshot the readings from the barometer he'd attached outside the kitchen window—dropping meant rain was coming. He was enthralled by the technology.

He'd turn on NPR or classical music, ask about my plans for the day, and rarely stand still for too long. His restless mind kept him moving, starting a conversation but completing it as he moved through a doorway, then back and then out and then back in again until, finally, he was released, and left the room to be with his thoughts, turn them into action, words, the book, scale that mountain, then another. He simply couldn't stay still for a conversation unless it was a subject he'd brought up.

I wanted him to stand still, but never asked. Maybe because he found it in him to sit still long enough with me, playing role-playing dice games and watching *Magnum, P.I.* or *The White Shadow* with me. If he was too wound up to stay in the same room for a conversation, that was a quirk, a glitch, a tell—the manic mind of Dad the creator whose mind simply never slowed, until later, when the day was done and it was time for the first pour of iced gin. He'd remove a bottle from the freezer and fill a clear blue glass with ice and a slice of lime and dip his index finger into it and stir and suck it dry. Finally, his mind slowed.

He'd read aloud to Nina from some item in the *Times* he'd found interesting, and she'd respond because she was interested or needed to pretend she was. That seemed like part of the deal they'd struck. The only edge in his voice would come with her, when he'd snap at her for not understanding what he was saying, or if he had to reread something he'd found interesting and she wasn't paying close enough attention, feeding Mason or putting groceries away or just needing a break from him.

He was the creator and mastermind and earner, and she was the agreeable support system, echoing, rarely if ever challenging, editing, child-rearing. She was unflappable and seemed to possess extreme tolerance for his bad behavior, which at the time, verging on stardom and riches once again, wasn't the worst arrangement.

But those were the good times, if not the best. What would happen if things turned, as they often did?

Not long before my arrival, Dad spent a summer living with Jeffrey MacDonald in Raleigh, North Carolina, during his murder trial. Every waking minute on the job, observing and engaging and jogging and eating and plotting a defense with attorneys and the defendant. That was the deal. He paid for that access.

While in Raleigh, he walked through the cramped, stuffy Fort Bragg murder scene alone, where everything remained as it was found on that cold, rainy horrific February night in 1970. The coffee table was still overturned. The copy of *Esquire* with the story about the Charles Manson murders. The blood-drenched mattresses. He saw the photographs of the two little girls, bright and glowing like his own daughters, and then their bloody sheets and bloodstained carpet, their lungs and throats punctured dozens of times with an ice pick, their little fingers sliced—defensive wounds. He was plagued by nightmares for months.

Maybe that's where his mind went on some of those hushed inebriated nights. He wrote about the nightmares, but never mentioned them to me. And maybe he sensed my gaze or the way I tensed up each time he brought his glass to his lips. I could have been there or not. It was another winter weeknight in Williamstown and another marathon day at the typewriter looming.

Most nights, after leaving him downstairs instead of finishing homework, I sat in my bedroom on the phone. I struggled with Latin and math and science and history and English. My new school had a lot of homework, and I wasn't doing most of it and wasn't sure why. I read *Time* magazine and *Black Beat* and *Cracked* magazine and *Sports Illustrated* instead of *A Separate Peace* and my US history textbook. I stole a library book about John F. Kennedy and ripped a portrait of him from the back and taped it to my wall. Dad saw it and told me: "Bobby, his brother, might be someone you'd appreciate more, given your concern for civil rights and racial issues." And he showed me a brushed-silver framed black-and-white picture of Bobby, signed to my father by Ethel, his widow. "She sent this not long after he was assassinated."

There was a world beyond Magill Road and South Street in Williamstown and my own thirteen-year-old ideas about right and wrong and pain and healing and girls and love and longing. My father was offering breadcrumbs and clues, markers on the winding path that I could heed or not. It was something, maybe enough, or not, but more than I'd have gotten had I not followed my instinct and moved there. And it made the nights with him, fading away in front of me, until I left him alone at the dinner table because I just couldn't take it anymore, almost worth it.

The bedroom windows rattled in the bitter winter wind, and I turned off the lights and in the moonlight that poured in I found NBA star George Gervin sitting on a throne of ice and he was smiling with a self-confidence I couldn't imagine ever feeling.

Maybe I should have had the confidence that came with the decision to move there, to leave what I knew and what was comfortable for a new school and new friends and my father, every day, finally.

But I also knew I'd been running away. That was always my little secret. In Philadelphia, I was sleepless in the same room where Dad wrote his first book. Faced with monumental challenges—for him, marriage and parenting, and for me, high school—I lay awake trembling instead of sleeping. I ran away to the very man who knew all about running away.

There was a loose, easy rhythm to life and aside from feeding Lucy, I did as I pleased.

I was grateful that Dad let me park myself in front of the TV with a Pepsi Free and a bag of Lay's and play video games for hours after school until he'd come down from his office make himself a drink and ask Nina about dinner. I still wondered why there was different wallpaper in every room and why the ratty red lounge chair made its way up from New Jersey.

Dad asked me about homework at dinner. I'd done none of it yet because I'd stuck around after school kissing Katie in the stairwell behind the auditorium stage. She played field hockey and lived in Manchester, Vermont. Instead of finishing homework in my room, I'd stay on the phone with her for hours. The phone bills were in the hundreds. I'd play the Michael Jackson song "Human Nature" on a loop and switch the receiver from my hot ear to the cool side and back again. She told me what a WASP was and that she was one. She asked what I was and I told her my father was Irish and my mother was Italian, though I wasn't entirely sure. Why did it matter? It didn't, she said. There would be long silences and I'd wonder why she was talking to me and kissing me and caring about me.

She'd suddenly say my name. I'd ask her, "What?" Then nothing. More silence, and that was how calls were with Katie.

There was Leila, whose dead father had been the Shah of Iran. She lived about five houses up South Street and had armed bodyguards who were always lurking when I'd go over after school. We listened to Def Leppard instead of Michael Jackson, because, she told me, he was gay. She wanted a nose job and I lied and told her she didn't need one. Her gorgeous older sister would drift through an upstairs living room in their massive estate and a trail of sweet perfume would linger. Leila and I each had larger-than-life fathers neither of us talked about. Only, mine was alive.

And Beth from North Adams, who called me "Joey" and her "little brother" and was theatrical and dramatic and busty for an eighth grader and liked a sulky boy named Peter, who didn't like her back.

And Melanie and Shannon and Mitzi and Patti. It was ridiculous. It was always about a girl. Only she could make me feel worthwhile.

I spent most nights on the phone with New Edition or Sugarhill Gang cassettes playing on my Panasonic boom box and weaving colorful fat shoelaces through the eyeholes of my new Adidas Forums. I was as much of a stranger to myself as my dad was to me.

When Dad mentioned my struggles with math, I told him I had something that might help. I produced a *Math for Dummies*–style book I'd ordered from the back of a *Cracked* magazine that promised to unlock all the mystery and confusion around quadratic and algebraic equations.

I handed him the softback glossy volume. I loved the way it smelled.

I'd mostly just open the pages and stick my nose deep in it and inhale and then marvel at the clean, clear boxes and the bold lettering of the word that appeared at the bottom of every page like some kind of cheat code: "Solution." It was all so easy.

He held the book at arm's length, peering down at the cover. I said it couldn't hurt.

He pointed out the cover: "They misspelled 'mathematics'!" He laughed and handed it back. I sank. I was sure I'd solved something, discovered a secret shortcut through the confounding thicket of numbers and letters and symbols. There was nothing malicious in his reaction. He was amused and didn't hide it. He was laughing at the publisher of the book more than me, his corner-cutting son.

He reminded me that if I wanted a math tutor, that was certainly something that could be arranged.

But he didn't insist, and I knew he wouldn't, and didn't mind at all. I was capable of more and was badly underperforming, barely meeting the expectations of a child with what I was told was a superior IQ. Easy enough would have been a tutor from Williams College and a new after-school schedule with homework at the dining room table that he could look over with me until I got back on track.

We were both home every afternoon. There was time. There was money. But it never happened.

"A little less time on the phone and a little more time on your homework," was as stern as he got with me.

He'd done enough damage, he may have decided. He wasn't going to criticize or condemn or raise his voice or punish me for some crappy grades. They were partially his fault, after all. He'd screwed us up from the start. Hardships were inevitable.

Or maybe, less charitably, and knowing now what I didn't then, having witnessed the experiences of Mason and Gavin: the part of parenting that required the work of consistent attention and energy, engagement and sacrifice, held little appeal for him.

Or maybe he was trying. Those hours spent with me at the kitchen table on a rainy Saturday afternoon playing Top Secret or Mr. President, and when the skies cleared heading outside for another seven innings of Wiffle Ball. Maybe that was the best he could do and it was pretty fantastic and more than he'd ever enjoyed with his own father and how good did I have it? What was I complaining about?

Fatal Vision weighed in at a hefty 663 pages, the longest book of his career. The back of the hardcover is a large black-and-white author photo set against the rich blue jacket. Nina took the picture. I'm sure they discussed it. His expression is suitably understated, no smile. Mere flecks of gray on the sides of his lustrous neatly combed and parted brown hair. No wrinkles, creases, or other signs of aging on his face. Until I looked closer. And then I noticed it: the shadow play in the picture. Half his face in soft gray light and the rest concealed in shadow. The two sides. Even then, peaking, the darkness loomed.

It was 1983 and NBC signed on to make a television miniseries based on the book. His next book contract would be massive. The eyes of the publishing world were upon him once again.

After a fourteen-year hiatus, selling his small New Jersey house to stay afloat, renting until the Williamstown move, an advance for *Fatal Vision* he couldn't touch because the first publisher dropped the book and the second paid him less, so he *owed* money while he worked, he was back on top. He received $495,000 ($1.5 million adjusted for inflation) for the paperback rights. The first installment of the television series would be watched by sixty million Americans on a Sunday night in 1984.

For all the money Dad was earning, he didn't feel compelled to circle back to my mom. One phone call to the bank and he could have paid off her mortgage. She would have resisted, but relented. She earned her nurse's salary and no more. They were divorced and the agreement of alimony until my sisters and I turned eighteen was never amended.

To do anything else, provide something more substantial in lieu of his new circumstances, would have begged another impossible question: How much money would make up for the pain inflicted? Wouldn't throwing money at her, at us, be unseemly? It was easier not to start.

There was a doctor in town who my father started seeing. Richard Dreyfuss was also a patient. My father said the doctor provided whatever Dreyfuss needed to keep him "on" during summer performances.

The doctor told my father he must get tense and that must interfere with his work and some Valium would help take the edge off. Dad, the high-functioning alcoholic, followed his advice and had his first highly addictive benzodiazepine prescription filled.

"He is a prisoner of his disorder and what he really needs and will never get is hospitalization."

That's what my father wrote about Jeffrey MacDonald in 1983. The biographical similarities between the two men were striking. Both my dad and MacDonald had been twenty-six-year-old married fathers with two little girls and a son on the way. When the pressure became too much to bear, my father left. MacDonald stayed, then snapped and murdered them all.

As with MacDonald, it became clear to my sisters and me and everyone who loved and cared so deeply about Dad that he was also "a prisoner of his disorder."

Both men carried within them emotional fractures and compulsions that went unaddressed. Each possessed deep emotional voids they'd hoped another person might fill.

As my father wrote in *Heroes* about my mother: "She thought I was wonderful, and she wanted to help me become a great writer. I loved her so much I thought I would burst. I had always been lonely, and so had she, and now we would not be lonely anymore."

When their demons weren't quieted by attaching to another person and starting families, their reactions were extreme. MacDonald, the sociopath, directed his rage outward and murdered his family.

The empath, my father, simply drank, then walked away and drank some more. Neither consistently devoted time or energy to helping themselves. They were ruled by their instincts.

Nina told my sisters and me that no matter how perilous his condition, Dad would never allow himself to be hospitalized like his mother.

He'd been an emotional orphan at nine and ten and every year that followed and every other time his mother went away. And again, every time his father left for weekends to drink in motel rooms. Yet he concluded that psychiatry and psychology and talking about feelings and remorse and his miserable childhood and his addictions and compulsions was too much work for too little reward. He knew the pain, sacrifice, and futility of it all and, unlike his parents, was doing just fine.

His achy knees didn't let him jog anymore, so he'd walk and often end up at Jerry's Liquors on Spring Street and then the pharmacy two doors down, to grab whatever would help him sleep or take the edge off or get him going or quiet the voices or steady the hands or ease the pain. He had it under control.

The drinking and Valium and Ativan were simply additive and celebratory, perks for the four years of torturous work he'd done to make *Fatal Vision* happen. He'd earned it. Life was good, and feeling good, a little high even, only made it better.

Midway through my second year with my father I decided to leave. My first pass at seventh grade was underwhelming, my transcript riddled with too many C's and B–'s and commentary about my abilities and potential and lack of maturity and focus. I'd asked my dad if I could repeat the grade, get it right. He'd agreed. My report card improved. I had a girlfriend, then another, and good friends and Lucy. And I couldn't escape the feeling that he'd be fine either way. Whether my grades sucked or were stellar. Whether I had a girlfriend or five. Whether I was there, or not.

I'd gotten restless and bored. The town was too small and too white. Winter was too long. The schools back in Swarthmore changed, the high school merged with another one nearby and started in ninth instead of seventh. When I moved back, I would be in the newly formed middle school for another year. I'd gotten what I'd come for. An impulse followed. Fear-driven flight. I escaped, was free to leave, and did just that. I was leaving again, when the impulse moved me.

My mother had held my face in her hands before the one-way flight to Albany. I don't have a similar recollection of my father when I left, not the night before, the morning of, or the trip to the airport or of saying goodbye. Maybe I didn't even fly back. Did he drive me down?

I left. The geographic boundaries he'd carved out were reset. And I was okay with it, like I was on the other side of something. He could be in New Jersey or across town or western Massachusetts or Los Angeles or Italy and it wouldn't matter.

My sisters and I didn't miss each other. Or maybe we did. They may have sent me letters or cards while I was gone. I didn't send them any. Or maybe I did. They may have been at the airport when I arrived home in Philadelphia, or at the house in Swarthmore preparing a Welcome Home dinner or party. Or not. Why should they? We were all just teenagers struggling with teenage angst, and I was the little brother, returning to reclaim my time in the upstairs bathroom shared by three women.

My mom was tired. It was only her and never my dad who had to listen to Cynthia run the water on blast in the upstairs bathroom to mask the sounds of so much self-loathing and hear Sarah coming home drunk on weekend nights and figure out why she couldn't or didn't want to do better in school. And then I was suddenly back and asking pointless questions about who missed whom.

I was stuck somewhere in between the world of my mother and sisters, who couldn't help but see me as a teenage version of my father—with his height and name and two years spent huddling with him in Williamstown. Like my father, I had left them behind.

I may have been a little taller than before, an inch or two closer to Dad's height. My voice was deeper, my facial features a little sharper, not as soft and young as when I left. I looked just like him, a neighbor said. Or maybe Sarah was the one who said it. When I made a sarcastic remark at dinner I sounded "just like Dad," she said. When I was slow to take the lead on a bigger chore than taking out the trash, like fixing a loose hinge on the basement door or cleaning out the garage, I was still, according to Mom, "just like my father." I was fourteen and home again.

Dad was distant by choice, content to have his children growing up somewhere else without him. He didn't need to see us every day. Now his son had come and gone. And he was, as far as I could tell, unchanged.

Something he never said to my sisters and me, but could have: he was doing more with and for us than his father ever did for him. We would have scoffed. We'd have pointed out the obvious: the distance he put between us from the start. He'd have said something about the emotional distance his own father put between them and how torturous and confusing it all was. And he was alone, no brothers or sisters with whom to share the burden, to confide in, to comfort or be comforted by. He observed and carried with him a lifetime of caged confusion and isolation, sadness, and yearning. Where does all that confusion and sadness and fear go? And when the brain chemistry is a product of two depressed addicts, is a rational mind even possible? So he drank. And ran and drank and ran and dabbled here and there in analysis, but fame came early and thirty-one weeks on the bestsellers list and the adoration of millions and Nina, why fix what ain't broken?

I'd read and forgotten most of what he wrote about his father in *Heroes*. I recalled only a few details, aside from the drinking. He had a potbelly and smoked a pipe. He was quiet and read detective stories and ran a failed travel agency. He was an orphan. He was raised by a Catholic monsignor. He bore all the traits of a victim, of a traumatized child unable to ever speak out. He fathered a son and the orphan had to figure out how to parent. And that son would do the same. And then it would be my turn.

So there I was at fourteen, taller like Dad and funny like Dad and my voice was deep like Dad and in a place where none of that worked to my advantage. I was still, or more than ever, on my own. Ill-defined and unmoored like most teenagers, I was ruled by an insatiable need for something I'd only found pieces of in Williamstown. Someone somewhere would give it all to me. They had to.

And once they'd started, and I was hooked, they'd better continue, because something else I brought back from Williamstown, or that may have been there from the start, genetically coded to emerge only under certain conditions, like powerlessness in the face of parental abandonment or adolescent heartbreak, or the hardships of a child I'd someday father, was gestating: a toxic cocktail of unchecked, disproportionate sadness and anger.

SIX

2016

AFTER

By fourth grade, Jayson and his Lobo teammates were better. They were winning games. They were passing the ball with more purpose. They were following basic directions and executing simple plays and keeping hands out of pockets and skipping sandwich breaks. They made the playoffs.

On a Starbucks napkin I illustrated the concept for Jayson: triangle and two. The opponent only had two players who could score. We'd put a defender on each of them and the other three would set up in a zone, one up top, two down low—a triangle and two. They'd get frustrated and confused because every time one of their good players got open there would be another defender in their way.

It was working! We led at halftime. The other team, who had beaten us twice in the regular season, hustled off the court to the locker room to regroup.

Tied late, Jayson stole the ball, drove the other way, and scored, and put the game out of reach. We used the same scheme for the next game and beat the higher seed. Then once more in the championship.

When the final buzzer sounded, some players were in tears. The boys all got big silver trophies. Jayson slept with his.

It was his eighth birthday. Jayson wore his navy blazer over a black kneeling Kaepernick T-shirt and a pair of black pants and Curry basketball sneakers.

"I'm so hungry," he announced to us in his little voice on a cool spring evening on our way from the car to his restaurant of choice, Ruth's Chris, to celebrate.

He held the large leather-bound menu in his little hands and read from it in dim warm lighting of our cozy booth: "I'll have the four OZ fill-it," and his mispronunciation was anticipated by Jeanine and me because he did it in February when we came for Jeanine's birthday and before that for my own. I held up my smartphone and recorded, because how long before he caught on, figured out that "oz" meant ounces not OZ, and the "t" was silent in "filet"?

The order went through without a hitch, the waiter understood and followed Jayson's little index finger planted on the entrée he desired.

Serotonin surged. I had words for it and understood what was happening and why. I'd done the work to be better. Where tears may have formed and my appetite vanished and the moment missed, new chemical additives kept me present as my eight-year-old son ordered his birthday dinner.

I was the father across the table from his child in his blue blazer and new sneakers mispronouncing from the menu on his birthday who got it. I understood just how precious the moment was, glorious and fleeting and worth all my attention. I was sure: I'd learned the right lessons from my father's failings. Where I'd been verging on losing out again, this time on my son, as I had lost out on my father, powerless in both situations. Except, no! I had agency this time. I wasn't missing out and neither would my son if I just fought for it and for us.

So I made the calls and appointments and took the pills and kept us going, father and son, the way it was supposed to be.

I'd convinced myself, as a dad, I wasn't just getting it right, I was nailing it. It came so easy, too easy.

The novel I wrote about a young married couple with a small child who gambled on the housing bubble and lost, their marriage collapsing under the strain, the one inspired in part by the novel Dad had given me, *Revolutionary Road*, was set up to succeed.

It had enthusiastic publisher backing, but through a single stroke of unfortunate timing, it was suddenly forced to share its publication date with an Oprah selection that had always been scheduled to publish a month later.

Mine was not alone among books published that suddenly impossible first week of August that suffered.

Planned reviews and interviews with NPR and *The Wall Street Journal* and *The New York Times* and *Entertainment Weekly* were canceled to make room for coverage of the Oprah selection. "It's a zero-sum game," I was reminded by my crestfallen editor. Books had a two-to-three-week window upon publication to break out or not. Every novel published on August 2, 2016, that wasn't the Oprah selection was doomed.

I'm not going anywhere. Fuck a book tour. What's the point? The book is dead, right? I could have emailed that, said that, acted like that. Had I felt that way, I may have. Just like my father.

As gutting as it was on publication morning reading the dead-on-arrival email from my editor before even getting out of bed, there was something propping me up, compelling me forward, a healthier impulse that I was answering to.

Despite the commercial kneecapping, there was a book tour and an opportunity I wouldn't miss. I did my due diligence. I planned and calculated and launched an ambitious plan. Barring the unforeseen, I could make it work.

Jayson lined up his stuffed animals along the base of the picture window, facing out. It was late afternoon and hot outside, but cool in our compartment. We were an hour into our trip. We started in Washington, DC, where Cynthia and her husband and my niece and nephew made the trip down from Philadelphia during their summer visit from Paris to help celebrate the publication of the book. Had he been alive, my father would have been there, too, even if he were forced to stay in the Best Western on the edge of the city, his Four Seasons days long over.

From DC's Union Station, Jayson and I headed first to Chicago. Then another train would take us west to Seattle and Portland, and then down to San Francisco and Los Angeles, where Jeanine would fly out to meet us.

It was the two of us: Jayson and me. We could hit all the stops, make them on time, and not miss a reading or interview. And we could do it together, father and son, just as my father had with me on that overnight train to Montreal when I was Jayson's age.

We ate dinner in the compartment and the attendant made up our beds while we walked to the snack car. He wanted the top bunk. He played his LeapFrog video game, and I pulled the blue blanket up to his chin and kissed his forehead and said good night.

"Where are we?" he asked. It was sunrise. I was standing and checked my phone and told him.

"In-di-ana," he repeated with wonder in his voice. It may as well have been India.

We raced around Chicago; ducked into a mall for new Steph Curry sneakers and Star Wars Lego sets; the Willis Tower, where he paused and deliberated and took deep breaths and finally summoned the courage to step out and onto the clear glass floor, a 1,300-foot drop to the city streets below; and we agreed we'd hop off the train every time it stopped in a new state so he could set foot in Wisconsin and Minnesota and North Dakota, and as we rode he told me about trap-door spiders with Montana unfolding all around us, and he panicked when I strayed too far at a stop in Cut Bank, fear in his voice, "Daddy, come on. Come on! They're going to leave!" and there was time, I promised him, we have plenty of time, superstar. But never as much as you think.

Seattle and another train down to Portland and if we timed it just right we'd get there, I knew this but didn't tell him and I checked my phone and there were delays but also time made up and with luck we might make it and we hopped the cab in overcast Portland and checked in to the boutique hotel with the giant game room, where we'd come back for billiards and ping-pong and foosball and PlayStation, but we had to hustle and the sun broke through and the city was bright and alive and it was a Saturday and I punched in some credit card information on the phone and the cab dropped us at the stadium and we joined throngs of green and yellow clad Portlanders in the queue and scanned the tickets and followed the signs and concrete walkway into Providence Park and down the stairs and down and down to the very first row of section 118, only the team benches a few feet below stood between us and the immaculate emerald-green soccer pitch. He took it all in, the capacity crowd already singing and the giant flags waving and I snapped all the pictures and sent them to his mother, Jayson with his head on his crossed arms resting against the low railing absorbing it as I absorbed him, a moment on a clear bright Portland, Oregon, afternoon in a stadium full of people, three thousand miles from home, just us, the only two people in the stadium, the state, the world.

And down to Los Angeles and the pier watching the men cast their lines and later into the crashing surf and into an impossibly golden-orange sunset that my smartphone captured that I later enlarged and printed and framed and hung on our bedroom wall: Jayson at dusk, a lone silhouette on the beach in midstride of euphoric retreat from a crashing wave, sherbet sky, and a single ray of sunlight finding him, our nine-year-old son.

It was a matter of scale. I didn't write a bestseller and then three more that earned me fame and opportunities and connections to powerful people who could make golden moments for my son. What I could do was figure out what might make him happy and try to pull it off. We bought Wizards tickets in sections close enough to the court that allowed us, if we arrived early enough, to get access to the tunnel where players arrived and left during pregame workouts.

Little Jayson, seven and eight and nine years old, his little hand stuck out for one more high five from John Wall or Bradley Beal and there's Blake Griffin and James Harden and Jamal Crawford, the jersey he wanted and wore when the Clippers came to town and there he was shaking their hands and getting their signatures on his jersey or trading card and pictures taken and each score another hit: waves of serotonin. And the jumbotron and a time-out during the last three minutes of a tie game with Toronto, and the stage was set: the emcee was looking for a couple of fans to get the arena charged and Jayson in his Wizards jersey stood on the baseline, the arm of the emcee wrapped around his little frame, the microphone at his mouth. *"Whatchu you wanna say, Jayson?!"* and his soft brown cheeks and sweet brown eyes filled the jumbotron as he leaned into the microphone and delivered an impassioned clarion call: *"Let's Go Wizards!!!"* And the crowd roared.

One more moment. One more high. This was the stuff of life, the reason for it all, the very best of existence. What could top this? How much more joy could I feel?

And none of it felt like compensation for something I wasn't doing. I was the piggyback ride to school from the car every morning. I was the goalie for any number of after-school penalty kicks, high-fiving each other for once again "closing down the playground" at dusk, the last two there. I was the pusher of swings, the provider of crisp bills and quarters for the ice cream truck.

It wasn't the playing field with the California Angels when I was nine or in the locker room with the Sixers when I was eleven or with the Patriots on the chewed-up postgame Orange Bowl playing field chasing after his friend in the organization, Dad screaming out his name through the throngs of media and players, keeping one hand wrapped around my arm so as not to lose me in the melee, and he nailed it, slid us into the tunnel and locker room to celebrate their victory in the 1985

AFC championship. By force of will he just did it. He had that power. And used it for good, for me, so I could feel something special. Rarefied places and moments that he knew I'd treasure. It was the least he could do, he likely thought. This doesn't make up for being a lousy father, *but how awesome is this?!*

He knew people everywhere and used those connections for shared moments he knew would thrill me. He used more connections later to land me a paid gig with the Clinton campaign or Rainbow Coalition internship via Jamie Raskin or asked Roger Ailes to speak to my college political science class or a six-minute stint on a national cable news program to promote my first novel with him next to me. "Just talk to the host. Keep your eyes on him and not the camera," he advised me in the greenroom.

I worked with what I had. Limited influence and access were my own making, the result of choices and priorities. Jayson would have to settle for what I considered my best. And I felt pretty good making that soccer match in time, scoring those front-row tickets, getting lucky with Amtrak, somehow arriving on time and that rare sunny afternoon in Portland.

At the final tour stop in Philadelphia. It was the question-and-answer segment of a reading, when I was sitting behind the table the store had arranged and in mid-response I watched him get up from his chair next to his mother and walk up the aisle and around the table to me and slip his little arm under mine and felt him lean into me while I spoke. His small hand on my back that first basketball practice. His eyes finding mine after all those jump shots. I looked at him that night at the reading, expecting maybe he'd say something or tell me he had to go the bathroom, but he just stood there, gently resting his hand on mine, letting me continue. *You did that, Jayson. A few short steps across a small room to stand beside me and you made me feel something no book or reading or review ever has or will.*

My mother and a few of her friends were there, too. Jeanine

brought her mother and father. Some childhood friends of mine and then a handful of strangers.

Sarah and her family couldn't make it, had a vacation in Florida they didn't want to cut short. She explained later, she and I having drifted apart, that she resented the way everything and everyone was expected to stop what they were doing every time Dad had a new book. We all had to pay attention and listen to his stories, and it was just this spirit-crushing one-way street of all Dad, all the time.

She had a life and children and a career, most of which Dad didn't give a shit about, especially when he had a new book, which was always. She certainly wasn't going to cut short a family vacation to celebrate her brother's second book.

It hadn't always been that way. She'd engaged my first book. She chose it for her book club. She'd hosted a baby shower for Jeanine and drove to Washington when Jayson was born, sat on the carpeted loft folding and organizing his little baby clothes.

But something shifted in her not long after. Maybe it was something I'd done wrong or hadn't done right. Maybe I didn't visit enough or ask enough about my nephews and nieces or her. Maybe I forgot one too many birthdays. Maybe I was just a self-obsessed man like Dad.

An email from her made her feelings clear. She felt "so sorry for Jayson" because he was destined for a "sad, isolated childhood." It was jarring and hurtful and didn't align with anything Jayson was experiencing. It was instead emblematic of pain and bitterness she'd carried with her for so long. That's how I read it. That's what made it easy to dismiss.

Dad's self-obsession and insufficient interest in her children and Sarah's life was long-standing. I was his namesake and a writer and a new Dad who was apparently doing it very wrong and hurting her in the process. And yet, she was my older sister and a happily married mother of three bright, kind children and knew more about parenting than me. Could I be getting it wrong? And how?

I reminded Sarah more than a few times I wasn't Dad. She was unconvinced. Give it time, she said. A flight impulse would kick in. My son would be jarred awake as I trashed the kitchen and threw laptops into pools and slammed the door behind me as I left.

But I wasn't going anywhere. Ever. I was hooked on my son, like an addict. I'd run like a scared kid only a few years prior in the face of commitment I was sure would suffocate me. And now I was high on my son and happily, obsessively homebound. Run or burrow in. It was all or nothing, life lived on the extremes.

The Italian publisher of my first novel wanted to fly me to Milan and Rome to promote the book. Jayson was eighteen months old. Jeanine insisted I go, of course. A once-in-a-lifetime opportunity. Ten days in Italy without Jayson? I feared the worst, some accident, the plane would go down. Jayson was too perfect, too pure, and life was too good to last. Nothing I felt was rational. I apologized to the publisher and declined the trip. Jayson, like Jeanine when I fell in love with her as a nineteen-year-old boy, was an uncut narcotic.

The high from watching him deliver his three lines in the fifth-grade school play, the smile I couldn't suppress, the dozens of times I watched the same clip on my phone.

That was the rush that devolved and became something with bite and an edge. The joy of Jayson was essential. It fed and sustained and lifted me. All I had to do was tickle him or read to him or watch him play or look down at his own shadow as he ran across the soccer field and I was high again. But it would take a little more the older he was. Existence and his essence weren't enough. Talents and innate potential emerged. Like the heroin addict who needs an increasingly potent product to get a better high, Jayson required a new type of attention and work from both of us to chase the new euphoria.

Jayson buried long-range shots. He spun around and sliced through defenders. I sensed the eyes of others on him and heard the murmurings and fielded the questions: "How old is he?" and I'd tell them and they'd shake their head or nod in wonder or even say, "Damn," and the other kids watched him as an eleven-year-old sank nineteen (!!) threes in a row moving left to right around the arc and ask out loud, "How does he do that?" I'd said something quiet and humble like: "He works hard," barely able to contain myself. *Goddamn, that's beautiful!*

I didn't make those shots, Jayson did. But I felt the pride of an artist, a creator of beauty, my child was my product just as my father's name was his brand, and every book he authored was him. Dad poured everything into each project, and the outcome, the success or failure of each, was a verdict on him, the man, the person, his life to date. Jayson was my child, but becoming my project, too. What if it failed? Came up short? Where would that leave him and, more importantly, me?

SEVEN

1984

BEFORE

Mom was home late from work and lighting a Vantage cigarette and Sarah was scoring weed on the aqua Princess touch-tone phone in the bedroom she shared with Cynthia who was still in the bathroom with the door locked and the water running to mask the sounds of self-loathing and Dad was on TV and I was alone in the basement watching him.

It had been a couple years since *Fatal Vision* and he was back on national television because of an appeal or some newsworthy development in the MacDonald legal saga. So I watched.

Or maybe it wasn't so bleak that night. Maybe that was the next blockbuster book or the one after that found us all separated and coping in our own ways, only me still tuning in with the same level of interest. Maybe that night we were all gathered around the television because it was a prime-time national talk show, just the host and Dad and calls from across the country and we were excited and proud.

We laughed at his bald spot when the camera angle shifted. He was poised and delivered his answers with quiet conviction. How does he do that? I wondered. Sit there and process and respond so coolly and convincingly, with appropriately placed injections of wry humor. Never once did he get flustered or stumble over words. He was warm and open, and people trusted him. I trusted him. And was convinced I always could.

I knew he'd call the next day from New York or Chicago or wherever the book sent him and he'd be sober and engaging and he'd listen like he wanted to be closer and mention the holidays and us flying up when the tour was over and then asking for Cynthia and then for Sarah and then Mom.

His big soft hands rested on the table, fingers interlaced in his understated blazer with elbow patches and button-down shirt and a pleasant expression and sober tone as he explained precisely how Jeffrey MacDonald folded back the blue pajama top to puncture the chest of his wife with the ice pick thirty-seven times. Or was it forty-seven? Our father was asking viewers to picture it: What would become of the flesh after twenty-five, thirty, forty punctures with an ice pick? And then his little girls. One after the next.

The host went to calls and we tried but couldn't get through. He sat there in the television studio in New York, in part, for us. It had to be, though how wasn't exactly clear.

When he was on another national talk show the next day, only Cynthia and I watched. Sarah missed it and said she forgot. The next day he was on again. Only I watched.

He did a hundred other television and radio hits because the book contract called for a massive tour. Millions of dollars was at stake, orders and foreign sales and television rights and actors and directors and network executives all working to squeeze as many dollars as they could from the story Dad listened to at a restaurant in Orange County in 1979 told to him by a nice-looking, smooth-talking Green Beret Princeton-educated surgeon looking for an author to make him famous after the vicious murder of his pregnant wife and two little girls.

Friends and teachers in school would say things to me like: "Saw your dad on TV last night," and I'd say "Oh" or "Cool," because what else was there to say? It *was* cool and I was proud that he was interesting enough to be on TV and didn't come off badly and even seemed as warm and likable as I knew he was. That was my dad and he was pretty cool and very kind and liked to drink too much and I missed him a lot, probably more than I knew at that point, not as far removed from the sobbing six-year-old version of myself as I liked to think.

Sarah came home drunk or high or both. It was summer and dark. She was sixteen and upset, had been crying, black streaks of smeared mascara on her cheeks. She appeared in the outside doorway of our screened-in back porch, not risking a front door entrance that might wake Mom. I turned down the volume on my boom box. I'd recorded the extended-play version of "Feel the Heartbeat" from the stereo in the living room on a blank tape over and over so I wouldn't have to rewind the tape when the song ended. I was sweaty and out of breath on the eight-by-ten-inch sheet of white-and-blue, floral-patterned linoleum I paid thirty bucks for at the MAB paint store across the street.

Who the fuck are you? Sarah may have wondered and likely did under normal, sober, less dramatic circumstances.

"You don't have to stop," she said that night, bloodshot eyes and legs crossed and a distant gaze.

I waited. A motorcycle engine roared and tore down the turnpike on the other side of the backyard fence. Sarah was the type of girl who would be clutching the guy riding that motorcycle, ripping down the highway for thrills. Maybe she had been and that was him, leaving her behind. Maybe that's why she was crying. One more guy launching himself, leaving her in the dust, when all she wanted to do was tag along, hang on, go wherever he went, no matter the risks.

I could have asked what was wrong, but I knew it was a boy. It may have been the brother of the one who I fought on the football field in sixth grade. He was calling me an "n-lover" because I'd had a crush on a Black girl and had Black friends and I "called him out," which meant we would fight that day. I'd done this twice before and for no good reason. I hated fighting. I never hit anyone other than my sisters and that was only a slap on the leg or arm. I didn't punch and never hit anyone in the face and couldn't imagine it. I'd only been chased, had bottles thrown at me, never caught or punched or kicked or knocked down.

I wore my white Lynn Swann Steelers jersey and the gold chain I thought was cool. He ripped it off and scratched my neck, pushed and I backpedaled, and he kept coming, short and determined with his greasy hair and angry eyes, and suddenly in one motion I grabbed his arm and spun and threw him down and pinned him and gripped his neck with both hands so tight his face was dark red and I told him to say it again, call me that again, until I felt the kicks from heavy boots, his dirtbag friends intervening, sparing him from the torrent of rage pouring out of me.

That was the little brother of the guy who had Sarah's heart tied carelessly to the back of his chopper. He used the same words as his little brother and she used the same words as they did. I called her out, too, but not to fight.

In that way, Sarah was the black sheep. Cynthia was dating a soccer and track star who happened to be Black and on his way to college. And I was playing out a Bronx breakdancer fantasy and devouring Richard Wright and fighting racists on the playground. Sarah, though, had a tolerance for a certain kind of ugliness in her boyfriends and social circles and language that I couldn't square.

I didn't know what to say. What did I know, other than I didn't need to drink or smoke to feel like shit. I knew she didn't like her bad grades and the way math confused her and the numbers were all jumbled and paying attention for too long was impossible and it was so much easier for Cynthia and me and that pissed her off. I knew I was the one male in the house and still wasn't angry at Dad like she was. I knew that even after I left Williamstown and had registered his seeming indifference, I felt neither anger nor resentment. And that made life easier because being angry and resentful was exhausting.

So I turned the volume back up and nailed a backspin and went for a windmill and almost pulled it off. But I was still her little brother and part of me was hoping she'd watch and be impressed and say something. When I finished spinning, though, she was gone. Back out into the dark summer night chasing after the boy and maybe something else, something Dad never gave her or would. Another chopper roared past. Was she on it?

Mom yanked the phone cord as far as it would stretch so she could pull the basement door closed behind her for privacy. This was how she talked to Dad about serious matters, Sarah's school troubles or Cynthia's pain. I may have come up that summer I couldn't sleep when I was twelve and kept waking her up and calling Dad and calling our family therapist and panicking and crying all night. Normal calls found her in the kitchen speaking mostly in a monotone and smoking a cigarette.

What I don't remember is Dad driving down from Williamstown to see Sarah or Cynthia or even me, for that matter, when we were struggling.

I verged on quitting eighth-grade basketball mid-season. I was frustrated and lacked confidence. The ball was in someone else's hands and I was fine with it. Tall and skinny and athletic. That's why I was the fifth starter. And I never wanted the ball. Too much pressure. I knew if I shot it wasn't going in. There was a reason I was so open. Practices were long and games mostly sucked. My light blue polyester shorts were too short and chafed the insides of my thighs. The jersey was too loose and I was preoccupied with tucking it in but not too far and could never get it right.

Dad and I spoke on the phone. I told him I wanted to quit. Sometime after I hung up, he typed a letter that included a story about his hapless experience trying out for the Holy Cross basketball team in college.

In the letter he told me: Whatever you do, don't quit. If I started quitting at fourteen, I'd learn how to quit, and it would become easier each time to simply walk away at the first sign of adversity. I followed his advice and finished the season with the team.

It just so happens that in the championship game, with the score tied and six seconds on the clock, the opponent inbounded the ball at half-court and I intercepted it and drove to the basket, making the game-winning shot as the buzzer sounded. Dad sent another letter with a color cutout of Superman stuck to the paper and a check for $100.

My mother left work early to be there and witness her tall, skinny fourteen-year-old son, who was just back from two years with his father, snatch a moment of glory owed to his father's words.

I spent a year at our local public high school, newly formed when the state decided Swarthmore High School was too small and would merge with a neighboring school. It was large and most of the students were no longer children of college professors and other like-minded townsfolk who generally valued the Quaker college at the heart of their village, but accountants and insurance adjusters. My social studies teacher told the class he slept better at night knowing Reagan had all our missiles on the ready, protecting us from the communists. Soccer and lacrosse boys were entitled alphas who played stickball in the cafeteria using balled-up electrical tape while kids tried to eat. No one challenged them. Cynthia and Sarah matriculated through and graduated. Not me.

There was a newer, small private high school in town founded by parents from the recently closed Swarthmore High School. The new school occupied a single long hallway and library and small gym that had once been my elementary school cafeteria. There were sixty-five students in grades 7 through 12. Tuition was a modest $5,000 a year, which my father agreed to pay.

There were barely enough athletes to field a varsity basketball team. But those who were there were talented enough to compete with bigger, better schools. I was in tenth grade. It was November after Thanksgiving, and I was sick with a fever and cough and managed twenty-eight points against Shipley School in my first varsity game.

I'm not sure how, but the points kept coming. *The Philadelphia Inquirer* printed an area scoring leaders list and there was my name, second on the list: *Joe McGinnis (always misspelled) Swarthmore Academy—27.7 ppg.*

My mother clipped and cut and pasted and amassed a thick book of stories and game recaps as the season and coverage rolled on about the tiny school achieving basketball success and the sophomore scoring phenom from Swarthmore.

I was interviewed and photographed for a story in the *Philadelphia Inquirer* sports section. Sitting on the worn red love seat in the living room, I could have told the reporter he was sitting exactly where Maureen the sixteen-year-old babysitter taught me how to French kiss when I was merely eleven or even ten while my mother worked the middle shift and my father was hiking around Alaska or in Los Angeles hanging out with a murderer or at home in New Jersey drinking his second bottle of red with Nina.

Instead, I talked about colleges I might want to attend (Oberlin, William & Mary) in the room where Mom hosted bridge games and chain-smoked Vantage cigarettes and tried to balance her checkbook and where, before that, my father once sat, bouncing his daughters on his knee, while I existed only in concept. Maybe he and Mom could make it work. Maybe another child would do the trick. What if it was a boy? He couldn't walk away from a son.

"You're still not angry?" Sarah would still occasionally press me about Dad and his distance and absence. "That he's missing all of this?" she said, referring to my run of local basketball shine. That he doesn't want to be here for it.

I had it figured out: we'd be different people if he were around. I didn't know how we'd be different, but his restlessness and resentment and drinking would be unbearable.

Neither of us discussed why he didn't choose to live closer, in town even. About his choice of New Jersey, he'd always said he preferred the proximity to Manhattan, as though his work as a writer of books required extensive time in the city. It didn't.

Sarah saw the bullshit long before I did. She was angry and sad, where I was merely sad.

I didn't hold him accountable for the damage he'd done to Mom and Cynthia and to her. I should be angry on their behalf, she said, or I inferred. That anger would come, she warned. It *had* to.

Straight A's and twenty-eight points per game, I thought. Oblivious was working. Anger from me at that point would have accomplished little. I didn't want to be bitter and cut off, resigned to superficial check-ins. So I put myself first and let him off the hook.

There would be a reckoning, she insisted. There always was.

Dad had a new book in the works, another true crime blockbuster. I never did ask him why the attraction to such grisly subject matter. I did know he was fascinated with the masks people wore, artifice and superficiality and what lay behind them. *Blind Faith* told the story of a wealthy father who hired hit men to murder his wife after a night at the casino in Atlantic City.

The plan was simple: they'd follow on the dark highway. He'd pull off to check something with the car. He'd get out, they'd approach and shoot her dead. He'd get a bump on the head, and they'd take wallets and jewelry and be off. A robbery that led to the murder of his wife. His motive was insurance money. She had a million-dollar policy and he'd get it all for himself to share with his girlfriend. He had three grown sons. The story, my dad decided, wasn't the run-of-the-mill murder-for-money scheme for which the perp—Robert Marshall—was tried and convicted, but the sons coming to terms with a father capable of killing their mother.

He'd rented a house in the summer of 1986. He had research to conduct. My sisters and I had a week with him in the Seaside Heights, New Jersey, house he'd found. Dad was grilling on the deck and Springsteen blared from the stereo. He drank beer and then gin and then beer again. He talked about the case, the Marshall family, the sons, the girlfriend, the appeals, the town, the attorneys. The winds kicked up. He talked about Roby, the youngest Marshall son, who refused to accept his father's guilt. He was the heart of the story.

My sisters and I downed burgers and chips and root beer and Nina dutifully tended to Mason and Gavin, seven and two. Dad had a mouthful of meat and swigged his beer and gestured as he spoke. "How do you process that? Your father hiring someone to murder your own mother for money? Roby can't. He won't. He just can't. Your father is a monster? How do you ever learn to accept that?"

His face flushed with a familiar glow of energy and booze and sunburn. He carried all these themes and ideas, and the page wasn't enough. He had to speak it, too. Articulate it and convince anyone who would listen that what he discovered, intuited, and concluded was in fact the thrust of the story and that it mattered and was worthy of the millions of dollars invested in its telling by the publisher and television networks who optioned it.

And his way of doing things, the big things, his professional calling, his passion, was working. He was, at the time, one of the most famous and highest-paid writers in the world. What was there to fix?

So he talked and talked and it didn't seem to matter to him that we only had a week together and there were the three of us with full adolescent lives, new friends and passions of our own and fears and stories from college and high school. The details of the lives of his subjects animated him most.

What existed behind the mask? The public face and what lay beyond it. That was what drove him to write. Selling Nixon to Americans. The truth behind the lives of supposed heroes. The real Alaska as lived by its residents. The narcissist sociopath and the stepfather whose world was shattered and who single-handedly pursued justice on behalf of his murdered daughter. After *Fatal Vision*, his next two true crime books were less about the actual brutality of murder, but the emotional journey of those directly affected: the son coming to accept his father's guilt in *Blind Faith*, the mother who survived the homicidal plot unleashed by her own son in *Cruel Doubt*. As grisly as the material was, Dad could identify a human story, a character whose journey would redeem the horror endured by victims and observed by readers. And with the commercial success of *Fatal Vision*, his true crime formula was wildly lucrative. While he swam in these polluted waters of his grisly subject matter, he did so by clinging to the life rafts that were the heroes within the tragedy.

He was living in that world, with those people who were strangers to us, but like family to him. And he'd better get it right. It had better be worth reading, spending $22 for a hardcover, or his grand reemergence would be short lived.

Even as obsessed as he was with such topics, he remained the warm and playful dad we'd always missed, and though we were teenagers, we still mostly enjoyed time with him.

He could be standing in the kitchen and I could pass through and playfully start throwing mock blows and he'd engage and cry out, "What is this? What is the meaning of this unprovoked assault?" while defending himself with his big soft hands, never quite throwing or landing a blow of his own.

And yet, always simmering beneath the surface and often bubbling up and spilling over, triggered by the most innocuous provocations, was the pressure of it all and whatever other demons were wreaking havoc.

So when a strong gust sent a single loose paper napkin into the air at dinner that night, Dad paused mid-sentence and, agitated, snapped in Nina's general direction, looking for someone to blame: "Everything's blowing away!"

We fell silent. Then burst into laughter.

"One napkin, Dad!" I held up the lone square paper napkin. "Everything is blowing away?!" And we laughed and he couldn't help but smile, too. We'd repeat the phrase to him, and about him, for years to come. And later, when things were at their most bleak, he'd tell me on the phone in one of the last conversations we'd ever have: "Everything really is blowing away."

He returned from New Jersey at summer's end to his new Williamstown home, bought with the substantial payments he'd received after *Fatal Vision*, its paperback and television rights, and *Blind Faith* contract and its television rights.

He was no longer just off campus with professors living next door, the house that I'd escaped to when I was twelve. He'd moved farther out of town, more isolated and peaceful. Buddhist monks meditated in a hillside monastery across the gravel road. Superman lived down the street.

Before Christopher Reeve's tragic accident, my sisters and I would check his mail. The five mailboxes were lined up for efficiency where two unpaved roads intersected. REEVE was spelled out in black letters on one box. Superman got junk mail, too.

The 3,830-square-foot, four-bedroom, four-bath New England Cape-style house lay on seven acres of landscaped garden and meadows filled with wildflowers and 360-degree views of Mt. Greylock and the mountains surrounding the valley.

It was all for Dad, and Nina—whose vocations were occasional freelance photography and editing Dad's work and raising Mason and Gavin. They had two dogs, including Lucy, graying and slowed, and a few cats who came and went.

Nothing was blowing away. He'd earned and purchased a writer's paradise. He was the rare author who'd broken through, beaten the longest odds, and nearing fifty, could safely say he'd done it all his way, never once having to do anything other than write to earn a living and provide for his family, while enjoying nearly universal acclaim.

No one traveling to his new house, visiting or residing for any length of time, even a long winter, could observe the hillsides and mountain views and farmland and grazing horses and cows and pastures and brooks and streams and foliage and see what he would come to see: the darkest, loneliest place on earth, a place he'd come to refer to as "Williamstomb."

It was like his childhood life in Rye, before he took flight and followed his passion to write; his quiet, isolated Williamstown home bore an eerie similarity when his career would crash and there was just him alone, not suffocated by his damaged parents but forced to face the people he'd damaged and all the ghosts and regrets that came to life absent a career, an obsession. Just him and the big, cold house in Williamstomb.

And he'd put himself there. He'd left the huge house near the center of things, on the edge of the Williams College campus with neighbors he knew and liked and a walkable distance to town, sandwich shops, a small movie theater, his liquor and pills. But he chose more distance and isolation, neighbors he would never bump into, wouldn't be forced to talk to.

Even on sparsely populated Oblong Road, he was only a five-minute drive from town and just down the gravel road was the Store at Five Corners, where he had an account, so he or Nina could scoop up the *New York Times* and *Wall Street Journal* and *Boston Globe*, all with "McGinniss" written in pencil and put aside along with some wine and ground coffee and a few croissants.

And there was a lady who would clean every week, landscapers who would mow the acreage and trim the overgrowth. What would later signify disrepair and neglect and the deterioration of everything, including his marriage and financial and mental condition, was at the time merely evidence of his lack of pretention and vanity. There was interior painting that came with the house, peeling and faded, that needed touching up. There was the crappy shower in the guest bathroom and faded pink wallpaper, the stained wall-to-wall carpeting. The electric stove and original cabinetry in the kitchen. There was a hodgepodge of unmatching furniture throughout the house. He had more than enough money to renovate and upgrade, but none of that mattered much to him.

Nina was similar, not materialistic at all. Dad would order exotic meats and good wine and a satellite television because cable hadn't reached them yet. An interior designer would have done wonders to the place. They had no interest.

There was the small pond along the edge of the property near the gravel road. There were bushes and tall grass surrounding it. Late one morning, when she was so tired, and it was time, Lucy calmly walked over to the side of the small pond and lay down and closed her eyes for the last time. That's what Dad told me on the phone.

There was an inground rectangular pool that came with the house, a laptop's throw from his office. No one ever used it. It was the Berkshires, and the water wasn't heated. There was an afternoon during which he was struggling with a malfunctioning laptop and became so exasperated that he kicked open the office door that led outside and hurled the device into the pool.

There was the sloping green lawn where the other dog (a small white dog named Moira, who Sarah had adopted, then gave up because she decided she wasn't a dog person), was mauled and killed by a neighbor's pit bull. And poor Gavin, barely a teenager at the time, was there to witness it, helpless, horrified.

There was a crawl space in the upstairs hallway where keepsakes and manuscript pages and galleys and magazines and collectibles and old clothes and luggage were stored. It's where Dad ended up one terrible autumn night, curled up and breaking down.

He possessed a uniquely dangerous blend of wild success and a compulsive personality disorder. And for thirty years, he made it work. His priorities were his own and he honored and pursued them with a vigilance that bordered on mania.

He'd call after dinner. He was immersed in the world of *Blind Faith* and the names and locations and developments that had nothing to do with my sisters or me.

And it was nighttime, so his filter dropped, and thoughts spilled over, unchecked. Sometimes I held the phone away from my ear and stared at the patterns in the linoleum kitchen floor of my mom's house trying to find a way out of the maze. He had so much to say and the names of all the players in his story spun in a dizzying irrelevant circle. For the first time I can recall, I was relieved he wasn't closer, that I wasn't with him, visiting or living in his house, subjected to this conversation at the dining room table.

The other message he delivered with every after-dinner call: this is what he spared us. Be grateful he's not closer or we'd end up like Mason and Gavin. We'd have been kind like them, like our father, but we'd have sat for dinner every night, watching Dad get drunk. And every night, another piece of our childhood would disappear. And we'd go about our night and the next day and the weeks and months and years that followed, a little farther from him each day. And the in-between times, the sober days of his obsessions and periodic, unpredictable explosions would punctuate our lives. We'd be left alone, free to roam and do as we pleased, with few guardrails or expectations aside from being decent humans, left to carry so much inside, all that we witnessed from the force of nature, the Category 5 hurricane of passion and rage and addiction until we were swept up in it, tossed some distance away, landing hard, dazed, wondering where and who we were. And at a certain point, one by one, we'd arrive at the same conclusion: the storm could be chased, but never caught. And maybe that was okay.

In that respect, as children, distance had been our friend.

• • •

If you asked him, downtown Los Angeles in 1987 bordered on dystopian. The Los Angeles County courthouse and the courtroom he was consigned to was its own circle of hell. For months, he was sentenced to be there, compelled to attend and testify in his own defense against Jeffrey MacDonald. The days were dreary and exhausting. He was questioned and cross-examined. He was challenged and accused and belittled and only occasionally defended.

MacDonald wanted $15 million for breach of contract. While writing *Fatal Vision*, Dad had written him letters that made him feel like my dad was an ally when he wasn't. The lawsuit argued that Dad had breached the contract they'd entered when he'd misled him.

To maintain his sanity, when Nina wasn't out there and testifying herself, he played on a loop the upbeat anthem of the summer called "Touch of Grey" by the Grateful Dead to and from the courthouse. He spent occasional weekends with Nina in a lush, oceanside Santa Monica hotel with a private cabana, working on *Blind Faith*.

The jury deadlocked. A settlement was agreed to in the amount of $325,000.

My father's attorney for the case told the *Los Angeles Times* following the trial: "I think the fact that the case even got to trial initially has an extremely chilling effect upon any nonfiction writer. Once you must defend yourself in a lengthy trial, they've punished you—win, lose, or draw. The writer is at the mercy of someone who has a lawyer that's willing to take on his case and has nothing else to do."

The punishment phase was over. He'd done what he felt was necessary to write the book he'd wanted to write and paid a price for it. The takeaway seemed simple: he'd lost, and MacDonald had won. More painful: no one had come to his defense. It made sense to me at the time, but barely. The literary world he had such disdain for, the pretentious Manhattan crowd he was proud to avoid, didn't come rushing to his aid. So what? He'd still prevailed. He'd still wrote the bestseller. He was still on top.

He was a prominent author defending the craft of narrative

nonfiction and journalism, the process of delivering the truth to readers, messy as it sometimes was, and no one wrote a word in support. He was the author of a modern nonfiction classic and a true crime blockbuster and not a single writer of prominence rallied to his cause. He was devastated. The indifference of his peers wounded him, and he never quite recovered.

EIGHT

1989

BEFORE

Two years had passed since the MacDonald settlement. His new book was publishing, a second consecutive big one, *Blind Faith*, and the celebration commenced on the Upper West Side of Manhattan on a frigid January night. And he wanted his children there for it.

Cynthia and Sarah were both home from college for winter break and the three of us took turns showering in the upstairs bathroom of our Swarthmore home, dressed, and waited in the kitchen, the front door open so we could see it arrive.

The white limousine was out of place on Magill Road. Except for prom nights and the rare funeral, Magill Road wasn't a limousine kind of street. It was sent by his publisher to ferry us to Manhattan for the party. Our mother was working middle at the hospital, likely not invited, wouldn't have attended if she were.

The gathering was attended by Bret Easton Ellis and Howard Cosell and Barbara Walters and publishing insiders and an Oscar-winning actress and literary types whose names meant nothing to me at the time.

The party was hosted at the West End Avenue apartment of Pulitzer Prize–winning author J. Anthony Lukas and his writer wife, Linda Healy. Tony and Linda were Dad's friends. Tony would later kill himself in that same apartment. His mother had done the same when he was a boy. Maybe he and Dad bonded over that, their fraught genetics.

We left the party with a dry-mounted poster of the book jacket and convinced the limo driver to stop at Burger King before we left the city. We'd see him again, maybe in a month, maybe longer. I didn't really care.

He'd call. He'd send postcards from book tour stops. I'd watch some of his television appearances. I'd miss him and sometimes wish he was closer, even then, after so many years apart. But we knew better. That was how it was, and who he was, and what choice did I have?

Just as MacDonald sought out my father to write his story in hopes of making him look good, my dad summoned his own killer. He needed to clear his name, lest anyone think he did something untoward in gaining access to his subject. He wasn't naive. He knew who MacDonald was when he met him—smooth and vain and almost certainly a murderer. But there was a big story there and he needed a big book. Just as marriage and fathering children saved him from the draft, a book about the horrific crime with its Princeton-educated Green Beret surgeon could revive his career.

As he did with Ailes and Nixon, he decided if MacDonald was arrogant enough to talk, he would do what was necessary to keep him talking. He'd convey to MacDonald what was necessary to get to the truth. The subjects of many of his books were mostly unsympathetic characters. They were killers and manipulators and narcissists. And without access to them, there was no book.

"Oh, Jeffrey," Dad wrote him, "total strangers can see within five minutes that you did not receive a fair trial."

And he added: "What the fuck were those people thinking."

And continued, referring to the time he spent with MacDonald sharing a house in Raleigh: "You spend a summer making a new friend and then the bastards come along and lock him up. But not for long, Jeffrey. Not for long."

The convicted triple murderer wouldn't have been blamed for believing the journalist was an ally.

The price paid for the misleading of MacDonald was two months of one summer in a Los Angeles courtroom and a bruised ego. The publisher's insurance company paid off the settlement. It cost Dad nothing professionally: he was under contract for *Blind Faith*, which paid him more than *Fatal Vision*. He was a millionaire and then some. MacDonald would still die in prison. And my dad would never have to set foot in downtown Los Angeles again. It was time to celebrate and embrace his status as one of America's premier authors.

But he couldn't resist. His integrity had been put on trial and not a word was written in his defense. He could have held a grudge. He could have worked it out in therapy and earned quiet satisfaction with the success of the next book and the one after that. But Dad was a provocateur who craved action, hungered for validation, to be told he was okay, he'd done nothing wrong and should be celebrated. Maybe he wanted grace from his peers that he could never expect from the children he left behind. Maybe his addiction was wreaking havoc. Maybe it was all of those things.

He directed his attorney to draft a letter and send it out to thirty journalists inviting anyone to write about the case, the chilling effect on the first amendment, etc.

Only one reporter responded: Janet Malcolm of *The New Yorker*.

Dad was hopeful. Malcolm seemed like someone who would empathize. She'd endured a decade-long legal battle with psychoanalyst Jeffrey Masson after being accused of fabricating and libeling him in a forty-thousand-word profile she wrote for *The New Yorker*. She was found guilty, but when the original jury couldn't decide what to award the plaintiff, a second trial was held. That jury also found that she had fabricated quotes, but that they weren't libelous and awarded no damages to the plaintiff.

She visited Dad at his Williamstown home. The plan was a series of conversations. They sat for five hours during their first meeting. It started comfortably enough, but the mood shifted not long after the conversation began. If I knew about it at the time at seventeen, I had complete faith in Dad's decision-making process. If he thought a writer from *The New Yorker*, which I likely confused with *The New York Times*, wanted to come talk to him about murderous MacDonald and *Fatal Vision*, it was a good idea.

He and Malcom agreed that journalists could and sometimes should befriend their subjects to get the truth. In the end, he'd argued, subjects consistently feel betrayed by what ends up being written.

MacDonald just wanted to control him, interfere with his life, Dad said. That was what the lawsuit was all about, not some high-minded moral question about journalistic integrity. MacDonald was locked up and bored and hated that he'd been exposed as the killer he was by a book that he himself had wanted written.

And there was my dad, sitting in the dining room with Janet Malcolm, seeking some version of what MacDonald had sought from him. But unlike MacDonald, Dad wasn't incarcerated and bored, but instead a free man at the apex of his career.

In the recordings of his conversation with Malcolm, his voice betrays him when she asks if he regretted letters signaling support that he'd written to MacDonald: "Oh yes, I sure do. I knew that he would break off contact the minute he found out that the book wasn't going to be what he had hoped for."

Hearing the conversation play out online, all these years later, crackling through my laptop speaker, I knew his voice well. He was home in the house near town, where I'd lived for two years. I could picture the deck on which they sat, the pale yellow, paint-chipped wooden railing over which I used to throw plastic parachute soldiers. And across the lush uncut grass, carriage house, and half acre, where

Dad and I played countless innings of Wiffle ball games, Lucy chasing and running off with the ball while I circled the bases.

MacDonald was a murderer, was the essence of what my father told my mother on the phone in 1979, within days of first meeting and spending time with his subject. A decade later he was telling Janet Malcolm how embarrassed he was that he fell for MacDonald's act. It was messy business, embedding with the sociopaths to get their story, their essence, their truth. It was messier still to be sued for misleading killers and then have your integrity publicly besmirched. Did he lie to MacDonald? Did he lie to Malcolm? Messy business.

He wasn't easily duped by anyone, much less an arrogant surgeon with a yacht he purchased in Huntington Beach after the murder of his wife and two little girls. Dad knew that in the darkest hours of that cold, rainy morning in 1970, during the amphetamine-fueled fight with his wife, MacDonald snapped. Dad knew that he'd accidentally killed his five-year-old daughter who had come in to see why Mommy was screaming.

He knew how it played out from there: when MacDonald the doctor realized his daughter was dead and he'd beaten his wife unconscious, he was finished. Unless. The *Esquire* magazine Manson murder story sat in the living room. A story of a home invasion by drugged-out hippies and slaughter. He found rubber gloves under the kitchen sink and a knife and ice pick in the drawer and headed back to the bedroom, where his daughter lay dead, his wife unconscious.

"Here's a guy who has killed his wife and kids and he's lying to me consistently and my goal then is to try to keep him talking to learn as much as I possibly can about what kind of psychopath he really is.

"Those letters are embarrassing. I'm embarrassed that I was so badly fooled by this guy," he told Malcolm. I know his voice well. The higher pitch when he's hedging, bending the truth. "I didn't know what the hell to think. He's writing me these letters."

He claimed he'd wished he'd "never written those letters. I'm embarrassed at how genuine the feeling in those letters is."

He asked rhetorically: "How do you get close to them without developing some sort of personal relationship?"

And once it's personal, the lines are blurred, the roles of journalist and subject have evolved into something murkier, where feelings and values and personal morals come into play.

Everyone has their own internal line that they will or won't cross. A boundary. The longer the relationship endures, the trickier it becomes. He knew early on, almost immediately, that MacDonald was a murderer. He could maintain the facade of allegiance to get the best story, or make his true feelings clear to MacDonald and lose access to his subject, risking the fate of the book, and his career.

What choice did he have? "I think you did it, Jeffrey. Now, where were we?"

"Do you want to open the window? It's getting stuffy," Malcolm asked not long after they'd moved inside and the tone had shifted; he'd become the subject, she was the journalist, and their fast friendship was dissolving in real time. He was sweating. He'd invited this and it was too late. He canceled future interviews. He said he wanted to put all of it behind him.

Malcolm contended that he "exhibited himself to her as a defensive, self-righteous, scared man." And brazen. "He left a record of the crime," Malcolm wrote. "The betrayal of the subject."

By the end of her *New Yorker* piece, Joe McGinniss emerged as a more heinous criminal than Jeffrey MacDonald.

It was "the murder of a reputation" according to Nina. That was her characterization of *The Journalist and the Murderer* during an interview for a television series about the MacDonald case and the cottage industry that sprung up around it.

"Joe lived big," Nina concluded. "He went into these things with his eyes open. So, if it's big and bad it was also big and good. You might as well do something big."

In Dad's unfinished memoir, he wrote that Malcolm carved him up like a turkey. Nothing he'd written prior mattered, and he had "only myself to blame." That last admission was a rare instance of him acknowledging culpability for his circumstance.

"Janet Malcolm trashed our lives," Nina said. "He never really got over that. Pilloried for what he thought was good hard journalist work. He lost respect," she said. "It's a tragedy. A small tragedy. It's not murder."

But in the end, it was the murder of a reputation, Nina concluded. It was a crushing blow to his ego and one from which he'd never fully recover.

Would Malcolm have written her story and subsequent book that so eviscerated him had he not invited anyone, her, to write about his case?

What if he'd left it alone? What if he'd been secure enough with what he'd accomplished: a true crime classic in *Fatal Vision*, millions of dollars generated, millions of copies sold, his career relaunched, a subsequent *New York Times* bestseller also adapted for television (in which he had a cameo appearance), and the only price paid was the "occupational hazard" described by Malcolm: a lawsuit settled and paid out by the publisher's insurance company. And a bruised ego.

The question of moral obligation isn't black-and-white. Who is the writer obligated to? Contractually, to the publisher. Morally, he maintained, to the reader, who expected the truth as the writer found it. What did he owe the subject, Jeffrey MacDonald, beyond one-third of all proceeds they'd agreed to at the start in exchange for full access to the defense team and defendant?

If telling the sociopath what he wants to hear keeps him talking, so be it. Politicians, advertisers, factory owners, entertainers and televangelists, the powerful: If the subject invites a writer inside to report what they find, should the writer pull the subject aside and disclose their feelings?

What Nina didn't disclose in the interview was that when the book version of *The Journalist and the Murderer* published in 1991, Dad was editing his third true crime bestseller, *Cruel Doubt*, that earned him an advance of nearly a million dollars (approximately $2 million, inflation adjusted), plus its subsequent television miniseries and whatever that paid him.

And beyond that book? Anything he wanted. He'd had his pick of subjects for which he'd be paid seven figures.

The murder of a reputation hinted at a victimization complex.

During the interviews, Nina never mentioned his net worth at the time of Malcolm's piece, and after. She didn't acknowledge all his self-inflicted wounds. She did, however, reflect on what Dad shared in the quiet moments, during the long, cold winter nights in Williamstown, after the second bottle of wine, how the club he'd never wanted to join had trashed him. To many of them, he'd become a con man, a liar, sloppy, putting his own interests, a big book, ahead of what was morally right.

It was jealousy. They resented his outsider status, that he played and won the game so young, and sustained it, without having to move in their pretentious circles. They resented that he'd achieved more success and notoriety and money than they ever would.

Nina reassured and reminded him, as she always did, that he remained at the very top of his profession. And my dad knew his own heart, his kindness, the decency with which he treated people, strangers and friends alike.

Dad was always going to be the lonely boy in his bedroom on Green Acres Drive in Rye, praying for friends, wondering when his mother would return from the hospital and what he had done wrong to make her so sad.

Vulnerable Dad craved validation. Compulsive Dad needed the chaos he'd invited. Afflicted Dad fed the twin diseases of addiction and depression without restraint. I was his firstborn son and his namesake and witness to it all, from afar and firsthand. And Mom had told me, at an implausibly young age, I was just like him. That still hung over me. It weighed heavier the further he spiraled and the older, taller, and more cynical I got. She was wrong at the start. When she'd first said it, it was pejorative. It was about her pain. Now I was nearing twenty-one and more acutely aware than ever that maybe she was right. My time would come.

NINE

1991

BEFORE

Two years after Janet Malcolm's *The Journalist and the Murderer* was published, *Cruel Doubt* made the *New York Times* bestseller list and made money and spawned another NBC miniseries. Dad was free and rich and unchanged.

I was at his house in Williamstown over Christmas break with Jeanine. We lingered in the kitchen snacking on gourmet chips and sipping ginger ale and Dad had his gin glass and heard me out because I was fresh from another hyper-intensive academic grinder of a semester at Swarthmore and still wired.

He showed us a galley for *Clockers* by Richard Price. It was about drug dealers and cops in New York. I scoffed, handed it back. "He's white?" I asked. "And these characters are Black?" We argued. I explained, with Jeanine standing next to me, that a white man can't write from the perspective of a Black man. "They can't *know*," I concluded. Dad thought it was preposterous. I knew I was right and loved knowing how right I was. More so, I loved Jeanine and showing off for her.

I told him he had no idea how many great thinkers and scientists came from the continent of Africa. *World's Great Men of Color*. Had he read it? He should. He threatened to stop paying my tuition. I told him it was too late, my indoctrination was complete.

Nina took pictures of Jeanine and me in the living room with Mt. Greylock in the distance, spare and cold under a gray December sky. Dad tended the fire and loaded another rotation of Italian opera CDs into the sound system, and when I had a chance I snuck a Geto Boys CD in and told him he had to listen to this track, it was incredible. He gave it a verse, then recoiled at the third "motherfucker" and we went back to opera.

There was no sense then that he was anything but cruising at the highest altitude, nothing but clear skies ahead. Any choppy air was his own making, aerial stunt flying, and he'd come through it. I still didn't know he was taking pills and which pills and how many pills. I knew he drank too much, as always, and that was it.

Jeanine told me two things after that visit. The first was that my dad was rich. I knew he was doing fine but had no concept of just how much he had. That was information he'd never share. The second was that he was intimidating. He spoke with authority and humor and had this big voice and confidence. And he was large, six foot three, and his mouth full of food and a gulp of wine and still he spoke, and if she did dare speak, she'd best be sure of what she was saying, or he'd make her feel like an idiot.

I reassured her that I could feel small around him, even when I was educating him about African history. I left him that week feeling like I often felt with him. He was doing big things and operating at a level I couldn't appreciate. What I didn't know was just how near the edge of the cliff he was.

Professionally, after three true crime hits, his attention shifted to his home state senator and a man about whom he'd written briefly in *Heroes*. Teddy Kennedy never wanted the spotlight, and nothing was ever expected of him until his three older brothers were all struck down. And Dad explained that it was all the fault of their fascist father, who did anything and everything, including sending away the daughter he allegedly raped to get a lobotomy so she would never talk. That's what Dad believed to be true. Or convinced himself he believed.

After the deaths of his first three sons, Joe Kennedy had only Teddy to carry the name forward; the legacy was in his chubby, awkward hands. Is it any wonder he drove himself off that bridge?

Self-destruction was easier than waiting for the bullet to strike him down like his brothers. To stand before the entire nation, crippled by the disdain and disgust of his own father, thrust forward when the only place he ever wanted to be was in the back, wisecracking and sailing and pouring the drinks.

Dad would write an authoritative biography of the last remaining Kennedy, the tragic figure, the reluctant heir to Camelot, the last brother.

Thematically, it made sense. Like the Ailes production that sold Nixon to the voters and the mask of the narcissistic sociopath that was Jeffrey MacDonald, the mythical Kennedys were showing their vulnerability with Teddy's personal unwinding in 1991, bottoming out during a night of drunken carousing with his nephew in Florida that ended with the rape of a woman (some asserted that Teddy himself was involved). *Time* magazine ran a story in April of 1991 headlined "The Ted Kennedy Problem."

Dad would humanize and empathize with ill-fated Teddy. It was as safe a time as any, despite the Kennedy family's remaining influence, to dig deeper. He knew what could ensue without Kennedy's approval. He didn't care.

He knew the risk when he invited Malcolm to interview him. He knew the Kennedy book would generate attention and maybe chaos. No one wrote unauthorized books about the Kennedys without controversy.

Maybe there was a reasonable path forward as an unauthorized

Kennedy biographer. Another author had written an unauthorized biography of Jack called *Reckless Youth*, which was published with some controversy, but was widely acclaimed and sold well.

But Jack was dead and gone and already the subject of countless biographies and assessments of his personal and political life and legacy. One more volume was hardly controversial. Teddy was alive, and if not well, still a sitting senator and the remaining heir to America's last politically dynastic family.

Dad's methods, experimental and boundary-pushing, had succeeded to date. Wildly so. Kennedy was simply next in line for the "McGinniss treatment." Only, the author wasn't in great shape. And nothing he did, despite a million-dollar vote of confidence from the publisher, was executed with the care and precision of his previous works.

He dove in. He was rebuffed by most potential sources. But the book had to be written. He made decisions about how to proceed that were at best unconventional and controversial.

Inferring thoughts that Teddy might have had at various points in his life: What was Teddy thinking when Bobby was gunned down? Was he walking on the beach in Hyannis? Did he consider walking into the icy water until it overcame him? Wouldn't that have been easier than the pressure of what lay ahead: all the expectation and responsibility thrust upon his narrow shoulders, the last brother?

When using passages from some of the sources he relied on for research, rather than footnote and attribute them conventionally, he relied on a sources-cited page at the back of the book.

Nowhere in the volume did he enumerate the number of prescription pills he was consuming daily while researching and writing the book.

Kirkus called it "oddly compassionate." He didn't have disdain for Teddy. Only Teddy's father, and the damage he was willing to inflict on his young, irrelevant son, sending him to ten schools by the time he'd turned thirteen. But *Kirkus* was almost entirely alone in their assessment.

Just as Malcolm had, reviewers and pundits condemned his methods and questioned his journalistic integrity. Months before the book was published, word spread that it was full of lies and innuendo, unsourced and plagiarized.

When it published, he was mauled. A *Charlie Rose* segment with three journalists and Rose (who was fired in disgrace years later for walking around nude in front of his young female assistants) dismantled him. Only Jonathan Alter came to his defense. And even Walter Isaacson conceded the book was "a galloping good read."

Rose invited Dad on the following week to tell his side of the story. Dad was brilliant and poised. Those who knew better, though, knew he was reeling. He'd rage on the phone or in the kitchen with Nina. The Kennedys were destroying the book. They'd teed up the negative reviews, they'd called television networks and told them not to book him or else they'd never get access to another Kennedy ever. They trashed his reputation, sent their lackeys out to call him a plagiarist and liar.

"You like to fly close to the flame," Rose said.

"I like to take chances with technique," he responded.

Critical good will he'd amassed from *The Selling of the President* and *Fatal Vision* and the subsequent hits was gone.

From the *Los Angeles Times* in July of 1993:

Wry, rumpled, best-selling Joe McGinniss is an author without allies. Worse, he is being condemned by peers and crucified by literarists with careers mightier than his. Their words for his new work are consentient poison: avaricious slop, plagiaristic, journalistic histrionics, unadulterated junk, salacious, mean-spirited and novelistic landfill. Yet here is rangy McGinniss, very much alive, fighting back in chinos and too-long shirt sleeves, Irish cocky and joking about meeting in his publisher's Manhattan conference room without windows: "They're afraid I'd jump out."

TEN

2018

AFTER

Starting sixth grade at a new school, Jayson had braces and was young for his class and looked even younger. He had new KDs on his feet, but a little boy haircut, i.e., no Black barber visits yet, no fades and sharp lines because he was still our little egg, not some middle school tween.

Suddenly and for the first time in his eleven years, he had acute self-awareness.

A boy on the varsity basketball team with Jayson's same complexion who wore all the right clothes and had his hair cut the right way and was all cool confidence told friends in the hallway between classes about Jayson's quite-basic little-boy hairstyle and kids' clothes, holdovers from elementary school. There was nothing about our little egg that said "baller."

In response to some teacher's observations about his lack of participation in class, we reminded Jayson that as uncomfortable as he was hearing his own voice, he must participate in classroom discussions. "Raise your hand and ask questions," we told him. "It gets easier the more you do it."

It was the same on the court. "Attack the basket the first time you touch the ball," I told him. It would get easier after that. "The introvert has an extra burden," we told him. Effort was required to feel confident. Hard work and consistency were skills he could develop.

He suddenly required help in a way he hadn't before. And I was there for it, convinced I knew exactly what he needed.

A teacher requested a meeting with me because "soulful, wistful" Jayson's personal essay about his previous school and how much he missed his friends and his teachers raised some concerns. He wrote about how much he missed afternoons after school, since kindergarten, Daddy there to greet him when the day was done, to hand him a snack for playground energy, money for the ice cream truck, to play goalie, to throw the football, to push him high on the swing until he was ready to leap.

I missed it, too, maybe even more than Jayson.

"Is he okay?" the teacher asked me. "Not too sad?"

"He's adjusting. He's very sensitive, like his parents. Sensitive with introvert tendencies. He'll get through it." There was no reason to believe otherwise. Children are resilient.

On his fifth-grade yearbook page, Jayson wasn't subtle:

My hope and dream for the future is to get into a private school called Sheridan. The reason is because Sheridan has a great basketball team and is one of the best schools in America.

He'd be fine. He was the bright, athletic child of two social introverts for whom undeniable talent on the basketball court would be liberating. Self-consciousness would melt away. Confidence would grow. Classmates would talk about that awesome new sixth-grade basketball player. He'd grow more comfortable in class, in his own skin, raise his hand, ask more questions, offer more opinions, clap back at mean-spirited eighth graders. I had it all figured out.

His long-term goal was to someday play basketball "for money."

He also wanted to play Division I. He wanted to play AAU. I told him anything he wanted, he could do. I believed it, too. He'd been labeled a high-IQ player and a "special talent" by nearly every coach who'd seen him.

There was a summer league game in fifth grade: his team with only four players against an opponent with five and a deep bench. On the right side of self-awareness, wholly in the moment, yelling parents and loud whistles tuned out, Jayson tallied twenty-nine of his team's thirty-five points in an overtime loss.

But competitive basketball is not for introverts. Attitude and confidence are essential. The game is fast and intense and intimate. There's nowhere to hide. At the competitive level, it was demanding: either contribute something or get off the court. There was no time to dawdle, pick your nose in right field, swing your foot at the ball should it ever find you on the far end of the pitch, take three wild swings at a ball once every couple of innings.

Jayson possessed innate advantages that let him enjoy the game more than most: exceptional hand-eye coordination and body control allowed him to dribble and shoot and move through and around defenders with relative ease. So, the endorphins kicked in early with every spin move and made shot. I was a decent basketball player. But Jayson had gifts I never possessed.

By the time he arrived at his new middle school, Jayson had played as many hours of basketball on various teams and camps as I had in four years of high school.

He'd also played many hours of video games and after-school soccer and "boys vs. girls," watched *Adventure Time* and *Phineas and Ferb*, and listened to nightly bedtime stories from Daddy and Mommy.

Gifted or not, Jayson would be nurtured and balanced, have as much joy and laughter and fun as he deserved. There was no harshness in his world. Basketball wasn't a refuge from uncomfortable realities, it became the uncomfortable reality.

Fall became winter and for the first time in his life in all the ways a sixth grader at a new school could, he was struggling. He wasn't alone, we assured him. We were a team. Together, we'd figure things out.

And of course, a work-around I was sure would make everything easier for him was fast approaching: the basketball season.

But a picture told the story. It was his first JV middle school home game. A no-cut roster of fourteen kids. A long row of plastic chairs lined up against the wall for the coach, his assistant, and the team. A few minutes into the game, having spent two minutes running up and down the court, getting rid of the ball as soon as he touched it, scared to dribble or shoot, he was yanked, and took the very last seat at the end of the bench, elbows on his knees with a faraway look in his eyes, staring into the middle distance wondering how it went so wrong, so fast.

He was in pain, lost and without answers. And when his gaze met mine across the small gym, what did he find? Comfort, reassurance, and confidence that it was okay, he was fine? Or the dreaded, ugliest expression: the stern, humorless visage of an utterly contemptible man, the type of father I'd always, rightfully, found so detestable?

For twelve years we'd lifted each other to heights I never knew existed. And when he needed me most, that November afternoon, I was gone, snatched and replaced with someone unrecognizable, someone ugly. He was hurting, and I was there to make it so much worse.

Nearly five years since my father's death and two years since my last book, I was well into my new novel, which revolved around a larger-than-life father and his alienated adult children coming to grips with his legacy. I dreamed about my father often.

But nothing was more important, and pressing, than witnessing Jayson falter at something that had brought him so much joy. I was powerless. I couldn't change my father, couldn't keep him closer, healthier, alive. I couldn't fill the void he left. And suddenly, the center of my world, the most pure, uncut high I'd ever experienced, was snatched from me. In its place: a new drug, darker and no less potent. And I was hooked.

I'd seen the other fathers at games, yelling at their sons to "attack the basket!" or "make a play!" or "hustle!" So many parents in middle school gyms screaming at their children, and occasionally I'd find myself swept up in the energy, the urgency, the *need* you could *feel* in the stands, all those parents with all their emotion, their child performing, the hours and money invested, the biggest most unrealistic goals, professional ball and college scholarships and top-tier high schools and AAU programs and immediate shine, that's *my* son and there I was joining the chorus: "Eyes up!" and "Hold your follow-through!"

Some kids needed a sport, or their parents thought they did, to escape dire circumstances, earn a scholarship to high school and then college and a shot at money, NIL deals, maybe professional ball somewhere, someday. It was unseemly, often ugly, and almost always a joyless affair.

Jayson didn't *need* it. And he was often going up against kids who did. And those kids were surrounded by kids just like them, so they showed up hungrier, seasoned, oozing confidence.

"He's on a different path," Jeanine said.

"He does it until he doesn't want to," I said diplomatically, but quickly added, "But if he quits because he's scared, what does that teach him? If he learns to give in to fear now, it just gets easier."

Fear was ruining something for my son that once brought him joy. It was my job to help him. How? He'd need to inure himself to the noise, the rough play, the joyless coaches and environment, and find his inner dog and unleash it. Who would help him do that if not me?

Quitting wasn't an option. "You don't walk away from something you love because it's hard," I told Jeanine, Jayson, anyone who would listen.

We found consensus. Jayson would push himself, with our support, to get the very most out of himself in the classroom and on the basketball court. Hardly groundbreaking. Jeanine delivered the message with an appropriate blend of seriousness and care. I, however, possessed a rapidly devolving delivery style wholly inappropriate for our child.

"You're too hard on him," Jeanine warned me.

"Not hard enough," I insisted.

"You don't know how much power you have," she said. "He can't take your intensity."

"Where else is he going to hear it, then? How else does he learn?"

"You'll break him," she said.

I had too much bass in my voice. My expression was too stern. It was too much for some adults, my wife, my mother, much less my twelve-year-old.

"He needs to have some fear of me, right?" I argued.

She disagreed.

"He's too sensitive."

"He's twelve."

"He's passing to Joey," I reminded her. "Joey's first sport is football. I think soccer is after that. Then basketball because his friends play. And Jayson devotes how many hours, how many nights, weekends to the game? How many nights are we driving out to PG County and down to Alexandria for another workout, another practice, and we ask, I ask, and he keeps insisting, he wants this, loves the game. But he's bringing the ball up and crossing half-court and the first hint of a defender and he's passing to motherfucking Joey?!"

"That may be, but he can't handle you."

But he'd have to because I wasn't walking away. We argued. She had to protect him from me. She was too easy on him, too permissive.

He was *twelve*!

I knew this, I saw it, I processed and resumed. The child would do as I had, face the challenge and pain and carry on. And unlike me, he'd have a father to help him through it, every day and night, and early morning, before the sun rose.

• • •

Beyond self-awareness, there were more serious signs of distress for Jayson. Two leapt out.

His mother and I were discussing family finances. More precisely, his mother was suggesting spending cuts: DoorDash dinners, Amazon Prime, Showtime, and Starz. We were already paying exorbitant rent for the privilege of living in the Spring Valley neighborhood of upper northwest DC and I hadn't earned real money for too long and my third novel was near completion, but not yet under contract. I wasn't insecure or feeling inadequate. Both of my books sold film rights, earned wonderful reviews, did well enough, and I was vindicated, having done what my father said I'd never do.

And I was all in as a dad, in ways I'd never dreamed possible. I'd made a deal with myself and may or may not have consulted Jeanine when I did: she was the Chicago MBA and finance guru who knew money and how to spend, save, invest; I was the writer and devoted dad who was bringing structure and discipline and motivation for our son and making him breakfast on weekdays and ferrying him to and from school and practices and training. It was fair, I'd decided.

But Jayson overheard too much talk of financial pressure and registered seriousness in our tone and internalized the stress. Externalization was inevitable.

One night not long after the start of sixth grade, sitting between us on the sectional, he told us maybe it would be better if he wasn't here. At all. Gone. It would be easier for all of us if he were dead.

We responded immediately with an impassioned no, never, ever, would life be better without you here. It would be infinitely worse. He was the best thing about our lives, we insisted then and repeated often.

The second red flag for us was during a homework session that same fall. He sat at the coffee table struggling to balance equations, pencil in hand. Jeanine patiently tried to explain, make it easier for him to process. To no avail. He couldn't make the particular problem make sense. His face was flushed and his nose and eyes twitched, a facial tick that seemed to worsen when internal stress rose.

It seemed innocuous enough at first, just his little-boy face and click sound or long-blink, mouth-twitch combo. He's a child, we thought. He's got quirks. I used to manically pull up my tube socks, wearing holes in them in elementary school. My friend, who is now a nephrologist, the child of Ivy League scientists, chewed the neck of his shirts all day, a dark bib of saliva-soaked cotton at the end of each school day. We were kids. We did weird things.

But that evening he snapped, and in one motion he gripped his pencil like a knife and drove the point into the back of his other hand, breaking the skin, crying out, exasperated.

We called his counselor with the golden retriever and reported both incidents: his talk of dying and his self-harm. She assured us: we were right to be alarmed.

What was broken in me that allowed me to continue, in light of that moment, with a tone and perspective so ill-suited for my son? But on I went.

"Maybe this isn't the sport for you, Jayson," I told him after another rough game. "The kids are having fun out there, chucking up shots, not giving a shit. They want to be out there. And you're out there looking like you'd rather be anywhere else."

That newly familiar faraway look in his brown eyes. His brain tasked with the impossible: processing big concepts from his suddenly serious stern daddy.

"Maybe you're too comfortable."

He said he wasn't. I knew better.

"That's my fault. I'm sorry. Maybe I need to make it harder for you," I said. I said other things, too, helpful things, comforting things. I reminded him how amazing he was, what a wonderful child, how bright and caring and talented he was. We'd found a counselor. He was doing well in school. He had old friends and new ones. He insisted he loved basketball and didn't want to stop playing. He was trying to please me, and when he spoke that way, he was. And I reminded him: I was terrified to get the ball in eighth grade. Please don't pass it to me, I thought, hiding in the corner during games. I looked funny when I shot and the shots never went in. So why did I play? I loved the game. It was cool. It gave me an identity. So I suffered in silence, no one observing, commenting, critiquing, demanding change, challenging or intimidating me into changing. My mom was at work and Dad was in Massachusetts. You're cursed and blessed, Jayson, I said some version of this. I'm here, and it's painful, but if I wasn't, would you work through it?

"You did," he said.

"It took years and I got lucky. And even then, I never learned the right way to shoot until college and I never pushed myself to learn to handle the ball well enough and didn't lift weights and push myself to be the best. I could have done so much more."

I spoke like this, seemingly forgetting he was merely twelve and not just some kid, but my son, vulnerable and struggling.

After one of his practices, I stood in the stairwell at his school and the coach was explaining that Jayson needed to be more aggressive on the court. He didn't agree with me about Jayson's talent and said he didn't see it. I was suddenly that parent, I realized. I was the asshole convinced their child was special and if the coach gave him the chance, he'd see it, too.

I relayed the coach's assessment to Jayson: "Either show it on the court or don't. That's in your hands. But nothing changes in terms of playing time if you don't."

It was bitterly cold in January and still dark, and he followed me to the frigid car. I didn't wait for the engine to warm and we drove in silence to Bethesda a little before six a.m. Inside, it was bright and alive and we walked up a few flights of stairs and down a narrow hallway and down some stairs and past the tennis and racquetball courts through a doorway and up one last set of stairs: the bright, clean, and empty basketball courts of Bethesda Sport & Health.

Throughout the early-morning workout, he was at turns frustrated, flustered, determined, pissed off, and pumped up. Leaving sweaty and exhausted, he listened to his father tell him: "This is how you change. Put in this kind of work and see if you keep passing to Joey."

With permission from the coach, I attended his next practice. I'd seen parents in the small gym before, milling about. Sometimes even rebound for the kids. I didn't want to presume, so I'd asked if I could watch.

I sat in a plastic chair, the only parent present that day. I pretended to look at my phone, glancing up only occasionally. Coach summoned me for help with a drill or two. I took my seat again. Then I stopped pretending.

I was there for one reason, one goal: radar lock on Jayson. As they had on the elementary school playground, his eyes found me after shots. That day, though, Daddy wasn't smiling.

"You will play hard. You will attack the basket every time you have the ball. You will try to make a play. I'll watch you until you do."

He played his ass off that day. I rubbed his sweaty head and told him I was proud.

The T-shirt I ordered for Jayson read: NOBODY CARES. WORK HARDER. I did care, though. Too much? About the wrong things? Or did I have the right idea, just with brutal execution?

These were questions I should have asked myself then, but didn't. I had a gut feeling, an instinct: my role as his father in that new season of his life wasn't to be hands-off like my own father, or to continue nurturing the little egg, but to challenge, push, prod, insist—set a goal and work for it.

Jayson was to me what a book was to my father. I would make it work and if it didn't I'd lose my mind.

When you meet resistance, do you quit or keep pushing? My role wasn't to bullshit or coddle him when it came to academic effort and basketball ambition.

I bought him a book by Kobe Bryant about his journey, work ethic, and basketball mentality. The son of privilege whose drive to compete and be his very best burned brighter than nearly anyone who ever played the game. He had all the comforts as the child of an NBA player. He'd made himself uncomfortable day after day, year after year, for the game he loved.

Jayson didn't read the book.

I reminded him: if you want to be great at something, comfort isn't your friend. Or it was, but the definition of comfort evolved, or needed to.

I hadn't learned that. I mistook whatever reassurances I offered him as a continuation of the comfort I'd provided for so many blissful years. It was the natural evolution of all the swaddling and tickling and stories and laughter that filled our first eleven years together. But now he needed something new and more sophisticated from me, an emotional maturity and wisdom I lacked.

There were elements of basketball, an activity he wasn't required to pursue, that were harder for him than most. If it was making him unhappy, he should stop. Why not let him? Or let him simply figure it out as he went? If he came to us with questions or concerns, we'd help as best we could.

If he decided competitive basketball wasn't his thing, he could stop, maybe try again later. Or find something else and move through that, too. As he could with so many other interests and phases. He could even find a new passion. That's how I did it when I was his age. So did his mother with competitive gymnastics. We had parents who never once suggested we push ourselves a little harder.

I had the time and energy. This was my job, maybe my calling. He wasn't going to face fear and turn away.

"If you learn to quit now, it gets easier and easier and then that's who you become." I told him what Dad told me. And unlike my father, I had a clear, sober mind and all the time in the world to devote myself to the project that mattered most: not a book, but my son.

There was progress. For him more than me.

He'd worked his way up on his school team after the rough start, having earned the respect and trust of his coach. He was essential to their team's success. The newfound confidence carried over to a summer all-star league tryout. He shined in the tryout and earned a roster spot.

Then they played a game.

Multiple coaches and referees and loud parents who could barely contain themselves because the stakes were high and formula simple: show out here, land a coveted spot on a major AAU squad, win a scholarship to any number of topflight basketball high schools, and then the coveted Division I basketball scholarship. This was the DMV. DC, Maryland, Virginia. The best AAU basketball in the country and it was brutal.

For the sixteen or so players and their parents, the road started there, that Saturday morning in the modest Cesar Chavez High School gym, Drake booming from the loudspeakers. And our little egg, who during warm-ups caught a pass, hit this quick hard crossover-dribble combo into a sidestep jump shot, perfect form, follow-through held like Curry . . . Swish! The net didn't even move! A couple teammates looked at this new kid like "Huh." Then he did it again, but from farther out. Smooth, flawless form. Tight handles. Who was this little kid?

They really didn't give a shit.

And why should they? They had their marching orders and mission. And they played like it: seeking contact rather than avoiding it, elbowing and pushing and cursing and calling kids names and laughing while they ripped the ball from Jayson's little hands and headed down the court for another layup and two more points, and the whistle he heard was the referee signaling a time-out called by his coach, who muttered something dismissive to him and sat him on the bench, where he'd begun the game, wondering if this was the sport for him, how much happier he'd be at home playing *Star Wars: Battlefront* on his PS5 with his mom bringing him another waffle and juice.

"You're going from a plush nest into a rough game," I told him in the car on the drive home. "There's nothing easy about it. But it's reality and if you want play at a high level you have to figure it out."

More advice, pre- and post-game, because he needed it and I couldn't help myself.

"Walk like a baller," I told him. "Chin up. Hands on hips between plays or during time-outs, not clasped together like you're nervous."

"Fake it till you make it" was another favorite. Most of the time, he did some of what I suggested.

When I'd see him trying, though, his little hands on his hips or pounding some dribbles on the sideline, he looked so determined, and I was flush with passing regret.

I suppressed any urge to stride out onto the court and scoop him up and whisk him away, drive us all back to Horace Mann Elementary and hop in goal and let him take penalty shots or go deep for Nerf football tosses like we used to until we heard the garbled soundtrack from the ice cream truck. And then piggyback him to the car at dusk and drive home for dinner and his bath and stories and bed. And do it all again the next day.

Instead, I was the parent in the car grilling their child about their performance, asking impossible-to-answer questions, always too stern, always inappropriate in tone and delivery and context. The game was over. Car ride debriefs were unfair and useless.

My father grilling me after a game? Implausible. He had more tact. He'd have complimented my hustle or my energy and pointed out what some other kids did well, or what the coach was trying to do with schemes and plays. And then maybe gently offer, "It's absolutely okay to take the ball to the basket. You're fast and more athletic than most. What's the worst that can happen? Guess what? Everyone misses. That's the only way to learn and improve. Mess up, keep going."

He'd reserve and direct anger at people who he felt deserved it, maybe a critic or publisher or Janet Malcolm. But never his children and never me. Maybe he felt he'd done a lifetime's worth of damage when he left and that any harshness would be nothing short of cruel. Maybe if he'd been present and invested like I was with Jayson, he'd have reacted similarly. Or maybe not. Maybe my raw and unfiltered emotion in the face of my child's distress was unique to me.

I was treating Jayson, and whatever glitch denied him and me the high we deserved, like Dad would a negligent or incompetent publisher.

My son felt bad enough as it was, having played poorly or scared, or both. What he didn't need or deserve was me making it worse. I knew this. I knew better. And did it anyway.

To his immense credit, over the course of his seventh-grade basketball season, Jayson didn't quit and eventually thrived.

He played mostly free and had fun. He earned the starting point guard role for the varsity team. He was clapping up teammates and getting knocked to the floor and hopping back up and knocking down foul shots and layups and threes. He helped lead the team to the championship game.

He looked little, but earnest and tough and committed, and when they lost, he was the one member of the team to sit with his head in his hands, tears streaming down his sweaty, red cheeks. I held him and kissed his hot forehead and told him how much I loved him. And simultaneously thought: he needed to be more aggressive, in the second half especially, only took two shots, missed both. They needed him to score more.

I insisted that we get in the gym immediately after losing the championship game. The next day we started after school. "Do this every season. Win or lose. The next day, you go to work. Next season starts now."

He worked hard that day. Shot after shot.

"I'm so proud of you," I told him, hugging his sweaty little frame. "You're doing it. Everything you wanted to do you're doing."

He was breaking through. He was almost thirteen. He wanted more and was just getting started. Then Kobe Bryant's helicopter crashed. Along with his thirteen-year-old daughter and two of her teammates on their way to an AAU basketball game, Bryant was killed. A week later the first cases of a highly contagious and often lethal virus were detected in the United States. There was no vaccine and no cure. Life, as we knew it, along with Jayson's progress, stopped. My descent into paternal malpractice, however, continued unabated.

I dropped the ball. It's that simple. When he was two and three and I'd struggled, I did what was necessary, finally, and got some help. No more tears in weird places. Chemical realignment so I could be present for our own little Golden Age.

But there was more work to do. A prescription and a dozen fifty-minute conversations with the provider—when he was three and I was a mess because it was all too good to last—was a start. I treated that like an achievement, if not a cure. Before long, after the psychiatrist fell asleep one too many times, it was just me, the daily pill and life.

Dad was dead and gone. That was always going to be the outcome without a course correction. His was a decades-long unraveling. A self-destruction he didn't hide and often shared.

I'd hung around his Williamstown house over Christmas break in college with Jeanine and pointed out all the ways he was screwing himself and Mason and Gavin. I would offer ideas and solutions and hopes for a better, healthier existence for him. And didn't he understand? If he was better, we'd all be better. If he tried at all, we'd all benefit. Wasn't that the point? The parent-child contract, the implicit agreement a parent makes with their children: I'll always put you first.

I'll do the work to be better for you. But Dad saw contracts, whether professional, marital, or paternal, as one more shackle from which to break free.

Instead of effort and improvement, he spiraled. When I spoke up, it made no difference. Thoughts kept to myself accumulated, always simmering, acid-like. Until I felt cornered in a hotel suite at twenty-eight by the love of my life and raged against the inevitable, ending up just like the worst of him. I'd do as he had. I'd feel awful, trapped, behave badly, resent and rebel and fail. Trying, evolving, making the hard choices to look inward held no appeal. He didn't and I wouldn't.

And even later, when he was at his most vulnerable and still infuriating me, I couldn't help myself. I had to try. And like always, nothing I did with him, no amount of arguing or pleading or empathy, helped keep him alive or even healthy.

Decades of that grueling dynamic with Dad wore and weighed me down. He loomed like an ever-present storm cloud. Earnestly and foolishly, I tried to tame it. What I carried in 2015, when he was no longer on this earth and I was the fatherless father to one son, was something toxic, dormant since May 1, 2007, when the words from the doctor echoed through the delivery room as she extracted my son from the womb, "He's a big one!" The spell was cast, the high induced.

Until, twelve years later, Jayson faltered. He needed me. And I hadn't done the work. I hadn't spent time making sense of Dad, and the resentment, regret, and anger I carried. I hadn't learned the right lessons from Dad's mistakes to be better for Jayson. I was cruising along and congratulating myself for handling the first eleven years of his life better than I thought I would.

I wasn't prepared for my child in need. It shocked, scared, and challenged me. I was suddenly unmoored, fathering in ways wholly my own, but with tendencies that bore a striking similarity to my father's worst personal instincts—lack of control, raging insecurity, and unchecked anger.

My high, as alcohol and pills did for my father, had masked so much. Jayson's challenges at twelve cut me off cold. He was vulnerable and I was powerless and desperate, like an addict without a fix, like my father in the wake of every professional crisis. Like my father, I didn't see it. There were children at stake. What more motivation to change did we need?

ELEVEN

1993

BEFORE

Chinese food cartons filled the table. An empty bottle of red, a second one newly opened, plates and glasses and unopened fortune cookies. An extra chair was brought in from the kitchen so that the six of us could sit together for dinner, Dad and Nina, Mason and Gavin, Jeanine and me. I was visiting toward the end of the summer slog that was the publication of *The Last Brother: The Rise and Fall of Teddy Kennedy*.

The previous months were punishing. Money didn't make the demise of his career better. There was no next topic or new idea. And if there were, so what? He was toxic.

Mason broke a long silence, which was rare. He seldom spoke. He shared a monotone sentence or two about something current like Bill Clinton's White House, where I'd recently interned, or maybe it was about Chicago, where Jeanine was headed for business school. To his credit, Mason tracked our lives and cared enough to let us know.

Earlier that afternoon, Jeanine and I had followed cheerful Gavin, who was seven, to the basement to play. It was a jarring image: the large and brightly lit windowless room was littered with every expensive toy and device imaginable. Drum sets and video game consoles and miniature cars and electric scooters and plug-in guitars and beanbag toss games and dartboards and electronic-scorekeeping miniature basketball hoops. There were piles of barely used pristine toys.

There was something unsettling about the image—so much money spent, any impulse or request granted by his father.

In lieu of something else? Structure? Expectations? Responsibility?

Everything and everyone would be fine. Mason's grades were stellar, and he'd have his pick of boarding schools. Gavin continued to delight. There was no end to the money because he had a few million and royalties poured in and interest accrued and there was always another big book and more money coming and if it took the boys a few years to find their way, what would be the harm?

But his name, in the wake of MacDonald's lawsuit and Malcolm's character assassination and the Kennedy machine, had become synonymous with deception, plagiarism, and fabrication. His last book may have already been written.

He was slumped a bit at the head of the table, staring into the pinot in his nearly empty glass.

"Everybody hates me," he said to himself.

The words hung in the room. The chandelier lights were too bright, and the candles were unlit.

"No one hates you, Dad," I finally said.

I certainly didn't. I cherished our political conversations and mining his deep reservoir of personal knowledge about almost any leader I'd ask about. We used to talk about sports, too, but he'd stopped caring because they were all corporate and corrupt and American football was militaristic and all the owners were rich assholes.

For my sake, he treaded lightly around Clinton because I was a fan and he admired Paul Wellstone, but there just weren't any Bobby Kennedys left. So, what was the point of engaging?

I was there because he'd always ask when I was coming up and say he couldn't wait to see me and I knew he meant it. Though less and less. Not because I'd done anything wrong but because his world as he knew it was crumbling.

During that end-of-summer visit, there was no spirited debate about Richard Price or African history. I didn't dare ask about next books.

He was wiping sweat from his brow. He ate kung pao and noodles and drank more wine. He'd already taken whatever allotment of prescription pills he was consuming. I mostly sat waiting for the right time to excuse myself with Jeanine.

It's a wonder he'd survived. Fifty-one-year-old men twenty pounds overweight with poor diets who rarely exercised and drank as much as he did were leading candidates for premature death. Those same men who mixed maximum dosages of sedatives with alcohol were uniquely vulnerable.

He felt radically alone. All his worst fears were realized: it really was all blowing away.

Mornings for Dad became noon and early afternoon before he could rouse himself to face another day. He was foggy and hungover. No good news would come in the mail or on the phone. If he were lucky, maybe he'd sleep through not just the mornings but entire days. Maybe he'd simply pass out one lonely night in "Williamstomb" and not wake up. Oh God, and the leaves were turning and falling and the days were shorter and colder and it was winter already, or would be, and that meant five months of frigid lifelessness on Oblong Road. Gavin's eyes always found his dad, always with that hint of hopefulness in them that made everything worse.

A looming decision hung over everything. There was no easy answer and all the options sucked.

Mason was turning fourteen. He was suddenly this tall, skinny teenager with greasy hair and a monotone voice and superior intelligence who remained undiagnosed with intractable socialization challenges. Dad and Nina knew his high school social experience would be a struggle no matter where they sent him. What choice did they have?

What did his pediatrician and therapist think? Were they consulted? Was there even a regular therapist?

There were three options: the local public high school; Buxton, a small, artsy private school down the street; and boarding schools.

The public school was, according to Dad and Nina, not sufficient for their children. But the same school had enough quality to host students of exceptional academic potential from underserved areas from as far away as the Bronx and Boston and Cleveland in a program called A Better Chance. During my time in Williamstown, I'd even befriended one student from Philadelphia and dated another from the South Bronx, each of whom would go on to highly selective liberal arts colleges.

The students resided in a house on the campus of Williams College and were assigned a host family, where they would spend Sunday afternoons hanging out, doing homework, playing with the family's kids or dogs or both, eating a home-cooked dinner. Could the high school that hosted these bright, ambitious kids have been so terrible?

Mason could have been home by four every afternoon. He could have had a tutor or therapy or both. He could have had two parents making sure he was getting through his classes as he should and meeting with teachers and working with counselors to navigate what was a uniquely challenging stretch of life for any adolescent, much less one with his social impairments.

Or maybe Buxton would have been a better, more nurturing environment. Maybe they explored the option, queried the school about students like Mason, whether it was a good fit for him. It was small and private and close to home.

Either would have kept him home with his parents. Either would have kept him living in Williamstown, home to one of the most prestigious liberal arts colleges in the world, with access to any number of resources. He would have his little brother, Gavin, and Lucy and the cats and both parents at home.

In a different state of mind, maybe Dad and Nina would have

volunteered as a host family for an ABC student on Sundays. Maybe that would have been good for Mason. Maybe it would have helped with socialization. It would have given Mason a campus ally, someone to look out for him in high school. Maybe it would have signaled to him and Gavin that they were a family, invested in one another, in the community, and that no matter the challenges their children faced, they would face them together.

They decided Mason would apply to and attend boarding school. They'd send him away for nine months a year. It was what Mason wanted, my dad insisted. And given what life with Dad was like those days, it was likely true.

They sent him knowing he might suffer in silence, that no one there would look out for him. How would he be treated by classmates? Would he suddenly be able to speak up for himself? Defend himself? Forge connections and make friends like the other students? Would he find help if he needed it? Was it even available?

They knew it would be rough. But he'd insisted: he wanted to be like the other kids and that meant the best boarding school he could get into.

He left home without a remedy or even a clinical diagnosis for his condition (what would later be labeled Asperger's syndrome). Maybe being forced to socialize in the dorms and with a roommate and classmates would shake something loose, trigger a breakthrough or even nudge him toward a new phase, something resembling normal?

As it was, Dad was hardly in any condition to help. And he'd maintained Mason didn't need help. He wanted to go! What kind of parent would deny their child the best possible education when that child wanted it?

There was no reason to worry. Grade reports would come, and they would prove he was fine. Straight A's as always. Stellar write-ups from his teachers. If anything went wrong, the school would let them know. He was only a couple hours away. It was a superior education. He'd have his pick of colleges when the time came. And who knows, maybe there would be medication by then that could help him.

For Mason, all was well. And Gavin was perfectly well adjusted, addressed them as "Mom" and "Dad" instead of "Nina" and "Joseph" and had lots of friends, and even if he had some academic difficulties in elementary and middle school, it was all manageable and nothing to worry about. And when the time came, they'd send him to the boarding school of his choosing, too, if he had the grades to get in. And even if he didn't, families who could pay could always find a school.

Behind the wheel of the Land Rover, the sprawling campus of Mason's new home in the rearview, Bob Dylan playing, Nina riding shotgun, Gavin strapped into the back seat, Dad pulled away, leaving his son behind. Was he sad? Worried? Or relieved?

Wasn't it so much easier for everyone without Mason's silent, ghostly presence and unresolvable weirdness skulking around the house? The embodiment of some kind of karmic retribution for the pain Dad inflicted on his first three children: a child of their own, he and his new wife, the one he left his family for—but their child wouldn't speak and refused to poop or call them Mom and Dad and only ate foods that were yellow and spent hours in the upstairs bathroom every night. What was he doing in there?

When Dad woke in the morning, with Mason gone and not back until Thanksgiving, how shitty did he feel for the relief he enjoyed not having his son in the house? He knew the likelihood was high that elite boarding school boys might eat a child like Mason alive. And they would.

The seasons wore on and Dad moved through the days, after late, hazy starts, mostly in his office or living room listening to the hundreds of classical and opera and Bob Dylan CDs he'd amassed with a fire crackling and the woodstove warming the kitchen and Gavin running around and Nina developing pictures in her home office, and there were book ideas and brainstorms and trips planned. If I didn't look closely and didn't know any better, even in the wake of Janet Malcolm and the Kennedy debacle, life at 244 Oblong Road may have appeared something bordering on idyllic. He was casting about, if not forging ahead. He was searching for something new, looking abroad even, where they didn't care about Kennedys and Janet Malcolm.

In the meantime, he had cabinets and freezers filled with wine and gin and vodka, and the money, millions, in various trading and hedge fund accounts. Desk drawers were scattered with translucent plastic brown bottles of mood-altering medications. There was no psychologist or therapist keeping tabs.

He was at once the patient and doctor and bartender and pharmacist and money manager. This was his new normal, a combustible cocktail of wealth and addiction and alienation and depression. Minus one set of eyes on him, his middle son no longer staring at him, silently, oddly assessing and judging him.

Life for his first three children unfolded in heartening ways. Sarah and Cynthia were getting married months apart to caring, stable men. I was graduating from Swarthmore. He was proud and likely relieved and maybe even a little surprised. Joe graduating from Swarthmore was likely not an outcome he considered when I was leaning on math-for-dummies books and repeating seventh grade.

Dad had no next book. And everyone still hated him. If he was going to resurrect a career and pay for boarding schools and college tuitions and weddings and health insurance and the mortgage, he certainly better find a project.

Spring had come late to the Berkshires that year. It was March and April and cold and only the sun setting a little later each week gave any hint that light and warmth was possible. Dad was casting about, hungering for inspiration.

There had to be something pure and disconnected in any way from publishing and even family. For years he jogged. Mile after mile. He trained for and completed marathons in Boston and New York City.

But his knees were shot. Even long walks were painful. Drinking and pills got him through the days and nights, but what would get him through the darkest season of life to date? Maybe nothing would. His grandfather had died in his twenties, his own father at fifty-six.

And then suddenly he discovered something that would transport him away from New York publishing and Williamstomb and everything that made him so miserable. He became possessed by a new, unbridled passion, if not compulsion.

This soccer thing was intoxicating! The unbridled passion of the people, the common folk and elite swept up in a game where time never stopped, the ball kept moving, always the buildup and anticipation of that ever-elusive score . . . Goooooooooal!!!

This game was operatic and orgasmic and had decades of history and cultural significance behind it. Americans didn't and couldn't understand it. Which intensified its appeal. Embracing soccer was a "fuck you" to the American elites and dolts and their beer-swilling "football" and dreadfully boring baseball.

The game was played by South Americans and Africans and Asians and Europeans. It was the global game of the people. It was as real and authentic as a lived experience could be. And for a man who was professionally dead and emotionally moribund, the discovery was a spiritual defibrillator.

Soccer possessed him and wouldn't let go, breathed life into a dying man. And who knows, maybe he could even find his next book there. Who gave a shit if Americans didn't read it. He had millions. Americans were idiots, and the country was rotten, and he wouldn't write it for them anyway. It would be for him, a testament to his full immersion in the passion that revitalized him and gave him purpose once again, a reason to go on living.

In the age before the internet, he drove to distant shops to find soccer news, magazines, whether in English or Italian. He would record matches at all hours, played in countries he'd never set foot in.

On a serene late morning in the Berkshires, Dad leapt from the couch, began screaming and waving his arms, all red-faced rage, spitting curse words at the giant television screen in the living room: a Bolivian goal against Germany was waived off. Seven-year-old Gavin cowered, frightened his father had become a monster.

Nina comforted him and explained it away. Dad was "just having fun, see, he was fine," and Dad might have forced a broad smile and falsetto laughter for Gavin while still spitting out another couple of invectives at the television screen. He wasn't a monster at all. But in many ways he was possessed by forces, chemical and otherwise, that rendered him uncontrollable and unpredictable.

He couldn't help himself. To anyone who would listen, Nina and all his children, he would talk incessantly about Bulgarian strikers and Norway's chances and Nigeria's attack and Baggio's brilliance. He would later write about the power of his new obsession: "The manic nature of my enthusiasm was evident from the start." No mention was ever made of what we'd all learn later was the insane amount of prescription pills he was consuming daily.

He rode the new high to Pennsylvania for Sarah's wedding. He was neither somber nor sulking. He was a well-dressed, beaming father, head held high walking his daughter down the aisle of the redbrick church in suburban Philadelphia to marry a professor of biology from Reading.

And Cynthia's wedding was later that summer in the South of France to an equally kind man with seven brothers and generational wealth. There was so much that was so good for his first three children. And he had a new passion. A reason for wanting to get out of bed in the morning.

TWELVE

1994

BEFORE

The Knicks were playing Houston for the NBA championship, but the prime-time broadcast we were watching was interrupted.

In the flat orange glow of Los Angeles twilight, cruising along a six-lane freeway at an unusually modest pace: a white Ford Bronco belonging to forty-six-year-old Hall of Fame NFL running back and movie star O. J. Simpson, identified in that moment by police as "a fugitive from justice."

Unfolding on the screen in real time along with the most infamous police chase in American history was Dad's road back to writing relevance.

Another horrific murder offered him what might be a last, best chance to restore his professional reputation and top the bestseller lists once again and earn ever more financial security for himself and his family. All he would have to do was commit to writing a book about the O. J. Simpson murder trial.

As I waited for my job at a political consulting firm to start, I spent too many mornings watching live coverage of the O. J. Simpson preliminary hearings, hoping for word from Dad that he would in fact write the book. All would be well. He'd be back on television and a household name and publishing circles would have to welcome him back because a monster book deal and huge sales would confirm once again that Joe McGinniss was a star.

On July 13, 1994, in *The New York Times*:

> "McGinniss Goes to Crown"
> For the past several weeks Morton Janklow had been hunting for a publisher for his client Joe McGinniss's next book which is to be about the O. J. Simpson case.
> ... The book was to be about far more than just Mr. Simpson. "His book, while examining all aspects of the crime and the trial, will more importantly explore modern-day heroes, sports mythology and the incredible power of the media," said Betty Prashker, Crown's editor in chief, who acquired the book.

The offer was $1.7 million for two books. The topic of the second book would be up to Dad, i.e., freedom, the status he valued more than any.

Whatever he wrote about the trial, the investment from the publisher guaranteed a massive publicity push, wall-to-wall television appearances, a national and international tour, and the sale of serial and film rights. And then he'd be free to write the book of his choosing. Anywhere in the world he wanted to go. Any topic, however obscure. Even soccer.

I told him on the phone from San Francisco that he'd earned and deserved it, reminded him what he already knew: one of the biggest publishers in the world wanted him to author the book about the "Trial of the Century." To make sense of the madness that was the media obsession with the case. He could help make sense of it for all of us. What it says about the country, people, everything.

I was, at twenty-four, still his loyal firstborn son. I knew the talents he possessed were rare. I knew he could produce something unique and savage.

His words would be cynical and smart. Like Tom Wolfe on the Ken Kesey bus, he would turn the cameras in the courtroom around and train them on all of us: the gawkers and tabloid junkies. This was who we were and we were only getting worse, something he'd been lamenting for years.

I told him to hell with Janet Malcolm and the Kennedys and everything anyone said about him. It was irrelevant. It was in the past. The trial and his book and name and brand were happening now. He was back.

Maybe I needed him back, too. Maybe everyone did. I was naive enough to believe that somehow this book would do it. The project would return stability and energy and career momentum. His name and brand would be restored. The rest of him would follow. He'd be forced to curb excesses and stick to a schedule. He'd meet obligations. He'd be an example. We'd be proud and he'd feel better because of it. We'd have more open and honest conversations about his health and well-being because he'd feel better about his condition, his ego repaired, his stature returned.

"I suppose," he responded with resignation in his voice. The call didn't last long. He'd only had a few minutes. It was halftime. Argentina and Nigeria were locked in a spirited match at the World Cup. He couldn't tear himself away.

These massive stadiums full of people losing their minds in unison, breaking out in song, cheering and laughing and dancing and crying, waving flags and igniting fireworks while twenty-two young men spent ninety minutes plus stoppage time working feverishly and desperately for a single moment of glory. Life was not simply being lived but celebrated. And after so much private suffering, he'd wanted in.

But the Los Angeles County courthouse in downtown LA, which he'd last visited to testify in his own defense against Jeffrey MacDonald in 1987, was where, contractually, he would have to be for the foreseeable future. Not in an outdoor stadium celebrating life with thousands of strangers or even in his living room joining from afar. He was suddenly obligated to report and write something familiar—awful people doing terrible things and the gross American media obsession and saturation that followed. Hardly life-affirming.

But he went to work.

He petitioned Judge Lance Ito for one of the highly coveted few full-time seats in the courtroom. He and Dominick Dunne were the only two writers granted daily access for the yearlong trial. He was positioned between Dunne and the family of one of Simpson's two murder victims, Ron Goldman. Despite his claims for the past year of career death, of professional cancellation, he was once again at the center of things.

The courtroom seat was further proof: Joe McGinniss remained a smart bet, worth the investment as one of the preeminent true crime writers in America. Only Gavin didn't know or care. He was eight and his dad would be leaving for months, if not longer, and that would suck, more for him than for Dad. What sucked most for Dad? All the soccer he'd miss.

I saw him again in France for Cynthia's wedding. He looked healthier than he had in years in the quaint old church in the countryside. He wore his linen blazer and pressed shirt and tie and slacks. He held his head high in pictures. He was in his element: the French knew soccer. Aside from the flaky couple from Texas who kept taking pictures of their food, everyone there was likely to be European and therefore as eager to talk about the impending World Cup and the European professional seasons that would follow. All thanks to Cynthia and her passion for French, which lead to her meeting Yves, the kind, funny Frenchman working in Boston at the same time she graduated from Boston College and landed a job in the city.

I didn't know then that Dad had taken Cynthia to the Preakness in Baltimore when she was ten. They placed bets and she won hers with a horse called Lemon Tree. He knew one of the jockeys from the many other races he'd attended. He loved the horses. The track, the betting. The rush and power and potential for glory, even at 10–1 odds. He'd once hitchhiked with a high school friend to the Kentucky Derby, snuck in over a high fence, pestered none other than Jackie Robinson for a dollar so they could place one more bet before heading back to Rye. His only novel, *The Dream Team*, was centered around horse racing. He introduced Cynthia to the jockey, who was French, and wearing shimmering pink and emerald silks that mesmerized her.

That sunny afternoon left an indelible imprint on Cynthia. The race won by her horse and the French jockey and those brilliant colors and Dad. She later wondered whether that magical day with him was the genesis of her love for French. She'd become fluent, study abroad, earn her master's in French from Middlebury, and find a job in Boston where she'd meet Yves.

I don't remember complaining to Jeanine about Dad in France. Most of my familiar worries were about his drinking. He'd endured a professionally hellish season that cast a pall over everything until he found soccer. But when I did raise concerns, or lament his obsession with the worst things people said about him, or wonder out loud how he could send Mason off to boarding school knowing how vulnerable he was, when I talked about all these things with Jeanine, which was more often than maybe was healthy for a young adult in the world, I knew she understood all about exasperating fathers.

Multiple sclerosis was ravaging her own dad. He couldn't walk without a cane and later a walker. Diabetes was blinding him. Untreated depression kept him dreamy and self-obsessed, phone calls and visits hijacked by his meandering thoughts. He was eating the worst foods and forgetting or refusing his medication. He was exhausting her mother.

He'd been an artist and a teacher and jumped out of a plane as a member of the 101st Airborne to protect the Little Rock Nine. She'd call home and hope her mother would answer. If it was him, she'd listen to meandering tales about poems or stories he was working on that she knew weren't real, or weren't really going anywhere. She knew her mother had to summon an ambulance because of a diabetic episode and on the way to the hospital he'd convinced the EMTs to stop at the sandwich shop for meatball subs. Her heart broke a little more every time they spoke.

What was it with our fathers? Maybe they were both doing their best. Look at the fathers who'd raised them, depression and drinking and decades of physical and emotional abuse. Weren't their lives and the children they'd raised evidence of progress? Wasn't that enough?

When Dad wasn't on the phone with his agent and assessing the numbers and the calendar and the monumental commitment he was making to a story that he already disdained, he was glued to soccer matches from around the globe.

He used the "soccer as love making" comparison more than once, all the buildup and stops and starts and, finally, a goal. *Magnifique!* he said over the phone or in person or both. He repeated himself if he'd been drinking, which was always.

And Baggio! This Italian maestro, the pitch was his canvas, and he was the artist. He was a Buddhist! Roberto Baggio was a man of peace and meditation and athletic brilliance the likes of which the world had never witnessed! Hyperbolic Dad had adopted both Baggio and Italy as his own. When the World Cup ended and the Italian professional leagues began play, he'd be on the first flight he could book to Rome or Milan. He may never return.

There was just that one nagging commitment he'd made to Random House and that farce of a trial in downtown Los Angeles. By happy accident he'd found passion, a life force. He'd been a dead man walking and suddenly, he claimed, he was never more alive!

• • •

After graduating from Swarthmore, Jeanine and I left for San Francisco because we'd reasoned there was no better time to try someplace new. We liked the way traffic slowed for pedestrians crossing streets downtown and that no one gave us, Black Jeanine and white me, a second look. Too soon after our arrival, a year maybe, between Costco trips for bags of frozen chicken breasts and ferries to Sonoma, all I really wanted to do was play pickup ball or hit North Beach with some new friends. And sometimes I did. And sometimes Jeanine and I argued about it because what came first? Our time together, us, or some random new friends and pickup basketball? Weren't we building toward something, even if unstated?

For the first time since meeting her I felt confident that I could make it on my own. That I could survive, even thrive, on my own in the world. At the same time my dad was feeling trapped in a downtown Los Angeles courtroom, I was similarly restless. The apartment I shared with Jeanine felt like a contract I wasn't prepared to honor. I knew my father's history well. I knew he'd rushed into marriage for all the wrong reasons and blew it all up soon after. I knew I was just like him. I sat outside on Columbus with my baller friends on a cool and misty Friday night sipping cappuccino and flirting with women and realized I was doomed to end up just like him.

Jeanine found another place in the same development, and we lent each other laundry detergent and I borrowed her car to drive to USF to hoop and she met her work friends for drinks and readied herself for her Chicago MBA. She left and I stayed. I was arrogant or oblivious enough to think that she'd be in my life forever, would be the woman I'd marry when I was ready.

The gold Oscar statuette was heavier than it looked. It was cold to the touch and smooth when I gripped it tightly with one hand and gestured with the other.

My acceptance speech was brief and heartfelt:

"None of this would have been possible, this house, this life, without the murders of multiple innocent women and girls at the hands of the monstrous men of *Fatal Vision* and *Blind Faith* and *Cruel Doubt*. To the murderous sociopaths, and O.J., who made this moment possible, thank you."

Sarah and Gavin offered polite applause.

We'd been in Beverly Hills on San Ysidro just off Benedict Canyon and a stone's throw from Sunset Boulevard and the Beverly Hills Hotel. It was our first night in our father's rented house: six thousand square feet, $20,000 a month, in-ground heated pool and Jacuzzi, mature palms and oleander, pool house and billiard table, Matisse and Picasso and Pollock on the walls. The house belonged to someone in the film industry and when we weren't jumping into the pool or soaking in the Jacuzzi or shooting pool or giving award speeches with someone else's Oscars, we were wondering how Dad could possibly spend so much money on a house.

He'd spent a couple weeks in the Intercontinental Hotel downtown, where the jury was sequestered. During a visit to Los Angeles, Cynthia had found some furnished corporate apartments not far from the courtroom that she tried to convince my father would save him thousands of dollars. They were tastefully appointed and modern with all the amenities. He played along. Humored his firstborn. The daughter who once called him on his bullshit about just how much he loved her. "You say that, then you always go away again," she said when she was six. And there she was, walking him through the savings if only he'd leave the pricey hotel for something practical, less indulgent. After all, there was no telling how long he'd be out there.

She couldn't begin to appreciate the depths from which he'd climbed, thanks to soccer, a double murder committed by a celebrity, and an arsenal of prescription medications designed to rewire the circuitry of his brain to not merely avoid depression but to feel good, if not chemically high, most of every waking hour, long enough until it was socially appropriate to enjoy his first pour of gin.

Neither a corporate apartment downtown nor a suite in a five-star hotel were adequate for the moment. The sprawling home of an Academy Award winner suited him best and was the only way he'd survive this assignment.

He had so much and what difference did a few thousand, or tens of thousands of dollars, make? He had millions. He was writing the biggest book about the biggest story in the world. If he needed a Beverly Hills estate to withstand the grueling days in the downtown courtroom, so be it.

A break from the cool, gray San Francisco summer was welcome. Driving along Sunset Boulevard through dreamy, warmer Beverly Hills at dusk in a rented convertible playing Tupac on the CD player, feeling more comfortable and at ease than I had any right to, and later drifting along 3rd Street Promenade in Santa Monica, laughing with my sisters and Gavin and my father as my stepmother snapped pictures like we were some kind of celebrity family, all felt surreal and indulgent. We were there for Dad and Dad was there because two people were butchered to death by a celebrity and our father had so badly mismanaged his career that the only way to resurrect it was to write a book he didn't want to.

I'd swim in the pool and splash around with my sister and her friend and Gavin and then we'd all eat Italian delivery from some Westwood eatery. I drove a rented convertible alone at dusk through winding hillside roads through the canyons and neighborhoods with names I knew from maps and television shows like Holmby Hills and Bel Air and gazed up at skinny palm trees and played Dr. Dre and U2 on repeat and soaked up the vacation I'd craved. I decided to head to Brentwood to the house on Bundy and turned the volume down and crawled past the ever-present collection of gawkers snapping pictures of the front gate and small alcove where the bodies were found, Nicole with her neck sliced so deep her head nearly came off.

That was the reminder, the stark cold reality behind these circumstances, the lavishness amid grotesque tragedy, that signaled for anyone paying attention: this wouldn't end well.

Maybe it was the illusoriness of being there, so out of place and for all the wrong reasons and strangely comfortable and entitled and removed, as though time was suspended, and anything could and likely would happen. Dad again cashing in on someone else's tragedy.

Being there with him made me nostalgic for something fleeting between us. Dad and me on South Street in Williamstown in 1983 talking about my new crush and school and what I wanted for dinner and the feeling that a life with him may have been possible after all, if only I'd given it more time, tried a little harder, grown more comfortable in my own skin.

I could have stayed and grown secure enough to challenge him about his drinking, push him to get help. I could have pushed him to help my mother. I could have tried to figure out why he required nudging to do it, what was wrong with him, a grown man, that required his child to remind him of his responsibilities?

I could have chosen not to run. I was fast developing a Dad-like tendency: in the face of discomfort or fear, flight was increasingly the answer.

He was struggling. The days in the LA County courthouse were long and slow, rife with sidebars that dragged on to the point that journalists made these little buttons with the word "sidebar" and a line through it and passed them around. No more sidebars! Get on with it for Christ's sake! He was slowly dying.

The prosecution spent countless hours deep in the scientific weeds, losing the interest of the jurors quickly. His notes were kept in a glossy Museum of Contemporary Art Los Angeles notebook that he mostly filled with his customary illegible scrawl and shorthand.

As the prosecution fumbled away the case with meandering technical and quantitative scientific evidence involving "lambda markers" and "Mini Gel" he wrote, "This is the hard way to disprove a conspiracy," and more to the point: "Yawn, Snore, Doze."

"Hard to imagine jury is following this much detail."

"I think I'll kneel in the center aisle and pray for this to be over."
"What does [prosecutor] Darden think about all day?"

Seated where he was in the courtroom, Dad listened helplessly to Ron's sister sobbing as her brother's butchered body was shown on a large screen. The defensive wounds on his hands and forearms, evidence of his heroic effort to fight back, were found in his bloodied knuckles.

He noted that he'd watched in disgust at the open flirtation between prosecutor Marcia Clark and the defense team. He'd endured the sleazy, racist cops and Judge Ito's growing ego, the most famous judge on the planet. He was sick of glimpsing Robert Kardashian leaning forward to whisper encouragement or snide remarks into the ear of his pal O.J.

Somewhere in all of this was a kernel of truth about America and race and celebrity and excess and narcissism and corruption and superficiality. Dad was going to expose it and call us all to task. He was expert at obliterating facades. It was grotesque farce, and he would write it like no one else.

There was no book I'd more eagerly anticipated. More than the Kennedy biography, which I'd wanted him to take on because I wanted my heroes to be real, flawed, but demonstrating resilience in the end, always arcing toward redemption, even if falling short.

I'd envisioned him presenting Kennedy as deeply troubled, traumatized, and wounded and having demonstrated horrific judgment in moments of crisis only to soldier on because of what was expected of him and then failing to meet expectations and eventually, with the burdens finally lifted, finding peace and calm in his final years. And most significantly, to have made the effort at self-improvement, falling and rising again.

There was dignity in the effort, whether it succeeded or not. Trying was the point. Dad's version of facing adversity of his own making was to keep writing, self-medicate, and search for the most appealing exit.

• • •

When he wasn't in court, he and Nina spent hours in their darkened bedroom in Beverly Hills with the blackout curtains pulled shut watching Italian soccer on a giant screen via a satellite package that delivered live Serie A matches on weekends. When he wasn't watching soccer, he was hosting occasional parties with all sorts of the O.J. media circus in attendance.

Sometimes the parties got out of hand. Another writer got so drunk that he dove headfirst into the Jacuzzi, shattered a couple vertebrae, and narrowly dodged paralysis. Another reporter, whom he was deeply fond of, Robin Clark, died instantly in a head-on collision on the Pacific Coast Highway. Dad hosted a memorial service for him at the rented home.

Life was fragile indeed. He had a job to do, but at what psychic cost? Life-affirming, passion-stoking soccer matches were waged on pitches the world over and he was trapped in a self-induced, professionally vital, contractually obligated circle of hell.

He left Los Angeles days after the verdict was reached. I'd watched him react, sickened, next to Dominick Dunne, with his mouth shocked open, the sobs of the Goldman family next to him, the gasps and harrumphs from Johnnie Cochran and the Simpson family members.

When he returned to Williamstown to write the book, suddenly all that mattered to him were Saturday and Sunday: British, German, and Italian soccer via satellite. That was surely going to be book two of the two-book deal. Something immersive in the world of the beautiful game. Italy was indeed calling.

Only O. J. Simpson and the soul-crushing burden of having to write the book and devote months to talking about it could bring him down. Hadn't he suffered enough in his $20,000-a-month Beverly Hills rental? Now he had to make good on the massive contract, too?

Despite his precarious professional standing, he felt no financial need to write the book. I'd later learn that he'd had at least $3 million in various accounts in 1995 (approximately $5.8 million today).

Years later, when I emailed him to check in about his self-care and addictions and how he was coping, was he doing what he was supposed to for himself, walking every day, eating better, tapering, he responded to me about his finances, his compulsion for action, admitting that it was the highs he chased with his money that were his undoing: "When I was down to the last million . . . " he'd written. The last million.

He was online in his home office with the traders who managed a Merrill account and money was moved around like chips on a roulette table between doses of whatever benzodiazepines he was shoveling into his mouth like candy. Anything to get through another dreadful week of trying to write an O. J. Simpson trial book and get him to Saturday morning, when he'd awaken at six or seven as European matches kicked off.

He was wavering. He was trapped. He couldn't do it.

"Write the book, Dad. Are you kidding me?" I told him from San Francisco. He was grappling with the question of "want" versus "should."

"I've got nothing to say about it," was his line.

After all the shit he'd been through with Malcolm and Kennedy. They committed to pay him nearly two million for two books. He'd already sat through the trial. He was home with the notes and time to just write. His reputation would be restored. He'd be on all the talk shows. He'd have the next book as a reward.

"I've got nothing new to say," he insisted.

"Race, Dad. Write about race in America. Why did Black and white people react so differently to the verdict? What does it mean? Rodney King? The riots? How did we get here? What about the media's obsession with the trial and why? If Nicole and Ron were Black, would the coverage have been different? You can't ask those questions and explore that?"

"There's nothing left to say."

"You have a contract."

"And nothing to write," he insisted.

"I'll write it with you. Nina, too. Just start and we'll edit and brainstorm."

"Thank you, Joe. I do appreciate your passion. I got myself into this and it's not your responsibility to get me out of it."

"After Kennedy and Malcolm, Dad. You'd said you were done in American publishing. This may be your last shot."

"Enough, Joe."

"You'll be totally fucked if you back out of this."

"Your concern has been noted."

I turned to Nina. She echoed my father—he'd tried to write it and had nothing to say. I pressed, but with less conviction. He was stubborn, she insisted. She'd tried, she said. Try harder, I said.

"Author Abandons Simpson Trial Book"
The New York Times (via Associated Press), August 17, 1996

He had nothing new to say. That's what he told his agent, his editor, and attorney. He wrote a letter to his publisher calling the trial and coverage "an utter farce."

After spending a year in the courtroom and away from Gavin, he spent four months at home in Williamstown obsessing about soccer while trying to write something about the trial and had nothing.

He forfeited the two-book deal.

He explained he had started out as a sports reporter and that's where his heart was. That was the new venture. He was fifty-three years old.

He told a reporter from the Associated Press after backing out of the deal and returning the advance: "I feel wonderful. I feel twenty years younger. The whole process of sitting out there was some sort of very expensive therapy. It finally enabled me to see that all I have in life is what I want to do."

All I have in life is what I want to do.

What do I want to do? That's it. That's everything.

What does one need to do? What is someone, in this case a father, obligated to do?

His own father sunk all the money he had into financing his dream: a travel agency that bore his name. I still have an unsharpened pencil on my desk, white with Kelly green:

McGINNISS TRAVEL SERVICES, INC.
LET US MAKE YOUR TRAVEL A PLEASURE
Essex House, New York 19, N.Y. Cl 6-1980

There's some letterhead left, too. An airplane and the trademark green-on-white wordmark. Nothing else remains. He lost everything he had. He died broke, nothing left behind for his wife or only son. Dad had slipped him secret loans so my grandmother would never know just how much he'd lost.

Do I want to spend time with my children? Do I want to be around my grandchildren? Do I want to watch my son play basketball? What do I want?

Do I want to secure the financial future of my afflicted son? Secure the financial future of the children I left behind with their mother?

Do I want to pick them up from school two days a week? Bring them home and play and help with homework and have dinner and drive them to their mother's house? Take my daughter to tennis practice? Watch her play? Attend her piano recitals? Take my other daughter to softball? Coach the team? Take my son to the zoo or to get his hair cut?

Or do I want to move ninety minutes away? Then six hours away? Can I be happy living days and weeks and months at a time without seeing my children? Who makes that choice? Who wants that?

He'd wanted that. He chose that.

It was enough, he'd decided.

After he abandoned the book, his agent dropped him. His attorney, too. He was no one's client and he didn't give a shit. They didn't understand. He was never prouder of himself. He had the courage to walk away from all that money, burn professional bridges, put his financial and writing career at risk for one thing: freedom!

He didn't spend a waking hour without chemical or alcoholic influence. He was high and buzzed and drunk and rich and without contract or representation. He was free.

Free to sleep until he woke up, hungover as always. To eat as he wanted, fried cheese and Diet Pepsi and meats and pasta and pizza. He was free to play with his money online, the gambler he was, research and track down and invest with hotshot hedge funds he'd read about in *Barron's*. He was free to chase the dopamine hits of a good return, a few thousand earned at the close of trading, twice as much lost the next day, a few thousand gained back, then more lost again. The action was the point.

He was free to spend the afternoon online reading about soccer. Free to channel his obsession into story ideas and an eventual book, only with a new publisher and new agent, both of whom would have to be willing to take on both him—a risky bet at best—and the subject, soccer, a topic about which American readers did not care. But at least he was free, he insisted. That was most important.

At the end of every boozy night and start of every sluggish day, he likely reminded himself: If I played by the rules, I'd be stuck writing an O.J. book.

Nina was deflated, defensive, and finally resigned to echoing Dad: he tried. He had nothing new to say about the case. Subsequent conversations and emails with him were a window into his daily existence. Soccer. That was it. He talked about nothing else.

He immersed himself completely, as he had with Roger Ailes and Jeffrey MacDonald. But there was still no book, no deal, and one more red flag next to his name.

Beginning in 1989, when Malcolm made him a publishing pariah, and after *The Last Brother* seemed to confirm his toxic status in 1993, and then in 1995, when he broke the Random House contract, his self-induced career unraveling seemed complete.

In the face of it, he was defiant. He believed, in part, that his ability to jettison professional obligations and family considerations was evidence of artistic integrity. And that was more valuable than any pedestrian obligation like book contracts and financial security for one's dependents. He had his life back. It was exactly as he'd wanted it. Every urge and impulse fed. He owed nothing to anyone. In his chemically altered state, he was never more alive. And never more a stranger to me, less my father than an aging man, who seemed more petulant and self-absorbed than ever.

THIRTEEN

1997

BEFORE

A winter night in 1997. Petersburg Pass. The winding, dark border connecting New York and Massachusetts. Black ice. Dad was at the wheel of his Volvo. Seat belt on. Driving alone. Bob Dylan turned up loud. He was returning from the Albany airport after sending Mason back to Penn to continue his lonely, dangerous descent in West Philadelphia.

It was what Mason had wanted, Dad told himself. Mason wanted to go to boarding school and wanted to go to Penn. They'd all wanted the same thing, but for very different reasons. Mason might find something approaching normalcy if he'd put himself in normal surroundings. Dad and Nina agreed. It was also easier. So much easier, like moving ninety minutes away from his three young children rather than staying in town and sharing parenting duties.

Dad took a turn at the speed limit, maybe slightly over, and that was all it took. *Whoosh!* Off and over the edge and down he tumbled, fifty feet of rocky mountainside, the sedan finally coming to rest in an icy stream, destroyed, and his scalp split open like a soft melon.

Only his headlights glowing through the sleet from the depths of the rocky ravine happened to catch the eye of a lone passerby, who stopped. EMTs who'd arrived on scene labeled it a recovery operation. No one survived that kind of crash.

The staples were hideous and yellowing and ran down the back of his skull to the top of his neck. He was the luckiest man alive, he'd said. He'd lost 45 percent of his blood.

I wondered but didn't ask if they tested that blood. What would they have found if they had?

He recounted the brush with death. The Volvo saved his life! The seat belt and the Swedish engineering of reinforced steel and the airbag and the headlights pointing up toward the road and one person happening to glimpse the light. It was the longest of long shots that he survived!

The accident was blunt symbolism: his life as a speeding car descending a dark and icy road. I'd been hopeful for him before the accident. I no longer was. And at twenty-seven without a job or direction, lying on the couch in my mother's den, the "playroom" where I grew up, the den where Mom and Dad had lunch and martinis with Roger Ailes and his wife so many decades before, unable to eat or sleep, wondering what I would possibly do with my life having left San Francisco with little money and no direction while Jeanine headed to Manhattan to start her own life, I may as well have been riding shotgun with Dad that night on Petersburg Pass, soaring with him over the edge and into the abyss.

FOURTEEN

2020

AFTER

Schools closed and seasons were canceled. People were homebound and helpless as hospitals were overrun and bodies piled up. The planet was overrun by a deadly, highly contagious virus with no cure. But three months after it began, a window of opportunity opened. It was May and cases were stalled, and even dropping. The cherry blossoms were in full bloom. Local case counts were dropping enough. Outdoor activity was presumed to be safe, for children especially. A Phase One reopening had young ballers back on the outdoor courts.

He was sleeping through his alarm, face down, sleeping bag hanging off the bed. His floor was all sneakers and unfolded clothes and foil Cheetos bags and half-empty Powerade bottles and last night's bowl of soggy cereal on the table next to the computer and gaming system.

I'd made his oatmeal with a sprinkling of pure cane sugar on top just the way he liked it. I put his vitamins and turmeric capsule on the counter and poured his orange juice and peeled and sliced a banana. He had a long day ahead.

There was a basketball workout on that sunny May afternoon. He was masked and rusty. His effort was poor.

When it was over, I told him to apologize to the coach and asked him: "How many shots should you make before we leave?"

"A hundred?" he said.

"Two hundred," I said. "And I'm not rebounding and chasing your missed shots. And you're paying for today's workout."

Some fathers would make their son walk home after such a lazy showing. They'd be assholes, of course. Monsters.

I'd left his outbursts of self-harm aside. They were irrelevant, I decided. He needed to learn how to coax the best from himself. That skill, in turn, would go a long way toward addressing the self-loathing and subsequent self-harm. I determined this on my own, without extensive psychological consultation. I had my daily pill and decided that was all I needed. He was talking to a clinical social worker with a golden retriever therapy dog. I was convinced I was managing his development as I should.

I asked him about the poor effort he made: "Why are you even out there?"

Before he could answer I added: "That didn't look like fun at all."

He said nothing, absorbed it, every toxic drop, because none of my words were delivered delicately or with the care and compassion he deserved.

I made him pay for the workout, $35, with whatever money he had in his piggy bank at home—an actual ceramic blue pig. He was so young and even less mature. I reminded him of the two high school basketball stars I grew up with whose father had them outside in the winter making shots over a broom he held high every morning before school. Both girls earned full scholarships to Northwestern and Michigan State. They had the grades, too, I added. They were Black, too. You have no excuse, I said.

I thought he might quit.

"What's your plan, then?" I asked. "If you don't play."

"What do you mean?" he asked.

"What will you do with all your free time? And all that energy you've been devoting to the game you said you loved?"

"I'm not sure."

"You wanted to play for money someday. Your words. You're allowed to change your mind, of course. Always. Provide us with that plan and then you can quit," I explained. He didn't.

He did, however, decide to repeat seventh grade. He'd been young for his class and with so much time lost to distance learning and no return to in-person school in sight we reasoned: What was the rush? Why not get a full year of in-person learning for seventh grade if he could?

I'd done seventh grade twice, I told him. And look how I turned out.

He was barely a teenager and enduring social isolation during a global pandemic. He was not immune to loneliness and sadness and confusion. In fact, he was more susceptible than most.

A few months passed and it was summer and fall when he bottomed out.

It would be later, when something close to normal life resumed, schools resumed in-person learning, teams reconvened, practices and games commenced, that I'd bottom out as well.

Thirteen was hard enough. Jayson being forced to say goodbye through a laptop screen to his Covid-stricken grandfather was harder. Harder still was getting a smartphone with few restrictions and discovering the hard way that he'd inherited compulsive tendencies, quickly becoming addicted; not playing the sport he loved for over a year; choosing to repeat seventh grade but doing most of it virtually; having his basketball season canceled; his genetic predisposition toward social anxiety; being a Black boy watching George Floyd being strangled to death by a police officer and the summer of protests and social unrest; being my son.

It had been the three of us under the same roof for the duration of the pandemic, before the vaccines and resumption of normal life, and I lost track of my son.

I was losing my bearings. I was suddenly unsure, like a self-conscious child on a basketball court hoping no one passes him the ball. How do I present myself? What does he need from me? When his brown eyes follow me, what do they see? Am I doing it right? Is he somehow scared of me? The idea that he should be only made my imbalance worse.

I scrolled through his phone. He'd met a German girl his age. They were in love. He said he'd fly there to see her. He also referred to his "idiot/annoying/goddamn dad."

I'd turned fourteen at the start of eighth grade. My mother was at work by seven. I skipped school and walked into town to the apartment building of a friend of my sister's. We did things my son was barely chatting about with his new German girlfriend. And somehow he was in worse shape, more vulnerable and at risk than I ever was.

He was messaging her instead of doing SSAT prep or the $500 online basketball meditation course or making three hundred shots a day in the driveway.

He was online at midnight, one and two a.m. He was awake at five and six a.m. while we slept, messaging her for hours until it was time for online school and then homework and then limited outdoor basketball workouts, and the teenage boy, according to his pediatrician, required a minimum of nine or ten hours of sleep each night.

He'd been clocking four at most. And bad sleep. We were somehow unaware.

There was another girl from Georgia. For her, he'd created an alternate persona. He'd made himself fifteen instead of fourteen, still Black, and moved his home into a non-gentrified section of DC, with assaults and shootings and parents who fought too much, with a father who was cruel to him, made him walk the dog on cold, rainy nights.

There was a particular exchange that stood out. Not for the

alarmingly dark portrayal of his own home life, but the verve and humor and wry style of his fictional voice.

I printed and reread it. Aside from the flashing red sirens that went off in my head about his loneliness and isolation and self-loathing, the innate creativity and energy in his storytelling was impressive.

His dialogue popped. His voice was wry and edgy and self-deprecating. He had named himself "Tired" and her name was "Liv." Printing it out, I saw the beginning stages of a novel: QuaranTeen. He had thirty pages. I'd tell him my thoughts later: that he should keep going, tell the story, and I'd help him edit and shape it and if he really wanted to, it could become something worth pursuing, finishing, even publishing.

Days later, Jayson stood before us in the living room on a Saturday afternoon addressing us both, tears streaming down his cheeks: "I'm not in a good place."

He was exhausted and depleted. His virtual girlfriends and sleeplessness and sadness and boredom and Covid isolation and hormonal changes were wrecking him. And I was making it worse.

I reminded him that any violence he was viewing on his device was going to haunt him. It would make him feel scared and depressed and hopeless. It would keep him awake and when he slept it would give him nightmares.

There was so much more to it, though. And even still, I was disgusted with myself: How were we having that conversation then? He wasn't even in high school. "I never wanted him to have a goddamn phone!" I thundered to Jeanine later.

We'd argued incessantly. She was too permissive. I was too harsh. We relitigated and accused and condemned and exhausted each other, again, and compromised again. And failed again. Pandemic isolation had done real damage. Our divergent parenting styles were doing harm. His brain chemistry made him vulnerable to depression and darkness. And I was ill-prepared to meet the moment. What would Dad do? I never asked myself because I knew the answer and what would result: Gavin and Mason were the examples. Jayson deserved so much better.

I snapped a picture, used it as backdrop for my social media pages: eight-year-old Jayson sound asleep on his top bunk, little hand wrapped around a miniature flashlight, eyes closed, sound asleep, soft cheeks resting on the open pages of a book.

There was an updated version of the same picture. Jayson at thirteen, sound asleep on the living room sectional, but it wasn't a book he was clutching: it was his phone.

"We're failing our child," I told Jeanine. "There's two of us and one of him and somehow we're losing."

Vaccines and testing allowed the resumption of something approaching normal life. In-person learning and socialization and basketball seasons returned. Jayson had survived a two-year global pandemic during which children suffered academically and emotionally, the degree to which we're still measuring.

To be safe, we'd hidden all medications and continued with virtual and in-person counseling and purchased a timed lockbox for his phone and removed the keyboard and mouse for his gaming computer nightly. We were improving his odds at something healthier.

He'd bravely agreed to speak to professionals again after stopping during the pandemic. We reminded him that the brain was an organ like the heart and kidneys and lungs. If there was something causing pain in any of them, we wouldn't hesitate to call a doctor. He agreed.

Further still, to his immense credit, he reasoned: if there was a pill he could take to make it better, he pleaded, could we please give it to him?

• • •

But it was also go time. A new season of pressure was upon him and us.

September of eighth grade mattered most in terms of high school applications and interviews. First-term grades were paramount. And looming: his final middle school basketball season, which, if he thrived, would help him gain admission and possibly financial aid necessary to attend the high schools he most wanted to.

And with all of that, there I was. Still lording over him. I reminded him: He needed to set priorities. He needed to decide where he wanted to go to high school and why. He had to think these things through and figure out where he might be most happy. And most of my questions for him were nothing more than thinly disguised commands.

What kind of academic and social environment was attractive to him? Did he want to go to the big local public high school, which was too often too rough, with fights and occasional shootings outside, but with a basketball team that won city championships and a wonderful coach Jayson knew? Or was there a better fit?

What kind of basketball player did he want to become? What about travel basketball? Get in touch with coaches you know, I said. Find out if and when he could try out. Were there workouts he could attend? Were his friends playing pickup somewhere? Why couldn't he arrange games with players he knew? "I used to stand in my mom's kitchen calling guy after guy I knew to see if they wanted to hoop. You playing today? Where? What time? I was calling people I barely knew. You have this smartphone and six different ways to reach anyone. Make it happen.

"Otherwise, you're just a kid staring at a smartphone who calls himself a basketball player."

A parent should know better. I didn't. But Jeanine did and reminded me more than once: the frontal lobe that handles decision-making and impulse control was a barely formed gooey mess in the teenage brain. And I was demanding and expecting a maturity from my son that was simply a neuro-bio-physical impossibility.

I didn't buy it. Hadn't I trekked two miles from my mother's house to sneak into the college field house every weekend, so desperate to play? Wasn't my frontal lobe also oatmeal at fourteen?

Can we address desire and passion? And comfort and coddling and laziness? I had every excuse to feel sorry for myself and withdraw and get high and drink and wallow in my sadness. What was Jayson's excuse? I had the same frontal lobe, but no father present to take me to any court or workout or pickup games anywhere ever.

I was on a tear. I had it figured out. Jayson would engage and push and grow and it would be hard and uncomfortable and suck, but it would all be worth it.

An awareness and even passing interest or curiosity about the world around him had to be there, too. After all, he'd just survived a pandemic that took the life of his grandfather, had witnessed a social uprising in the name of Black lives like his. Articulation of who he was, what mattered to him and what motivated him was a priority.

I gave him books to read over the summer, *Black Boy* and *Manchild in the Promised Land*. We gave him *New York Times* articles to read and discuss with us.

I'd sought those kinds of things in eighth grade, books and American political news, without my parents feeding them to me. But I also didn't have the internet and a smartphone and pandemic-induced social isolation at his age.

Ignored was the reality: at fourteen I was so much like him. Video games and mindless television and hours on the phone and obsessing about clothes and shoes and girls was my default.

"And you cannot expect to get into Georgetown Day or Maret or Sidwell without something to say," I told him. "You have to play your way onto the lists of coaches, and you have to have a clue about the world around you. Not just good grades. But curiosity, ambition," I repeated myself. He was weary, but there was no rest. He was alone with the two of us, no sibling to guide or protect him.

Jeanine set up a large whiteboard in the living room. All the schools we'd targeted and deadlines for every phase of the application process. Dates and names and check marks and scribbles in blue and green and red. There was a plan, and we were engaged. I was fathering my son like a helicopter in thick fog, flying fast and low.

FIFTEEN

1998

BEFORE

I was staring at Richard Nixon's knowing smirk on a pack of cigarettes. It was an image on a poster for *The Selling of the President*, black-and-white dry mount, frayed and creased and yellowing on the corners. It rested on a secondhand IKEA shelf in my Washington, DC, studio apartment.

Dad was calling because it was October and I was turning twenty-eight. Phone calls from him were rare. He preferred email.

My Netscape and AOL boxes were stuffed with nearly daily notes from him addressed to "All." He'd cc Cynthia and Sarah and Gavin and Mason and sometimes Nina and other writer friends or his attorney. They were filled with color and commentary about European soccer, its players and managers and owners and fixtures and standings and scandals. He seemed convinced that his obsession was our news.

I'd stopped reading most of them. Sarah asked him directly at one point to remove her from the cc'd emails. If he wanted to communicate with her and find out how she's doing, please do it directly, one-to-one, she said. She rarely heard from him after that.

During our phone call, I sat at my simple though sturdy IKEA plywood table that took too many hours to assemble and stared back at Nixon while Dad talked.

"You know what I realized?" I finally said after listening to him relay a litany of factoids about Italian soccer teams and players whose names meant nothing to me, and it was after dinner and I could hear the gin in his voice.

"I'm turning twenty-eight and you'd written a *New York Times* bestseller when you were twenty-six."

That's where my mind was. Not on his condition or career or the scar where the staples in his scalp had been, but my own general lack of direction.

I don't recall his response. It was later, in a letter, that he reached me.

He offered a sanitized version of decisions he'd made at key points of his life and distilled and crafted into an intimate, wise, and heartfelt counsel to me, his firstborn son on his birthday. The birthday letter from him was on paper, typed and printed, folded and sealed in an envelope and stamped and stuck in a mailbox.

He'd written letters to me for a few of my other birthdays. The one he wrote when I turned twenty-eight was on "Joe McGinniss" embossed letter stock.

On the seventh floor of the redbrick apartment on Massachusetts Avenue, as I'd embarked on an expensive public policy graduate program despite waning interest and tens of thousands of dollars of student loan debt, I read the letter from my dad:

> So among the many other genes I've passed along to you (including what may be the most important of all, the sense-of-humor gene) there's one which quite possibly will impel you, from time to time, to take a plunge into the unknown: as when my father abandoned his hugely successful career in the architectural business and proceeded to lose every penny he had while fulfilling his long-time dream of

owning and operating his own travel agency (to the point where I had to pay all my own tuition, room and board for my last year in college and then, after *The Selling of the President* turned out to be such a surprising success, to secretly loan him thousands of dollars so my mother would never know the full extent of his financial failure). Or, on a happier note, my own decision to quit the "dream job" of being the youngest full-time big-city newspaper columnist in the country in order to write a book whose potential was by no means obvious. Or, later, to wander around Alaska for a year on the gamble that I would come home with material for a book. And, much later, to take off for the most isolated region in all of Italy without speaking a word of the language in order to hang around with a minor league soccer team instead of collecting my guaranteed million for a book on the O. J. Simpson trial.

I remind you of this heritage of yours at this time because I know you are frustrated and perplexed by not knowing what will come next. When you said on the phone that when I was your age I'd already written a successful book, I laughed and quasi-jokingly said words to the effect that yeah, that was the upside but be grateful for all the downside you've been spared.

He left home for a year in Alaska. Home being New Jersey with Nina, not Swarthmore with or near his children. The feeling that none of the downside that I'd been spared had anything to do with that year away from me. Or most of every month of every year no matter where he was.

Three years had passed since he'd broken his contract. He'd found a story he wanted to tell about a soccer team in a small Italian city. He'd researched, architected, and nailed a pitch about an obscure topic with limited commercial appeal to secure a new agent and a contract with a well-regarded publisher.

An eight-page proposal secured him a deal to write the book he'd wanted. From a guaranteed two-book $1.7 million contract, he secured a one-book deal worth $250,000.

It was much easier to give back what he never had, he argued. And he didn't need the money. He had two or three million in his various accounts. A quarter million to write the book he'd have written for free was a win, he'd insisted. A major publisher was paying him to leave America and O.J. and the Kennedys and Janet Malcolm behind and move to Italy for a year. He was flying high again, solo and chemically dependent, and again leaving Gavin behind.

He found an apartment in Italy. He immersed himself in all things Castel di Sangro, the bland little city near the equally uninspired Abruzzo region.

Gavin was twelve and missed him. But he was also accustomed to seeing Dad leave, whether ducking into a town car that took him to Boston for a flight to California or Milan or drifting away nightly at the dinner table. Gavin didn't have a choice, and the images of his father during those formative years were indelible.

Could his father have stayed home in Williamstown and written the book for which he'd already sacrificed nearly a year of life with his son? Instead, Gavin watched helplessly as his father insisted: he had to leave again.

His immersion into the world about which he was writing moved him ever farther from our lives. He was living out his fantasy: thumbing his nose at convention, the establishment, the publishing industry, responsibility, expectations, aging, near-death experiences, and lost years in courtrooms with vile people.

He was defiant. He followed his instinct and gut and always knew best. Another among the genes I'd inherited, and for Jayson's sake, would need to keep in check.

Jeanine's Chicago MBA and JPMorgan gig put her on the Upper West Side of Manhattan. She was ascendant. I was living alone in DC, and though nearly broke most of the time, I was free and convinced I was happy.

Where my dad was boxed in by his O.J. contract and soccer freed him, public policy graduate courses couldn't compete with novel notes I wrote in the margins of my notebooks during evening classes. Fiction was my Italian soccer. The freedom to create something from nothing was intoxicating.

The goal was a novel. The plan was simple. I'd finish the story and find an agent who would sell it to a publisher. Defiant and free like my father: I'd be a writer.

I visited him that Christmas. He'd come home to Williamstown from Italy to see Gavin and Mason, likely pressured by Nina.

He gave me a present. It was a cardboard box stuffed with old, used Castel di Sangro scarves, replica jerseys, ill-fitting hats and sweaters and shorts. They smelled like body odor. I laughed, then realized it wasn't a joke. He didn't give a shit. He was home for a spell, then headed back.

There was nothing for him in America. Life was in Italy, with the soccer team, the players and managers and whoever he was having an affair with. There was frequently someone else, I'd later learn. Besides, all was well enough stateside with his offspring. As well as he cared to know.

Cynthia and Sarah were starting families and enjoying stable and loving marriages. I had my master's degree and a new interest in writing and a woman who loved me, and you'd better not blow it with her, he'd said.

Mason and Gavin, though, were struggling, if not spiraling. Each were in school, but barely. Mason was failing out of Penn, no longer able to get himself to class or manage the workload. His Asperger's was wreaking havoc on his ability to meet even the most basic expectations. There was no easy answer. And Gavin's academic performance was uneven and boarding school offered more freedom than he could handle.

The well-being of his sons was something Nina would manage. Someone had to make money for the family.

After first and second passes with his editor, he was assured: the fun Italian adventure tale, which took a surprisingly dark turn at the end, could make a splash.

A follow-up to it would emerge and he'd pitch that and secure another contract because of the solid relationship he'd forged with his publisher. All was well. And he never had to write a word about the O. J. Simpson trial.

And the money? Hundreds of thousands of dollars was burned living in Beverly Hills for the trial, but he was in survival mode then and anything less would have wrecked him. He'd barely survived as it was, he'd argued. What he didn't seem to struggle with, or at least I don't recall ever hearing him lament, was time away from his sons that he wouldn't get back. "I miss my guys" were words he never spoke or wrote.

The addict and self-destruction savant with his newly self-diagnosed post-traumatic stress disorder following his nearly fatal car accident, plunged into his escapist soccer obsession and managed to create a book called *The Miracle of Castel di Sangro*. In it, he described his soccer obsession, from which the book was born, this way:

> I retain clear memories of what my life was like before. In many ways, I suppose I was better. My children respected me. My wife and I shared numerous interests. I had friends. I enjoyed music. I read books. That I would grow suddenly obsessed with "football" ... seemed no more likely than my becoming an astronaut. (p. 19)
>
> My doctor, who was also a friend, watched a preliminary match in my company and at its conclusion only half-jokingly attributed my condition to a ministroke, one that—while leaving all motor functions intact—had apparently disabled that portion of the brain that normally protects Americans against any appreciation of soccer or even interest in the sport.

> In retrospect, I can see that a less alarming explanation might have been that for a variety of reasons of no great relevance to this story, I was psychically ripe for a consuming passion that had no connection to any of my previous experience. (p. 20)

But there was pressure. Never more than in 1999, the months prior to publication and the need for the book to do something, to at least earn out its advance. It had been six years since *The Last Brother* disaster. If *Miracle* failed, he'd really be finished. That was his thinking.

He was higher than ever. And in the worst drug haze, he spent his waking hours feverishly chasing dopamine hits from his Merrill trading account. He rode the roller coaster of the markets as everything soared. Tech-sector stocks and pharmaceuticals and whatever the traders suggested. He threw more and more of his millions at the market while his Italian soccer book was readied.

Maybe he would win back the money he'd passed up. Maybe he'd win back the money he'd spent in Beverly Hills. Maybe he could shut everyone up and really stick it to them.

And then it happened. His publisher was destroying his book!

It was the era of exclamation. It was 1999, and for him, everything was a crisis. It all hung in the balance in ways most of us didn't know. Only Nina. The money was burning and the book was being set up to fail. And he was higher than ever.

The first hint of trouble came with early attempts at cover art for the book. It was a laughable rendering of an old Italian woman leaning over a bassinette: tucked in under a blanket was a black-and-white-checkered soccer ball. And he lost his mind.

He didn't send an email rejecting the cover art and asking for some new ideas that didn't include a soccer ball. Instead, he authored an email blast to his editor, agent, publisher, marketing team, entire family, and a few friends for good measure.

That first letter and each that followed throughout the production process read as performance art. They usually ran at least a page or two, sometimes longer, and were often peppered with odd historical references and Bob Dylan song lyrics and f-bombs and were sometimes hilarious, always lucid and crafted cogent arguments about just how badly the art department and publisher were handling the packaging of the book.

Had they even read the book? he queried.

He was biting and funny and acerbic.

He FedExed photos and scarves and team color schemes that could be incorporated into cover art that would announce itself as urgent, passionate, would leap off the shelf or screen, that would burst, almost orgasmic!

No more Italian caricatures of little old women and soccer balls and clichés. Contemporary Italy is Milan and modern design. *Think 1999 not 1399!* he wrote to his editor, publisher, agent, lawyer, friends, family. He cc'd the world. This was just the cover art.

Most of these messages were authored at night, when he was highest, gin offering fresh fuel for the raging chemical fire in his brain. He emailed on weekends, too. He wrote so much. Too much. To too many people. He was exhaustive and exhausting. He was without filter or muse or self-control.

And it only got worse as publication neared. The length and frequency of his emails increased. So did the recipient list. At one point during the marketing phase of publication, fifteen people appeared on his mailing list.

He was at war with his own publisher months before publication. There was no escaping the fact that the book revolved largely around the sport of soccer—a widely unpopular subject in America. He argued that soccer was merely backdrop, a vehicle for his relatable and universal fish-out-of-water tale, the one his editor had insisted could make a splash.

He and Nina wrote the book jacket copy. An American goes to Italy and kicks around for a year and meets charming, beguiling Italians that so many Americans idealize and then he brings them to life and, of course, as was trademark for his work, discovers and reveals a dark, all-too-human twist.

Soccer was not the point of the story, he insisted. In fact, if the word "soccer" or any reference to soccer appeared in the marketing of the book it would certainly fail, he argued. To the publicity and marketing and editorial teams he'd email more than once: *No soccer! This is not a sports book. Think Paul Theroux! This is bigger than sports. If you stick a soccer ball or label it a sports book it'll be dead on arrival.*

Then, as if some corporate overlord had pulled the publishers aside and sternly whispered into their ear, *Make him happy*, everything turned.

An aggressive marketing campaign was laid out by his editor. He was thrilled. He'd gotten through, had been heard. They weren't promoting it as a soccer book. His agent at the time, whom he would later fire, echoed his optimism and seemed to validate his methods (embedded in an email update to me), if not his madness:

> *I think Michael's new plan looks mighty damn good. All of your and my hard work, of "working on" Michael and Sarah has borne some fruit. Frankly, from the tentative tone I've heard from Michael of late I didn't think they'd be backing the book this way. But it looks like dogged persistence on our part got their attention. I hope you're feeling more optimistic about things. I certainly am.*

His closing words to me in that triumphant letter:

> *So once again the lesson, never never quit, even when you KNOW you're making a pain in the ass of yourself.*

> *Ciao & un abbraccio,*
> *Dad*

Maybe the book without a soccer ball on the cover would take off after all. Maybe his decision to break his contract to do what he wanted to would pay off. Maybe never quitting even when you're being a pain in the ass was the right move after all.

Maybe Gavin not having him around for those two years wasn't such a big deal after all. Maybe he was better off. Maybe the addictions and temper and bouts of rage were better left unwitnessed by a child.

But his dad wasn't a tree falling in the woods with no one around to hear it. Whether at boarding school or home, Dad was all noise and fury, and it was terrifying. And for Gavin, it was devastating to witness.

During the prepublication phase of the book, another email from Dad. A fellow writer had written a letter to *The New York Times* about *The Last Brother* and referenced plagiarism and the technique employed throughout the work imagining what Teddy Kennedy may have been thinking at various points in his life.

He was livid. He wrote that he happened to know of at least two men the writer's wife had slept with while the writer was out of the country on assignment. But he wasn't going to divulge that because *that* was beneath him. But he insisted they were all arrogant suck-ups, fragile hypocrites who would destroy him and his new book.

> Oh Joe, the well is poisoned, and now they'll just lie in wait for a chance to ignore or attack the new book. It's a disgusting business when practiced by the arrogant who feel their special status exempts them from any obligation to the truth. And these, all with close friends among the Kennedys, exist primarily at the NY Times, Boston Globe, Washington Post, Newsweek, Time, New York Magazine, The New Yorker and NPR. Of course, since as a group they have the unchecked power to determine what succeeds or what fails in the arts—be it a book, a movie, a play, a ballet, a pop album—this omnipotent octagon shapes the cultural life of America according to its own narrow and

oh-so-prestige-conscious range of tastes (and, worse, depending on the favors owed to or owed by certain practitioners of the arts).

The poisoned well. The culture-shaping omnipotent octagon that paid him a million to write *The Last Brother*. That offered him $1.7 million to write the O.J. book and another of his choosing, and the $250,000 to write about a minor-league Italian soccer team in the wake of breaking his own two-book blockbuster contract.

They were aligned against him, Janet Malcolm, her new best friend Jeffrey MacDonald, and Teddy Kennedy leading the charge, behind them a cocktail-sipping army of pretentious Manhattanites scoffing at that morally indefensible, plagiarizing, email-blasting buffoon McGinniss.

There were delays and publicity targets missed for myriad reasons. An initial print run of 100,000 had been scaled back to 45,000. Two weeks after publication day, all advertising and promotional work ceased. His editor emailed him that any further work done to promote the book would not, by design, involve him.

He authored a five-page email to the publisher. Halfway through he asked if the Kennedys had intervened to kill the book. He was screaming into the abyss.

Sales were sluggish. American readers in 1999 were not going to be convinced to give a shit about soccer, much less plunk down $25 for a hardcover from an author whose last book was six years prior and universally reviled.

I forwarded good reviews I found online. There were many.

The New York Times called it "an engaging tale well worth telling, rich in comic incidents, delightful characters and dramatic surprises. In the end, we long for our own season in Italy, where, as elsewhere, the holy and base walk hand in hand." (June 6, 1999)

The Washington Post said it was about "obsession and delusion as they appear in certain aspects of the American consciousness . . . Part

Jamesian novel, part Hemingway lament." And concluded: "This is a narrative about knowing it all and knowing absolutely nothing. I wonder if the author realizes it." (June 18, 1999)

But reviews didn't sell books and he'd taken a blowtorch to his own publisher. I reminded him that he wrote the book he wanted to write. I pleaded with him to calm down. Maybe log off. To wait until morning to click "send" on his emails. I stopped reading them. I stopped emailing him. There was nothing left to say. It was over.

SIXTEEN

2000

BEFORE

Freedom was always an impulse that drove him, he explained to *Holy Cross Magazine* in a cover story entitled "The Rebel."

> I was an only child and raised by parents who were, to put it mildly, overprotective. And while I made my own freedoms in high school, basically it was still kind of a sheltered life. The desire really to be free, to be independent, just to break out to be really on my own, free from these eyes looking over my shoulder, was a very strong one. Books provided the perfect solution . . . because I could be totally independent. I could do whatever I wanted. It was independence and freedom, I think, that I was after from an early age.

About *Miracle*, he explained:

> When I went over there, I was 53 years old and I'm reading my Holy Cross class letter and a lot of people 53 years old, they're being pushed into early retirement or they're thinking things are sort of

winding down now, the kids have been put through school, their careers have peaked, and you can get this sort of sense of creeping twilight coming in.

Italy and soccer are two huge new loves that have entered my life at the age of 50. I think by that time a lot of people's capacity for new love and adventure is sort of dwindling, if it's not entirely withered and died. I believe for most the people in my class, adventure was the furthest thing from their minds; security and consistency and knowing what life would be like five or ten years down the road was about their highest priority. Whereas for me, it wasn't a priority at all. I would've shuddered to think that I might have known what life would have been like five or ten years down the road.

Journalist and author Michael Wolff summed it up in *New York* magazine on October 4, 1999, in a story entitled "Publish and Perish."

[F]or various reasons—a guilelessness and certainly an extraordinarily poor sense of his profession's politics among them—he has tended to walk into literary disasters . . . It didn't take much to see this as something more than just one writer self-destructing, indeed, to see it as another indication of the career of writing itself going up in flames . . . It's a journalistic truism that when you want to learn what's really going on, you look for the least-stable person—the crazy lady—who will tell you things that others, for reasons of decorum and self-interest, hold back . . . McGinniss became a crazy man.

Fall and winter found him home in Williamstown. He would wake up late on most mornings. He'd stack some logs in the woodstove. Days were short, the light was flat and fleeting as temperatures plummeted and stayed there and sleeping it off meant a mere handful of hours of sunlight for him.

There were no calls from agents with ideas or proposals or good news. He had no agent. There was no word from anyone at his publisher, no plans for a paperback or further discussion with the publisher of the toxic book. He had no publisher.

Meanwhile, though, his daughters had healthy and beautiful children of their own. He wrote letters and sent cards and toys and books and clothes. A new chapter had begun. There was another grandchild on the way! Then another!

At his best, he had his head up, he'd insisted. He started a comic thriller of a novel about genomic scientists racing across Europe. He had hopes for an eventual Italian publication of *Miracle* so the people he cared most about over there could read it. There were Brits who loved the book. There was one who even paid ten grand to option it for a feature film. Clooney could play me! he offered. But still, he insisted he was finished with America.

"I no longer wish to live out my days in this country . . . " began the message he sent. The millennium bore down. He had a new course to chart. He was in throes of addiction. He was a publishing pariah. He'd rather be in Italy, or maybe London, than endure another season of professional and personal despair in "Williamstomb."

He had new ideas and energy only for a new horizon and a reason for getting out of bed in the (late) morning (or early afternoon). He was determined to follow his heart and gut and instinct. He was ready again to leave it and everyone and everything behind. Even Gavin. Again. Because all he had in life was what he wanted to do.

It was a bright, crisp autumn afternoon in the Berkshires. The soccer match was between two amateur squads: a large well-financed boarding school and a significantly smaller private day school, Pine Cobble, where Gavin was enrolled. He was in sixth grade and not on the team, but attended the match with a friend and Dad.

A goal was scored by the home team. A whistle sounded. The referee waved it off. No goal! The ball apparently hadn't crossed the line. My father saw it differently. He exploded. He let fly a barrage of Italian obscenities and gestured wildly. He told the referee what he missed:

the ball clearly crossed the goal line, hit the net, and came back to the keeper! It's a goal!

He was on the pitch, in his red-and-white checkerboard-patterned Croatia soccer jersey. He looked like a lunatic. He was a madman. It was theatrical rage. He was a raging clown, more Monty Python than violent soccer dad. It was humiliating for Gavin just the same.

"Get the hell off the field!" the referee commanded.

"Or what?!" he yelled.

"Or I'll throw you out."

"Where? Down the hill?!"

"Get out!"

He wrote a letter of apology to the Pine Cobble principal the next day. There were no more middle school soccer matches for him.

The only truly effective treatment for depression is pharmacological, which strongly suggests that the cause is harbored deep within the chemistry of the brain. That was what he explained to all his children in a six-page letter authored and emailed after Christmas in 2001 when he was too depressed to see anyone, including his grandchildren. He wanted to apologize and explain.

External factors were real and impacted his state of mind to be sure, he wrote, "but to enumerate them runs the risk of self-pity." The same events may not impact another at all. Brain chemistry is the difference maker, he wrote.

He'd sought out a psychiatrist with whom he apparently formed a bond and in his words was "the best and only truly helpful shrink I'd ever talked to." (Unfortunately, this doctor died in 1995 while my father was in Los Angeles for the Simpson case.)

The deceased doctor had a partner who took on my father. His assessment, according to my father: "Of course you're depressed, given all you've got to be depressed about." That was Dr. M___. Beginning in 1995, he was one of the doctors who prescribed massive amounts of highly addictive medications for him.

Dad paraphrased Samuel Johnson biographer W. Jackson Bate: by 1764, and for at least another three years (ages 57 to 60) verging on breakdown, and only by the most heroic effort, exerted day after day, could he pull himself together . . . "What was making the situation so serious for him," my father quoted from Bate, "was not any one thing—the more shattering experiences of life are rarely so simple for anyone—but the convergence of several, all of them reinforcing each other."

His doctor told him it wouldn't always be like this. He mentioned gray November skies giving way to clear blue bright winter days, and beyond, the dawn of a glorious spring. And he planned to be here for it, savoring and enjoying to the fullest with each and every one of us!

> So here I sit, taking my pills, most of the time finding it difficult even to talk on the telephone, email my only lifeline to the world. Fall of '93, you could almost hear them from here: all the pens in New York and elsewhere, crossing my name and number out of address books. And so, I am convinced I would have a happier life in Italy. Convinced. Or even in England.
>
> But you see we can't just up and move to Italy, or even England, because of Mason. Oh, this year, Gavin's first away from home, would not have been good anyway, but we could now be actively planning for next fall, except we can't because of Mason. We simply cannot leave him. Yeah, we could fly over for a week, maybe two, but as for living in another country? It's a dream now reduced to the level of fantasy because Mason, such a sweet, loving, and oh-so-kind fellow, can barely manage unpaid part-time work in a Philadelphia used furniture store run by the other social outcasts of Uhuru.

Most of all he was grateful to the three of us.

> For far too long I've given you far too little and now it seems too late to make it up. I often think that if Tony Lukas had children, he

might not have killed himself—although that didn't stop his mother from committing suicide when he was eight years old. Talk about bad genes. Hey, I hope I passed a few good ones along, too: somebody sure did, or the three of you wouldn't be who you are, although I'm not a believer in genetic predetermination.

It was summer. I was in Los Angeles. On the rickety wooden rooftop deck of her Hermosa Beach oceanfront studio apartment, Jeanine sat in a white plastic chair, seagulls riding the steady cool ocean breeze overhead on their nightly commute up the coast, the sky over the Pacific deep orange with a purplish hue unlike anything we'd ever seen back east.

I'd resisted and occasionally raged against a lifetime commitment because I knew there was no such thing and imagining myself during the inevitable unraveling paralyzed me until the last possible moment. We'd never been out of touch, even when we dated other people and lived in different cities. I went to Manhattan to watch the 2000 Super Bowl with her. We had a snowball fight on Columbus Avenue. It felt like the moment I fell in love with her my first year at Swarthmore a decade earlier, her hands on her hips, taunting me as I missed and missed again and I laughed and kept laughing. When an opportunity with Accenture in Los Angeles arose, I helped persuade her to go with a promise that I'd join her when the part-time tutoring job at the university concluded. She took the job. Months passed. She commuted from Malibu to Laguna Beach and back. Her days were long and lonely, while I dithered back east, convinced the moment I set foot on that one-way flight to LA, if the plane didn't go down, surely I would.

She finally told me she was done.

I flew out from Dulles three days later with the ring that Dad's mother left for me when she died. Under a mesmerizing orange sunset and waves crashing and gulls drifting overhead, riding the breeze, I lowered myself to one surgically repaired knee and asked for something I wasn't convinced I deserved or had earned.

Unlike Cynthia's husband, I couldn't offer generational wealth. Though Jeanine certainly deserved it. In retrospect, I wasn't sure what I was offering. I'd insisted the novel I was writing would succeed, would find a publisher. My tenacity was a quality she admired. I made her laugh. She saw in me a passion and kindness and vulnerability.

She was the daughter of educators, a family of readers and writers and a faltering father. She navigated harsh and merciless corporate cultures and still possessed the same generous, loving vulnerability I'd fallen for at nineteen. Fear of ending up just like my father weighed on me for a decade until I saw the tears in her eyes and the winds seemed to wrap themselves around us under that magical coastal light on the first night of the rest of our lives together.

SEVENTEEN

2021

AFTER

I succumbed first and worst to the pressure of the season. Eighth grade and the resumption of in-person learning and the most important phase of his academic and athletic life. If Jayson wanted to get into any of the five schools he chose that we wrote on the whiteboard in the living room, it was time to earn it.

"Any underachieving is because we let him," I told his mother. "He has a phone because you bought him one. Why does he eat crap? Because you buy it for him. We can't keep doing the same shit and expect a different result."

This could have been a weekday morning running late for school or a weekend afternoon when he was still upstairs playing video games instead of working on his game or reading the articles I set aside for him and asked him to read the night before. And it was the bass in my voice that she would not tolerate. We argued some more. I blamed her for his phone and nutrition woes and slide into what I perceived as underachievement.

She blamed me for being too hard on him and too harsh and too mean. I was doing real damage, she said. She had to protect him from me. So she was lenient and permissive and indulgent. She gave him what he asked for and they got along better as a result. I was the big, bad dad who was making life hard. She was there to nurture and heal. We needed better balance. I needed more restraint, to treat Jayson less like my father treated his publishers and more like a loving parent should treat a child.

He was dragging. His shins ached from the basketball workouts we'd been taking him to and paying for. He was exhausted. Despite new technology restrictions and resumption of normal life, he was still restless, sleepless, and lonely.

He wore his hair in twists. They hung low to minimize what he was convinced was a too-large forehead. I reminded him that I wore bangs until I was in my twenties for the same reason, and guess what? No one gave a shit about my forehead. But he didn't want to hear it.

We'd been in the car for forty-five minutes, driving through a thunderstorm. Satellite radio hip-hop streaming and Instagram basketball highlight reels cued for him on his phone to stoke the flame, and my words were half sentences and the tone measured, light but energized.

"You got this," I concluded. And the words drifted and faded, and he didn't respond.

"Right? You got this. Do it early and it gets easier," I said.

I was trying too hard. It had to come from him or it wouldn't happen. I hadn't learned that pregame and practice car ride speeches and demands from me did more harm than good. There was no substitute for organic motivation. If it was going to happen, it was on him. I said some version of that on the way to that first practice.

"One chance to make a first impression," I reminded him. We'd spent more than a year working on confidence, projection, aggressiveness, playing free.

"Yep," he said and exited the car, jogged through the driving rain and into the brightly lit gym for the first practice of his new AAU team.

• • •

I wasn't going to watch. But I couldn't help myself.

Jayson was a mess. The shin-split pain and lack of sleep made him slow and tentative. He made bad choices. He gave the ball away quickly rather than made plays. It was ugly.

It was one practice, one forgettable moment on a Tuesday night in September.

So why was I pulled over to the side of the highway, hazards flashing, losing my mind?

A window was closing, opportunity slipping away. Jayson needed to impress the coaches at the schools we were targeting. And to do that, he'd have to find the dog in himself, an edge that wasn't there.

Or else what? Then what? I was going to somehow love him less. Maybe that was the fear: disappointment in him would breed disdain. The nurtured boy who didn't want to fight for what he'd insisted he'd wanted, who settled for comfort and ease rather than doing something special because special was hard.

"You wanted this! You wanted me to take you to this! What was the last thing I said to you before you went in?"

"One chance to make a first impression," he managed.

"Exactly. Be aggressive! Active, all positive energy. That's it! That's all you have to do! Warm up right! Clap it up! Energy! And what did you do? You did none of that!" I screamed.

"I know," he said, barely audible.

"Why not?"

He stared straight ahead, searching for words he didn't know, explanations beyond his grasp.

"I don't know," he finally managed.

"What is your malfunction? Why are you even bothering with this? That phone! You lose yourself in it and the video games." I snatched his phone and stuck it out the open window. "It's gone if you don't give me an answer." I was a lunatic.

How could he answer that? It was simply not possible. Who could ever answer anyone in the state I was in, much less a fourteen-year-old?

Much less the son of a father he thought he knew and trusted would always be the safe harbor, the reader of bedtime stories and provider of tickle bugs and knee football and ice cream truck money and swing pushing and goalkeeping and the life he deserved, the joy and nurturing of a present, passionate, ever-loving father.

I crushed a plastic water bottle, half-full, and whipped it at the windshield and it exploded, spraying everything, including him.

"Tell me!"

He struggled and stammered. He was terrified and should have been.

I'd started driving, pulled back onto the ramp that led us to the highway, even though I was nowhere near calm.

I was doing seventy and still demanding answers. None came. I snatched the phone from his hands. Big rigs and speeding cars kept pace on all sides of the rain-slicked highway. There was no margin for error.

My father drove his car off the side of a mountain road, likely with something in his system, chemicals to be sure, if not alcohol. Black ice and darkness and excess speed and he lost control.

But he was alone that night. He didn't have his young son in the passenger seat.

Jayson pushed back, finding his voice. He called me an asshole and insane.

I was the one with the malfunction. I wasn't a drinker nor an addict nor the only child of an orphaned boy. I had only myself to blame. I was aware and engaged and on a low-dose SSRI, the same as Jeanine and my mother and sisters. I had every advantage and no excuse. No financial pressure or son lost to mental illness haunting me. Not yet, anyway. It was as though something organic and elemental had roared to life and seized control of me, as though embedded in my hardwiring from gestation, finally showing itself in all of its horrific glory. But that's letting myself off the hook. As though I were powerless, when in fact, I had all the power and more critically, responsibility.

• • •

Instead of tossing it, I dropped the phone on his lap. And then, with him staring at me with shock and fear and confusion swirling like the wind roaring through the car, I placed my index finger on his warm forehead and told him "something's broken in there. I just don't get it."

Of course I was wrong. He wasn't close to whatever the hell I meant by the label "broken." He was pure and beautiful and becoming. I was the damaged one and breaking him in real time.

At home he explained to Jeanine what had happened. I stood there like a petulant punk. I justified myself. How many hours did we just spend so he could dick around on the court? Driving through a storm for something he insisted he wanted.

"He hit me. He pushed my forehead with his fingertip. He threw a bottle of water. He's an asshole."

"You hit him?!" Jeanine said.

"I pushed his forehead. Like he said. I did not hit him."

"You're the worst fucking father ever! Because you didn't have a fucking father, so you don't know what the hell you're doing!" he raged.

He wasn't wrong. Reasons didn't matter. Not the pressure of the season, the struggles of adolescence, the social isolation of a pandemic, or the deadening effect of technology. All that mattered was the damage inflicted by the father, the harm I was doing.

In the wake of my worst moment as a parent, life resumed. It had to. Applications couldn't wait. School was in session. Homework had to be done and done well. Basketball had to be played. Families were resilient. Even those with a parent behaving terribly and hurtfully. Especially when the other parent provides calm and nurturing. Enough conversations were had, and apologies offered, to broker a temporary, workable peace. The stakes that season were too high to do otherwise.

His out-of-network counseling continued, racking up thousands of dollars we were afraid not to spend. We were grateful for it. He enjoyed talking to her, so I drove him to DuPont Circle every Tuesday night and waited in the dark car or perused books at Kramers. I should have been in there with him. He needed his privacy, his safe space. But I needed to sit in a room with him to help undo the damage I'd done.

His post-traumatic stress was real. Sleeping was harder for him. Obsessive thoughts and habits continued. Still, he reached out, craving light and laughter and connection with his parents.

Want to watch something? was the text message he sent out almost nightly to us.

Three of us and our shepherd mix on the sectional with snacks and the remote. We played occasional Texas Hold'em on Saturday nights at the dining room table with the fancy chips I bought, and every summer since he was five, back to Rehoboth Beach and Funland. So much shared laughter and running jokes, references to punch lines and scenes and characters made in passing, and those glances from him, that impulse he couldn't deny; looking for and finding me, ever-present and intimidating in ways I still couldn't process. The malfunction was always mine. He needed me to be better.

I told him at the start of his last middle school basketball season: "You're the only one on the team who has played varsity. You were the point guard for a team that went to the championship. You work harder than anyone. You're the most skilled player in school and it's not even close. Remind yourself of that every time you step on the floor."

They won every game. Jayson shined brightest. He led the team in scoring. The championship game was played on their home court. When he was introduced, he went down to one knee so a teammate (Joey!) could pantomime crowning him. He was a team captain and held in high regard.

The small gym was packed. All the kids and teachers and parents at Jayson's school watched him shoot his first shot, a three-pointer: Bang! The next time down the court? Another one: Bang! The next trip? Another: Bang! Three threes in a row to start the game! The other team didn't know what hit them. Then another! Four three-pointers in the first minutes and it was over.

I saw none of them.

I was walking alone outside with my phone turned off because Jayson had asked me, told me, pleaded with me to not come to games. My presence was too distracting. Accepting his wishes was the least I could do. So that day, I walked outside alone in the cold. I resolved that when the outcome was decided, either way I would tell him how proud I was of everything he did and how he did it.

I wasn't a public prick, barking at referees, or like some parents did, for the coach to put their child in the game or for their child to shoot the ball. It wasn't my behavior *during* games that made it hard for him. It was simply my presence. And after and before.

After their triumph, as the celebration quieted, with the conference championship flag draped over his shoulders, I asked him:

"Doesn't this feel good?"

"Yes." He was smiling, taking it in.

"You earned this."

He nodded.

"Remember the day after you lost the last championship game in sixth grade? And the season after that?"

"Yep," he told me.

"What did you do?"

"Got up shots."

"Right here. In this gym. With this day in mind. You did this." Despite me, I thought.

The next day he was there, in the same gym, getting up shots. Alone.

EIGHTEEN

2001

BEFORE

It was early autumn and Dad was drinking alone in a sixth-floor apartment overlooking a highly trafficked road in Perugia, Italy. He'd found a teaching job at a nearby university and continued with his madcap novel. He'd left it all behind once again. Escaped. Broke, without a next book and his marriage to Nina crumbling and his sons reeling, slipping into addiction and off the radar completely. But he was free.

He sent group emails to Cynthia and Sarah and Gavin and me about the disintegration of his marriage to Nina and the pain she was inflicting upon him by choosing not to join him in Italy. Instead, she was staying home with Gavin and pursuing her degree at Mount Holyoke, which happened to be a considerable drain on their suddenly meager finances.

It was October and my birthday approached. My wedding was set for the following June. I was writing and tutoring and sending emails back to Dad, trying to reassure him, still invested in his happiness.

I'd suggested he come home and get help, get sober, reconcile with Nina. He said it wasn't time for rash actions, even though within the span of a few weeks he'd found the teaching gig, packed, and moved to Italy alone.

Nina had been talking to a therapist, and they'd agreed it was more than reasonable for her to pursue the degree and for him to support that goal. He wanted her in Italy. They were at an impasse.

He said he was angry and sad and amazed that Nina was claiming he'd mistreated her. Time and distance, he said. Step by step, he said. Calmly, he said. Day by day was the best way to proceed. He'd be in close touch. And my love meant more than ever.

In his spiraling state he claimed he was "clinging to your support and declaration of love for me like a life raft."

He was ready again to run. But to where? Who would have him anymore? He was a man without a country, he'd told me and my sisters and Gavin, merely fourteen years old, reading letters from his father that blamed his misery on Gavin's mother.

They needed to sell the Williamstown house. He'd burned through all but a hundred thousand dollars of the millions he'd lost in two years. The house was in disrepair, paint peeling, and carpets stained. Gavin was getting high most days and nearly failing out of boarding school and suffering panic attacks and missing and fearing for his father and comforting and defending his mother as best he could.

I was verging on thirty and a new chapter, finally, becoming some kind of man in the world with a woman who wanted to spend her life with me. I'd been like Gavin once, a confused and insecure teenage son of my father, wishing and pleading for better from and for him. I was powerless, too, once. But no longer.

Dad and I wrote past each other. Nothing registered with him. He was never more a stranger to me. Then come the fuck home, I said. He didn't. Get help. He wouldn't.

Cynthia and Sarah didn't respond to his emails. They'd reached their breaking point. There was only so much they could bear. They had children. They were pregnant. They'd survived Dad-inflicted pain in childhood and adolescence and earned peace and stability and love they could count on, that returned what they gave, with spouses and children of their own. Only Gavin and I were responding.

Dad wrote that when despair was one's only companion sometimes one acted from that despair. He said Perugia was beautiful and would be a fine experience if only he sensed love at the other end, six time zones away, from Nina.

> *You keep on loving Jeanine, working as well as you can, enjoying your life. I'll continue to cope with mine, and I'll be in touch molto frequentemente. I love you, Joe. And you're loving me has never meant more.*
>
> Dad

I wonder if he was standing at the open window six stories up, pitched forward, dizzy and sobbing. He would always be the boy who hid in his bedroom praying for friends. Just as he would always be the man who rushed into marriage and parenting for his own reasons, and when it suited him, shatter their hearts because he wanted something else.

He would always be the father to a son, Mason, who never called him Dad and who never hugged him and rarely laughed. He raised a child who was unreachable and unknowable and completely vulnerable in the world. And he let him go, out into that world, where the worst could happen and did. He would always be the father to his youngest son who called him Dad from the start and revered him. And he set himself on fire in front of him.

Maybe alone in his fugue state he looked out over Italy and down to the dark empty street below at a blur of dim streetlights and the occasional passing car and the cool autumn air against his sweaty face and pulled off his worn polo shirt and let the coolness wash over him, welcoming and inviting.

Maybe it would protect him, wrap itself around and lift him, hold the weight of not just his body but his lifetime of worries and regrets and fears if only he'd trust it, have faith, accept grace and take one last leap. All those haunted versions of himself, those villainous roles, would die once and for all. And he'd be no one. He'd feel nothing and be nothing. Just gone.

It was a Friday night. He'd emailed Nina in Williamstown something ominous. She responded with calls to him that went unanswered. She called the school in Perugia and then the local police. He'd later admit to consuming 80 milligrams of Ativan that night in Italy when he emailed everyone with the subject line: *unhappy update*.

Three Italian police officers smashed down his apartment door while he slept at one a.m. He described one of the "sronzos" throwing a punch at him and him retaliating by throwing a chair at the officer. He was told he had to appear in court on Monday morning and would have to leave Italy immediately thereafter.

He told us it was Nina's hasty phone call to the police that meant he would have to leave Italy that night and deny them the $20,000 he was being paid for the semester that he was earning to pay for "her thrills at Mount Holyoke," money they needed.

He complained that another credit card provided by Nina was declined because of the money she was spending. He said he knew for certain he would never lay eyes on the Williamstown house again. He said he had gotten rid of his cell phone. He no longer needed his laptop, either.

He was heading off on his own, he declared. No roof over his head, no country to call his own.

He said his hope was that it wouldn't come to this, but alas, one day he just might feel like he couldn't take it anymore. There will be pills to take that would put him out of his Nina-induced misery forever.

She'd taken everything else away from him, he wrote. The only way to stop it was to stop himself. Then he'd no longer be the burden to her that he had so clearly become.

He said he would love us all forever and hoped somehow, he'd see us again. And he signed it "from here to eternity—Dad."

A woman from the university arrived the next morning to find him outside the building hailing a cab. She tried to slow him down. He pushed past her, slipped into the back seat of the taxi, and disappeared.

From my studio apartment in Washington, I called his credit card companies. It was a crisis. I was his first son and a solver of problems. I could find and save him. It was all in my hands. Finally, something to do, concrete, to bring him closer to me. It was something with him I could finally control.

He didn't have his phone, so he couldn't be tracked. The woman from the university wrote down the license plate and number of the taxi and the driver reported dropping him at the train station. His apartment was in disarray. A note was found informing the university that he could no longer teach there. Another note was found for Nina in which he described his intention to kill himself.

A sympathetic supervisor at American Express disclosed that his card was used at a hotel in Rome. Or was it Naples?

Nina drove three hours to Boston to fly to Italy to find him, but forgot her passport, had to drive back to Williamstown to get it.

There were flights to Rome and Naples from JFK and Newark and Dulles all departing at night and getting me there in the morning. United 924 from Dulles at 10:15 p.m. would get me to Rome via London by 2:50 p.m. the next day for $1,119. There was another flight through Munich that would get me there by late morning.

My brother-in-law and Cynthia lived in Paris and could meet me. We could find him together and bring him home. We could figure out where to send him from there. I couldn't afford rehab nor could he. But Cynthia and Yves could make it work. Just had to get to him in time.

He hadn't canceled his credit cards. Everyone agreed that freezing or canceling them could alert him that we were tracking him.

But still I asked the same sympathetic Amex supervisor agreed to attach a note to his account should he use the card again: "Please contact your son. He is concerned."

Dad tried to get cash twice. So he was still alive. Where? She told me the Rome Airport Hilton at 11:42 a.m.

I called the police in Rome. I needed justification for their intervention. I was told I could fax something.

I called and told Nina what I knew. She was at Logan. She was flying over that night to bring him home if she could. If he wasn't dead.

"He wouldn't check into the airport hotel if he was going to hurt himself, right?" I said.

"I don't know, Joe."

"Logically it just seems he wouldn't head to an airport with no intention of flying somewhere," I said, more to reassure myself. He'd tried to kill himself just days prior, drinking an entire bottle of grappa and swallowing 80 milligrams of Ativan. He wrote a suicide note to Nina. A hotel was an ideal place to kill oneself.

Only an extraordinarily high tolerance allowed him to survive his first attempt. He was only checked in for one night. He hadn't used a credit card to reserve or purchase an airline ticket. Signs were ominous. I broke down. I cursed him. I called him names like "coward" and "fucking pussy" and "piece of shit." I said his name, then screamed, and was screaming it into pillows in my seventh-story brick box studio until I was all screamed out and just a body lying face down on a mattress. Then I resumed the search.

I reached the hotel in Rome and explained that my father was there and "in distress." Could they have security, or the police, check on him please? Stefano was the manager who spoke fluent English and agreed to have someone check the room. I could call back in a couple of hours.

I did.

"He is all fine," Stefano told me from Rome.

I drove Jeanine's black Sentra up to Swarthmore from DC. I was on my way to Williamstown to be there when Nina brought him back.

Apparently, the flight back from Rome was a nightmare. He'd lost it, panicked, screamed about September 11 and hijackers—this was a mere two months after the attacks. Had there been smartphones, he'd have gone viral. "Author Joe McGinniss losing his shit, screaming about hijackers on Boston-bound flight from Rome." He was restrained and held until the plane landed. His first night in Williamstown was another crisis. He lost his mind. He destroyed anything within reach. The police were called. He resisted arrest. He was handcuffed for the second time in two weeks, this time in his own home. He was dragged down the stairway by two Williamstown police officers. He'd destroyed the kitchen, ripped cabinet doors from their hinges, thrown the microwave across the room, shattered a dozen glasses, stacks of dishes like it was a Greek restaurant.

He was detained down the road in a North Adams facility for psychiatric emergencies and charges were pending. I had to get there, and would be there, to once and for all confront, and possibly save, my father.

Jeanine was ready to go when I parked on Pulaski, a block from the housing project where the men catcalled her, "Hey dark and lovely," when she walked to Chelten Avenue for some relaxer. And she was ready before I got there, that morning, and the day before, and the moment I told her days earlier about his dire situation. She was always ready for me when I needed her.

She'd wrapped up her work in Los Angeles and was home in Philadelphia and walking with her mother daily in her mother's effort to lose weight for the wedding, while managing the health of her own deteriorating father.

The redbrick building loomed over the black asphalt lot. Gray clouds hung low, and the breeze was cold, more bite than the air I left in DC. We stood in a loose group, Nina, Jeanine, and me along with Gavin and a friend of his who accompanied him from boarding school for support.

I felt Gavin looking at me, the older brother he needed. Mason remained in Philadelphia. He never answered his phone and never returned calls. Gavin was tall for his age, but had his dad's sad eyes. His uncombed brown hair was long and full, tangled and unwashed. He was gentle and quick-witted and cynical and taking all of it in, to heart, his father leaving his mother for Italy, then breaking down, almost dying twice within a few weeks' time.

I was never more grateful to be thirty-one. Jeanine and I knew it then: as hard as it was for all of us who loved Dad, this would be hardest and most formative for Gavin, at that most awkward stage of adolescence, never sure of himself to begin with, then forced to watch his father self-destruct.

I signed in. An orderly lead us silently to a gray room with a heavy door and a small thick-glass window. Dad sat alone in yesterday's clothes—old, stained khaki pants and worn-out red polo shirt, no shoes, no belt, nothing with which he could hang himself. His metal chair wobbled, and he sighed and looked up at me and said, "Welp."

He was ashen, with white hair and purple under his eyes, and his polo shirt stretched across his belly. I remember thinking: This is how he'll look when he dies.

He'd pledged to Nina in the past, during his descent: If you ever hospitalize me, I'll kill myself.

"So here I am. Just like my mother," he said.

I didn't have words for it.

"We have to get you better, Dad. It's up from here, okay?"

But he was discharged with no plan. Cynthia and Sarah weren't there. They had children and work and life. What could they possibly do anyway?

I imagined getting him to rehab, with long, peaceful days of small-group therapy and caring doctors and counselors who would help him, first wean him off the pills and, finally, the alcohol. It was fantasy.

Gavin had to go back to school.

It was Dad and Nina, Jeanine, and me and the dogs and cats in the house on Oblong Road, across the gravel road from the Buddhist monastery. Go there, I thought. Walk up the hill and knock on the door and ask whoever answers if you can stay. The gulf between Dad and tranquility was never wider.

I made a list of friends and family. I found the names of some reputable rehabs. But he had no health insurance. The doctor who oversaw his stay and authorized his discharge from the North Adams facility was useless and told me to call if needed and wished us well. He told me that Dad was no longer his responsibility.

Was he mine? Nina's? He was certainly responsible for himself. Or was he? He was an addict. It was a sickness, a disease no different from what Jeanine's father was succumbing to, or Dad's father dying from cancer, or his grandfather dying from the Spanish flu. And Nina? How could the enabler be responsible? And the child, me, responsible for the parent when the parent wasn't even sixty and unafflicted by something physically debilitating? Who had how many opportunities and resources available to heal?

There was no answer. My motivation for being there, wanting so desperately to help, for him to not just feel better, but be better, came from somewhere else inside me and would almost certainly go unsatisfied.

You can't live someone else's life for them, was a phrase I'd picked up in my hours online reading about addiction and rehabilitation during my father's breakdown.

It was late in the day, back home on Oblong Road. He was quiet and his eyes scanned the kitchen, everything somehow back in its right place. The house was eerily still. Hushed and lifeless. Even the animals were subdued, unsure when the next explosion would come. He showered and changed his clothes. He was hungry. We all were.

Nina ordered a pizza. I poured Diet Pepsi over ice for Dad. We ate in silence. I wondered when he would drink. At one point I left the room and gathered all the bottles of wine and vodka and gin, then slipped into his office and bathroom and collected all the pills I could find and carried everything upstairs to the guest room and hid them under my clothes.

It was late. He stirred downstairs. He paced the kitchen and hallway that led to his office and bedroom. He didn't speak. He had to make it through the night. Morning would come. Then a new day. We'd figure out a plan together.

I couldn't sleep. I listened to him shuffling around downstairs in the dark, likely looking for something to drink, some pill to help him sleep. I wondered what he was capable of without either. Would he have another seizure? He'd had one in Italy and another on the flight home. Maybe he would be gone by morning. Maybe he'd leave. Maybe he'd kill himself.

He called up the stairs for me. Startled, I didn't respond. I looked at Jeanine.

"Could you come down here please?"

I found him in the kitchen. Nina stood behind him, off to the side. Jeanine was beside me.

This man. Who was this man? My father, I scoffed. Dad. I felt nothing for him in that moment. Nothing healthy. Nothing loving or kind.

I wanted a solution. He was a problem that needed solving. I was the problem solver, the hero of this story. Where everyone else failed or didn't bother trying, I'd succeed. Then I'd start my own life, buoyed, confident in ways that would resonate for a lifetime. Finally, Dad would be better. And that would bode well for me, because I was just like him.

"What?" I asked. "Are you looking for something?"

He needed something, at minimum, to drink. Whatever they sedated him with at the hospital had worn off, was hardly enough to begin with.

"Where is it?"

"You're not taking anything. You're not drinking."

It was late and no one had turned lights on, so the four of us faced one another in the dark kitchen.

I didn't understand, he said. Some of the pills I'd hidden from him were essential. "It would be dangerous otherwise."

"I don't believe you."

"I don't care." His voice rose.

"Sorry, Dad. Not tonight."

"Get out!" he thundered. "Of my house!'

"I'm not leaving," I said.

Nina said nothing. Neither did Jeanine.

I wasn't leaving Nina alone with him. I wasn't leaving him alone with himself.

"Throw me out, then," I dared. I was thirty-one and strong, all those years of lifting weights and playing ball, adding muscle to my tall frame. I was engaged and would be a husband soon, then a father.

He was fifty-nine and heavier and I wondered if he'd do it, try to force me out like another piece of furniture or appliance he'd totaled before either of his arrests.

"I can't let you have it, Dad."

"Then you can get the hell out of my house!"

"I can't do that either."

Only the dim orange light from the stove provided any light at all. He was a shadowy, disheveled, and desperate stranger. Only a drink could save him. A couple of Ativan. Something to let him lie still, if not sleep.

Tomorrow would be different. Tomorrow we'd talk. Figure things out. That's what he should have said. But he didn't offer that.

"This is my house!"

"Barely. And no I can't leave you here with Nina. Not after what you did."

"Get *the hell* out!"

"Joe," Nina tried.

"That's ridiculous. You're not throwing Joe out of the house," Jeanine said.

"With all due respect, Jeanine, this is none of your goddamn business."

"Don't talk to her," I told him. "You need to go to bed. Sleep it off. We'll deal with it tomorrow."

Nina spoke up. "Joe, he needs something. It's dangerous otherwise."

I didn't know how chemical dependency worked.

"Tell me what he needs," I said.

"Ativan."

"How much?"

"Two."

"Stay here."

I went upstairs and expected him to follow, but he waited in the kitchen. I returned with two yellow tablets and handed them to Nina.

"Good night."

I lay awake that night, bedroom doors that didn't lock, a large kitchen knife under my pillow. I listened to him moving around the house in the darkest hours of the night, pacing, sleepless and agitated. I could have gone downstairs and put myself in front of him again.

"What's going on?" I could have asked and waited for his unseeing eyes to locate me and he'd process the question maybe after I repeated myself.

"Nothing good."

"You want to keep living like this?"

"Of course not."

"So let's do something different, then."

"Like what?"

And the conversation would have ended there even if we kept talking. He had a line he wouldn't cross, and near-death experiences, suicide attempts, arrests, and detainments couldn't convince him to cross it.

So I stayed in bed and waited for sunrise. I thought about June and white wooden chairs. Simple, clean, and elegant. That's what Jeanine wanted for the wedding. Under the lush green canopy of Swarthmore's outdoor amphitheater. Perfect.

• • •

"You can back out any time." I should have offered that. This wasn't how I'd end up, I may have said. Or asked: Is this how I end up? It couldn't be. I was ascendent. I knew what I could offer Jeanine, what kind of husband I would be. Fatherhood was a different question. I wouldn't end up like him, I told myself, and mostly believed it.

When he was thirty, he was jogging daily and writing and drinking and brimming with self-confidence and battling bouts of crippling insecurity. He was a history maker and celebrity author and father and husband and ex-husband and deserter of children and funny and wildly intelligent and self-deprecating and wore unwashed pants and T-shirts and flannel and hiked and read books and newspapers and magazines and listened to Bob & Ray comedy records and Hank Williams and called old friends late at night and missed his kids and often lay awake at night, trembling. If he was ever a man at peace, it wasn't for very long.

The trip there, standing over him in the hospital, confronting him in the kitchen of his house, leaving on my terms, felt like an inflection point. I was planning a wedding and writing a book and starting a life. There was compromise and balance and responsibility expected, and I felt ready for all of it. And he was stripped of everything in that moment, money, reputation, direction. I was the only one of his five children there for his worst. And he knew when I left, after he refused to commit himself to changing, he could no longer cling to my support like a life raft. He was a drowning man, and I was sailing away.

NINETEEN

2002

BEFORE

"'What I am often amazed by is that well-educated people often don't get very good medical advice and they don't seek it out aggressively. They don't seek out a second opinion,' says Kay Redfield Jamison, a professor of psychiatry at the Johns Hopkins University School of Medicine and herself a manic-depressive who wrote about her illness in *An Unquiet Mind*." (*Washington Post*, July 20, 1997)

"For reasons known only to him, he refused to do his best to save himself."

This was written not about my dad, but author and friend of his, J. Anthony "Tony" Lukas, who'd hosted the *Blind Faith* publication party to which Cynthia, Sarah, and I rode in the white limousine to Manhattan.

Lukas said, when asked about his often-crippling clinical depression: "All writers are, to one extent or another, damaged people. Writing is our way of repairing ourselves."

From a story following his suicide: "You know what they said about Tony, highly accomplished psychiatrists and experts in the field, he didn't try hard enough. He didn't talk to a psychologist and only visited a medication prescribing psychiatrist once every six months. The writer William Styron, who suffered crippling depression, who took it upon himself at his lowest, most perilous moment, to inform his wife that he needed to be hospitalized to prevent killing himself. Styron knew Lukas and was angry. He could avoid this fate, he surmised. Had he done the work." (*Washington Post*, July 20, 1997)

I sat at my IKEA table staring at my laptop screen. It was a gray November Saturday in Washington. Jeanine was back home in Philadelphia. She'd be headed back down to DC soon. For the wedding, we had invitations picked out and a cake design and honeymoon ideas, but nothing confirmed. Guest lists and musical arrangements were taking shape. A string quartet and a zydeco band for the reception.

Dad sent an email to all five of his children. He had a list. It was comprehensive and broken out chronologically. All the prescription drugs he'd been consuming in the years and months preceding his breakdown.

He noted: never was he on fewer than three of them simultaneously, mostly four or more, and all at or near maximum dosages. He'd embedded the list in a three-page confessional update.

Any that ended in "azepam" were tranquilizers. They had the same effect as a bottle of 100-proof alcohol. "Whatever I feel, the world will feel!" he said. And for him, he explained, 90 percent of the time it was rage and not joy. Everything else on his dizzying list was an antidepressant or a sleep aid or mood leveler.

"Allora," he wrote.

"*1993–1995 (Until after the OJ trial and breaking of the contract): Diazepam, Prozac, Paxil, Temazepam . . . "

I'd never heard of most. I later learned that temazepam can cause paranoid or suicidal ideation and impair memory, judgment, and coordination. When combined with other substances, particularly alcohol, breathing slows and the possibility of death increases. Temazepam is intended for short-term use only, a couple of weeks at most, to aid insomnia. He consumed it for years. Along with everything else. And drinking as much as he ever had.

"Desipramine, Zoloft, propranolol, Wellbutrin, Lorazepam, Diphenatol, Oxycodone, Ambien, Effexor."

*1996–1998 (While researching and writing *The Miracle of Castel Di Sangro* and encompassing the night of the accident in which he drove his Volvo off the side of Petersburg Pass a few miles from home): Lorazepam, Effexor, temazepam, propranolol, Zantac, metronidazole, Oxycodone, propoxyphene.

*1999–2000 (During the publication of *The Miracle of Castel Di Sangro*): Lorazepam, Effexor, temazepam, Zantac, Celebrex, cytomel, clonazepam, Seroquel, Oxycodone, triazolam, Celexa, Remeron, trazodone, methylphenidate, Neurontin, Risperdal.

*2001 (When he'd returned to Italy for the short-lived teaching job): Lorazepam, Effexor, Wellbutrin, Remeron, buproprion, temazepam.

It wasn't the insane list of drugs he'd been consuming for the past decade or even the tens of thousands of dollars he admitted blowing on them that left me cold.

It was the performative tone. The clever asides that made it eminently readable. His retelling of the first Valium, which he said "started all this," was prescribed by a trustee of the Williamstown Summer Theater Festival, who said, "You're a writer, you must get tense in a way that interferes with your work sometimes, these Valiums should help take that edge off." More controversially, this trustee was known to be supplying "notorious cokehead Richard Dreyfuss with what he needed to keep his edge on during performances."

"I am more a condition, a disorder or a syndrome than a person," he wrote.

Weaning himself off the drugs nearly killed him. Sleep was impossible. He was prescribed sleeping pills, which made him sluggish and foggy, but still he couldn't sleep. Because of their side effects he was unable to drive. He dozed off in forty-five-minute spurts. He walked into doorways and walls. He was dizzy and scared. He had a seizure. Then another.

Gavin and Nina were there for the worst: his bouts of violent rage and breakdowns and tortured recovery. Sleepless dad, pacing dad, dizzy dad, sleeping-all-day dad, frightened dad, convulsing, seizing dad.

What remained of the wiring in his brain was being stripped and restored. Did a version of him even exist that wasn't chemically altered? He'd been chemically dependent for decades, an alcoholic since he was twenty. He was a stranger to everyone and himself. Whoever he had become was unbearable. Whatever hybrid version of himself, should he survive sobriety, was welcome.

There was more reference to Samuel Johnson on his struggle with debilitating depression.

> *Well, no one ever said it was going to be easy, at any age. And day after day I will continue to exert myself to the maximum, if that is what is required. The grimacing November sky eventually will surrender blue crystal of clear winter days, and beyond that, to the dawn of a new and glorious spring. I not only plan to be around for it, but to be in shape to enjoy it to the fullest. And that means the most time possible spent with each of you.*
>
> *I love you,*
> *Dad*

It was more a personal essay than a heartfelt letter to his heartbroken children. He was working to persuade, put his own struggles and dizzying descent into historical context. I wanted honesty and vulnerability instead of three well-crafted pages passed off as a confessional essay for *Vanity Fair*.

He could have written that he was an addict and would embrace recovery. He could make amends or not.

I was part of "a doomed tribe" not just of writers, as Frederick Busch once said, but of my heritage, a chemically imposed death sentence carried out over a lifetime, slowly then suddenly then nothingness, blackness. Unless I don't start, I thought. I don't take medication. I don't drink, I thought. I'm stronger than you. I'm not you and never will be, I thought.

I have some agency.

His struggle, he insisted, was to survive the blackness and reach out and hold on for dear life to any light, whatever form it took. I was doing just that. And it all made sense. That was the cycle, the natural progression we could all expect, each generation more evolved than the last. Awareness was half the battle. By thirty, I was painfully, exhaustingly aware.

But where, Dad, was this struggle you keep referencing? Struggle implies fight, implies resistance. When did you fight?

He wouldn't go to rehab. After the trauma of watching his mother carted off to hospitals to get happy, he vowed he would never do the same.

He'd never change. The pattern would repeat. I wasn't sure why it mattered so much. It was his life, not mine.

But it did, still, and I carried the weight of it, the generational debt passed on and never paid off.

At minimum, I'd be better off for having gone to him when he was at his lowest. And standing up to him and speaking the truth before it was too late, before he was gone and I'd have to carry it with me, the weight of it all. As if speaking released something, lessened the burden I'd face, the cross I'd bear that I couldn't even imagine then.

In the hero's journey, a confrontation with the father seemed essential. I could feel something shift, our paths diverging. I'd trailed quietly and dutifully behind him from the beginning, grateful for the times he'd slowed and paused and hoisted me up on his shoulders.

I came to believe that night, that period, was the reckoning. If not final, then at least determinative. I wasn't him. Whatever demons I'd inherited were somehow exorcised.

I expected to feel better, a burden lifted. It would pay off. I'd be better later, when it mattered more. When I was the father.

Dad emailed me part of a Bob Dylan poem in December. It was brief and stark, about a trembling sky and the need to leave. He paraphrased the poet and told us he had nothing to live up to.

> *It's taken all the life I've lived so far to bring me to that point—nothing to live up to—and I'm delighted to note that part of that insight brings with it a deeply relaxing sense of inner freedom.*
>
> *But right now I want to hear from you, so how about it?*
> *With a love for you that is a part of me wherever I am*
>
> *—Dad*

He was off again, leaving Gavin, seventeen, barely hanging on in school, smoking weed daily, helplessly watching Dad slip into the back seat of a town car to take him to Boston for a flight to Los Angeles, where he'd spend a year teaching at a place called Soka University because he was broke and because his marriage to Nina was over and because the house was being sold. And because he'd somehow, at some point, met another woman who also taught there and he'd wanted to be with her, was apparently in love with her.

She was twenty years younger and taught anthropology. Before flying out to California, he'd buy her sex toys and erotic books on Amazon.com, leave his virtual receipts open on the desktop computer in the living room for Nina and Gavin to see, which they both did.

• • •

Dad was in California with most of his possessions left behind. What he needed, he hired Gavin for $25 an hour to pack and ship to him in Aliso Viejo.

Dad insisted he was still trying to make his comic novel work and might write a book about the college where he was teaching. He was putting his life together, piece by piece.

From the man who asked for and even demanded empathy, there seemed little thought given to the damage he'd done and was doing to his son, left behind again, distraught and adrift and addicted and longing for a version of his father that no longer existed and may never have.

Gavin was turning eighteen and his dad wasn't there for his birthday. He was instead in California with the new girlfriend. He told Gavin on the phone, "It may not be a car in the driveway, but I've taken care of you on your birthday!"

Arriving in the mail that day was an Amazon gift card worth $500.

Did he consider flying back for Gavin's eighteenth birthday? Could they have met in New York? Or Boston? Could he have arranged with Nina to be out of the house, or could they have agreed to make the weekend of his visit for their son's eighteenth birthday about Gavin and do their best for their troubled, fragile son, who'd endured a devastating psychological stretch for the previous two years, all at the hands of his father?

Aside from packing and shipping his dad's shit, Gavin's plan for the summer was to find work after a long-planned cross-country drive to California with a childhood friend. When he hatched the plan, he'd had no reason to think that Dad would be living there. Now, under the worst possible circumstances, the dissolution of their family and the sale of his childhood home, he was heading straight for him.

It was sunny and clear in late June, but the heat stuck and the breeze refused to blow.

White wooden chairs in the outdoor amphitheater under a canopy of elms and great oaks. Where we'd both been handed our diplomas. Where LBJ addressed a graduating class. Where Bob Dylan played a free concert. The chairs were perfect.

But they were left in cardboard boxes in stacks at the very top of the venue. I had to unbox and arrange a hundred of them. I had to buy the speakers at Radio Shack and hope they'd connect to the sound system. It was noon. The ceremony began at 4:30 p.m. I hadn't eaten breakfast. Inside, I blamed everyone else, but knew it was all my fault.

Dad and Nina and Mason and Gavin were all heading to Media to hang around Sarah's house until heading to Swarthmore for the ceremony. Sarah was tense. She hated hosting Dad, especially after everything he'd just been through. It required so much energy to pretend.

The last time he'd been there was Christmas. He'd driven down with Nina to check on Mason, who was living in Southwest Philadelphia and working at a meatpacking plant, one of the few jobs he was suited for because of his condition.

Dad was rarely down that way. Only Nina would go into the city to see how Mason was living and buy him groceries because he refused to see Dad. Reasons were never provided though I suspected it had something to do with Dad's addictions and gambling away the family's money and losing the house and his mistreatment of Nina and the breakup of the family.

Sarah graciously prepared snacks and sodas and the television was turned on to a random college football game until Dad found a soccer match and lost himself in it. It didn't matter if it was Italian or British or Spanish or even Brazilian or French or German. It didn't even matter if it was live or a repeat. He knew about some player from some side or a coach and even bothered to let anyone within earshot know.

His conversations with Sarah and her husband seemed superficial at best. Dad's presence was more a reminder of what wasn't possible and the increasing distance between him and everyone else.

Sarah the fourth-grade teacher, who spent money she didn't have on classroom materials for her needy students, who showed up early and stayed late, had so little in common with Dad. She was a mother of three who read Jodi Picoult and *People* magazine and watched the Eagles on Sunday and never lived anywhere outside the state of Pennsylvania. What was there to talk about with him?

She once wrote a short children's book complete with illustrations called *Hugs Make Me Happy*. It was well crafted and effective and moving. Children need to know, to feel, that they're loved, secure, and safe. Hugs from a parent or a grandparent or a sibling can do that. There was some discussion with Dad about how she might get it into the hands of a publisher. Nothing ever came of it.

He understood and appreciated, intellectually, that her profession was mostly thankless and exhausting. He was certainly proud of his daughter. And he said the words and asked about her class and the kids, and while she answered it wasn't a surprise to catch his eyes shifting toward the television screen. Pretending was a two-way street.

So the prospect of hosting him on my wedding day was an unwelcome chore. She had young children to prepare for their roles, beautifully performed, as flower girl and ring bearer.

And Dad wasn't there to help her. He was there because he had to be. I could snap a picture of Sarah in the doorway from the kitchen to the living room with another plate of cheese and crackers and read her mind: *This will all be over soon.*

Three o'clock, ninety degrees and humid. The wires slid into the back of the amplifier and the sound was clean and clear. Bono's voice filled the amphitheater and I sat with my best man on the stone wall of the grass stage trying to keep it together.

He told me the white chairs looked good. I took in the scene, the ascending aged stone seating and steps and towering trees and sunlight flickering through the canopy when the wind shifted, and it suited her, I thought, this simple, natural, elegant beauty. This was who she was.

• • •

The house on Magill was empty except for me and my mother. She met me upstairs in the small hallway into which our three bedrooms and shared bathroom opened. The space in which I played Nerf Hoop alone or with sleepover friends, the space in which my sisters glimpsed their outfits one last time in the narrow closet mirror before school in the mornings. The space through which my father walked after a day spent at the desk in his home office that would become my bedroom after he left. The space where he wrote and plotted his escape while his daughters napped in their shared room, only a thin wall separating them. Through that space, another day's work done on the bestseller to be, on his way downstairs for his first reward, the first pour, and maybe a walk to the pay phone across the turnpike to make the call to Nina—*was she at the house yet?* He'd already told my mother he had an event to attend in Manhattan, so it was all set, she suspected nothing. Dad walked past the same bathroom door behind which Cynthia would spend so many tortured hours because of him. The door behind which Sarah would smoke when Mom worked middle. The door behind which I'd once felt so distraught for vague but crushing reasons, I held a handful of pills and wondered how long it would take once I swallowed them, would I throw up or sleep? And then what? It tantalized me at fourteen, the prospect of life after death, finding out.

That was another lifetime. All of it behind me. Life was for living and I was starting the rest of mine in an hour, more ready than Dad ever was.

I straightened my new silver tie in front of the too-short mirror on the closet door. It cut off my head, so I had to duck to see my face.

My mother stared at me. I was him. There was no avoiding it. It had to be disorienting for her. I looked just like him in that suit, in that space. She never said it, though. She simply asked if I was ready. I hadn't eaten or had much of anything to drink all day. I refused sedatives or beta-blockers. I'd gotten everything done just in time, with barely an hour to spare. I told her I was, indeed, ready.

• • •

Half an hour before the ceremony, Dad met me on a narrow campus road that ran between the amphitheater and an old gray-stone dormitory. We were dwarfed by the enormous, full white oaks, the branches that still refused to move, the air so thick and still.

Before coming to Swarthmore, he'd been in California, then a stop in Williamstown, sleeping in the guest room, the same bed where I'd laid awake clutching a knife under the pillow after he'd been released from the hospital.

The trial separation from Nina was formalized. The house was still on the market. Nina had been staying up until all hours ripping carpet from the floors and doing the painting herself because they had no money to pay anyone to do it.

"I can't give you a lot of good advice about marriage, as you know, for obvious reasons." He stopped. "I'm so proud," he said and hugged me tight. I wished I'd felt differently then, but I was somewhere else, further along than before, and not behind him or by his side, but a different place and direction altogether.

He gave me a letter. It was printed on glossy heavy-stock cream-colored paper. In gold fourteen-point font, he wrote that he failed me in many ways because of his imperfections and worse. But he never failed me from a lack of love and never lacked the burning urge to do all he could for me.

He was gripped by that for thirty years and would remain ruled by it until he died, he said. "Sadly, much has been lost in translation," he wrote.

The care he took with the paper and colored font made me sad. It was all so compensatory. Much had been "lost in translation." I didn't know what that was supposed to mean.

I imagined him composing the letter. Maybe he was sitting in his new girlfriend's house, probably having a pretty nice day, the Southern California sun shining, a steady breeze washing up and over the hillsides from the Pacific. He'd have a sandwich from that gourmet shop in town and spend a couple of hours online reading about Baggio and Italian soccer and call out to his new partner about someone in a story he knew from Castel di Sangro and he'd send emails to his new agent and old editor, who was pushing the book about Dad taking a cruise around the world where he boards a ship filled with the uber-wealthy and circles the globe with them and writes about the predictable ugliness he finds and then maybe he'd tinker with his madcap novel, but not really because it was more of a mess than he wanted to admit and his partner wanted to go for a hike and then dinner and then try something with the toys he'd sent.

And his first son was getting married in a couple of days. His second son was still living out a tragic, lonely existence in a non-gentrified section of Southwest Philadelphia, victimized and afflicted with illness, and his third son was getting stoned nearly every day and almost failing out of school and would be heading to California in search of him. So he wrote to me. Then he flew back east to watch me get married. He went back to California to be with his new girlfriend and new life, and his youngest son, still reeling from the trauma of being his child, was driving through the night to find him.

It was somewhere along a flat and lonely stretch of highway in Ohio. Gavin was behind the wheel with his childhood friend asleep in the passenger's seat, making his way to Dad. He missed him. He was distraught and feeling lost. He needed to know that his dad was still reachable, somehow; maybe at the end of the three-thousand-mile drive, barely eighteen, he would somehow find him again. I could have told him, but he needed to find out for himself.

Dad called and I listened. It was sometime before Gavin made it out there. He explained that he was in recovery mode. After what he'd endured, the mere fact that he was getting out of bed in the morning, much less producing work, the novel, the book proposals, finding teaching jobs, were not bad for a dead man walking.

He had sunshine and warm breezes and a woman who only knew him from today, not the past thirty or forty years. She made him feel new and renewed and valued. He made her laugh. It was the stuff of survival. And he'd been in survival mode since 2001. And really, since 1989 and Janet Malcolm's savage attack that would have ended the careers of lesser men.

That phrase stuck, "lesser men." He knew all about them. He'd devoted a career to them. All the lesser men whose lives he explored and demons he'd exposed. Nixon and Ailes and MacDonald and the other murderous men and Kennedy and the corrupt Italian soccer bosses. And he was them, lesser too, an addict, an adulterer, a deserter.

But his lesser parenting was more than his own father ever managed. That was a concept that I struggled to process, much less accept and give him credit for. But it was true.

And wasn't that something? *Could you, Joe, wrap your head around that? The Tintin museum and the overnight train. The Wiffle Ball and tents in the yard and Alaska and snowball fights in July. And lullabies and Lucy and don't you know I had none of that from my father when I was a child?*

He could have asked me that. Made a case for himself. I'd have found it compelling. I may have felt something flicker, a fleeting warmth of understanding at the sound of the words that held special meaning to me, those moments he recalled and made possible.

I had a father who tried. He had a father who was orphaned at three and raised in, at best, unusual circumstances. Dad didn't explain any of that to me, or my sisters. He could have tried now, but I wasn't really listening anymore.

Gavin made it to California. Dad's house didn't look lived in. A desk with a laptop, no food, nothing in the fridge. He wasn't living there at all. He was living with his new partner. That's what Gavin figured out when Dad took him and his friend to Whole Foods upon their arrival, filling three carts with an insane amount of food.

It was on Dad's laptop that he found the letter Dad penned to his boarding school dean, pleading for leniency for Gavin and his grades. "Gavin is no genius . . . " And it was later, at night, when Dad slept, he and his friend heard the screams. Dad crying out, "No! No!" And again the next night. Dad took Gavin to an interview at a local college. He hammed it up during a group tour. Gavin bombed the interview. Dad was indifferent. Gavin's friend was ready to leave. So was Gavin. None of this was surprising, but was no less hurtful. Eighteen years with him, under the same roof, and he was never more a stranger. Dad with his youngest child, treading water after a three-thousand-mile journey to find him, was unmoved and unmovable.

Dad and Gavin were giving me a glimpse—a version of me with a future son of my own. I wouldn't have believed it then. Or even later, for the first eleven years of Jayson's life.

TWENTY

2003–2007

BEFORE

Dad was two days from his next port of call, alone in his cabin, sailing around the world to gather material for a book. He was trying to convince his new partner to meet him. She was reluctant. He didn't take it well.

David Rosenthal, then the publisher at Simon & Schuster, was a fan of Dad's work. They'd brainstormed and arrived at an outrageously appealing idea: a cruise around the world with rich Americans. It would be allegory and brilliant and funny. But Dad's partner had doubts.

I'd asked Gavin about Dad's madcap novel about genetic scientists racing around Europe. Gavin had glimpsed some pages.

"It's bad," he told me.

"How bad?"

"It's madness. It's a mess. It's just this meandering fucking mess."

"Even now? Sober? It's not any better?"

"He's not sober."

• • •

When his new relationship faltered, Dad dropped the cruise book and the novel remained a mess.

Gavin was called to duty once again. The loyal and loving son helped his father pack his belongings in California and drive back east. They stopped at the Richard Nixon Museum in Yorba Linda. They went to Nixon's grave, where Dad stood and wept.

Gavin was nineteen and did most of the driving and was forced to listen to inconsolable Dad breaking down, lamenting through tears the loss not of Nina, but his girlfriend. The house on Oblong Road was sold. Dad had a new book idea that allowed him to rent a place in Saratoga.

He was contracted to write a brief, well-reported story about a long-shot racehorse. David Rosenthal would publish *The Big Horse* for Simon & Schuster for a modest payment.

The late David Carr generously profiled Dad in *The New York Times* upon the book's publication. The title was "A Writer Is Back in the Saddle after His Fall from Grace" (July 28, 2004). In it, Carr addressed Dad's struggle with "Ativan addiction" and self-control. There was much he mercifully left out.

Carr had been an addict himself, crack and cocaine, not pills. He could empathize. Dad had weathered his own storm.

The publication was cause for celebration, modest as it was. There was a party at Elaine's on the Upper East Side. I attended with Jeanine. Nina and Gavin were there, too. It was awkward because it was as though Dad and Nina had never separated, there had been no affair, no breakdown and suicide attempts and house sold and fortune squandered, children traumatized. She was just there. Life resumed, as Dad wanted it.

Cynthia sent her congratulations from Paris. Sarah had nothing to say. The "Dad has a new book" routine was dead to her. She had a life to live. Besides, he didn't give a shit about her career, so why should she be expected to care about his?

There was no limousine to ferry anyone up to Manhattan.

His former editor Michael Korda was there and suggested a new book idea: Dad would go to the one of the world's most distant islands to live and write about what he saw and experienced. Mere talk of a next book for Dad left me feeling more optimistic about his writing career than I had in years.

I still clung to the fantasy that some sort of professional equilibrium for him would bring everyone a little more peace. One more rise from the ashes could somehow allow him a serenity that would soothe us all.

Weeks later he was in his rented Saratoga house and emailing suicide threats to his former partner in California and ordering pills online promising to swallow them all.

I went through the motions, made the calls, sent the emails to all the right people and it played out in a familiar way—police summoned, denials offered, crisis averted, and everyone worse off than before.

I didn't drive there. I didn't make a list of names for an intervention. I didn't find a rehabilitation hospital. I was done. Instead, I invited him to visit. He said he would. It would be years before he did.

A writer's paradise of my own was being constructed in Washington, DC. Jeanine walked to work along the quiet, tree-lined street, past dogs being walked and babies being pushed in strollers to one of the playgrounds, and I spent the day writing my novel.

By six, when the day was done, I walked our puppy to the back of the Fannie Mae building to meet Jeanine and walk home together. I'd give her pages. She'd give me notes. I was prickly and simultaneously overconfident and painfully insecure. I processed criticism and questions poorly. My fuse was short at thirty-four. I'd thought the pages were better than they were. I apologized. So many apologies. Maybe another reader would be healthier for our relationship, she offered. I heard my father in my voice, the tone, the quick trigger, a knife's edge.

The way he habitually snapped at Nina, the way she took it. That was a saving grace for me: Jeanine didn't take it.

Dad and Nina were back together in Massachusetts, in restoration mode. She demanded consistent counseling. There were no more pills, aside from antidepressants. The drinking was in check. They financed a modest new house on a tree-shrouded roundabout in a town called Pelham, minutes from Amherst and Northampton.

Despite poor sales of *The Big Horse*, Dad retained the support of David Rosenthal and continued to brainstorm book ideas. He'd survived his crashes and relapses. He was rebuilding. There was calm and optimism for the first time in years.

Gavin was in college. Sarah and Cynthia were healthy, and their children were beautiful and their husbands were present and nurturing as partners and parents. No one drank. No one smoked. No one abused prescription pills, and no one mistreated or neglected their children. Only Mason remained at risk, an unreachable victim of his untreatable condition.

I had every reason, with Jeanine's love and support, to believe that the best was to come. I'd emailed Cynthia in Paris and asked her rhetorically whether it was possible to fall even more in love than ever in the years after the wedding.

Jeanine had the conviction that I was capable of being the caring parent any child of ours would deserve. We laughed after, too, because something about the moment felt different. We'd been married for four years. We knew.

I'd long suspected, before the afternoon of the amniocentesis, that I'd feel a flight impulse when I learned I had a child on the way, a cold dread, a genetic glitch that compelled me to run when the pressure was on. *I can't do this. I can't. West. The desert. Arizona or New Mexico. Tucson or Santa Fe. An apartment. Any job and just keep writing. The endless skies and ancient red rocks and open roads for late-night and sunrise drives to clear my head. I'd circle back eventually, when I was ready. On my terms.*

When the long needle pierced Jeanine's smooth round belly and she squeezed my hand and I kept repeating, "You got this. You're good. It's good."

And the news: healthy. *He* was healthy!

That's when the anxiety melted away. Everything cleared. There was nothing more important in life than your soon-to-be-born, healthy baby boy.

Dad wrote me after I shared the news. His voice reminded me of what I'd always thought were healthier times, before his descent and crash. But he'd been an addict for so long I didn't know what he was supposed to sound like.

Gavin was at their new Pelham house with his girlfriend. He said they spent most of the prior night talking about me and Jeanine and the "baby-to-be."

He asked if we had a due date, if Jeanine was past her morning sickness. How was I doing? Was I scared? Did it seem simultaneously overwhelming and exciting? These were the questions of a man who was grounded and living in the moment. A stranger to me, but welcome.

He said he was curious because he had been so much younger when Cynthia was born. He had been twenty-three, not thirty-six. He imagined that many of my feelings and reactions were different from those he had felt.

I had a novel publishing and my first son on the way. Obama was the president, and everything felt possible.

Jayson was due. My mother came down to help, as did Jeanine's parents.

May 1. He was born. I went to the delivery room and held Jeanine's hand. We paid extra for a private maternity ward suite. I wore baby-blue scrubs and held her hand and spoke softly into her warm ear while the anesthesiologist made jokes and read a book. The room was cold. Beeping and directives and affirmations from nurses. A tugging sensation. Jeanine's eyes went wide, and she squeezed my hand.

"Woah! He's a big one!"

For three nights I stayed with them in the hospital and slept in the condo with my mother and Labrador. Then I brought Jeanine and Jayson home. The next morning, I was awake early. And six days passed, and unlike Dad after bringing me home, I was still there.

TWENTY-ONE

2010

AFTER

Sarah Palin was from Alaska, a place Dad knew and wrote about in *Going to Extremes*. The 2012 election was on the horizon, and she might just run for president. The timing seemed ideal. She'd be the subject of his next book.

Gavin followed the process closely.

I consumed updates from both Dad and Gavin about his search for a publisher and some kind of income and, of course, Italian soccer. Though he wasn't abusing prescription pills any longer, he was drinking a lot.

This was the same time I'd emerged from a stretch of depression. All the joy and beauty of my own son and life was too much. I couldn't be in the same room with him without tears forming. I got some help because the alternative was unsustainable. I ignored my father's lifetime struggles and what that portended for me and was convinced I required no more work than a pill a day.

The good news finally came in for Dad. After nearly a dozen

rejections, he got an offer. He'd be paid $200,000 to research and write *The Rogue: Searching for the Real Sarah Palin.*

"Thank GOD!" Gavin messaged me upon the news.

The next time I saw Dad wasn't in Alaska or Massachusetts but in a hospital waiting room in Philadelphia on a cold and gray January afternoon. He and Nina were there for Mason, who was thirty-one and near death. Dad sat next to Nina, their expressions as grim as the dingy fluorescent-lit room. Jeanine and I were there to see Mason, if he'd let us. He wouldn't. He'd only see his mother.

Though Mason was no longer a child, when he first saw Nina, he'd told her he was a "bad boy." Mason had always been and remained acutely vulnerable to exploiters and others who saw his condition as an opportunity, since the age of fourteen, when he was first sent away to school. The worst could happen and did, over and over again.

When he was released, Nina drove Mason back to his apartment. Dad said Mason didn't want to talk to anyone, wouldn't let Nina do his laundry even though he was too weak to walk without assistance. The laundromat was six blocks from his one-room apartment filled with books, including a worn copy of Basil Liddell Hart's *History of the Second World War* that he spent a summer immersed in when he was eight years old along with the Bible and Homer and countless books about Afghanistan.

Mason wouldn't let his parents talk to his doctors or social worker or case manager. Another infection could be fatal, Dad said. Mason refused money. He'd rather die than let us help him, Dad said. So they left.

He and Nina tried to convince him to see the doctors and get the treatments necessary, but legally couldn't force him. He was their son, but a grown man living in a different state who harbored so much anger toward Dad that he refused to speak or communicate directly with him. Who wasn't angry with Dad?

• • •

He left for Alaska to research and write the Palin book. The house he rented, unlike the Beverly Hills estate he inhabited for the Simpson book, was modest and rustic. It was dwarfed by the neighbor to the left, whose towering lakefront new-construction estate was the envy of Wasilla, Alaska. Only a six-foot wooden fence separated the two properties. The owner paid him a visit within days of his arrival.

Todd Palin, then husband to the former governor Sarah Palin, knocked on Dad's door. They exchanged pleasantries, though Todd seemed leery of Dad's friendly disposition. He simply asked what he was doing there. Dad answered: writing a book about Sarah. And Todd turned and walked away.

That very day Sarah welcomed him, her new next-door neighbor, with a Facebook post wondering what he would gain from peering into her daughter's bedroom.

> Yes, that Joe McGinniss. Here he is about 15 feet away on the neighbor's rented deck overlooking my children's play area and my kitchen window. We're sure to have a doozey to look forward to with this treasure he's penning. Wonder what kind of material he'll gather while overlooking Piper's bedroom, my little garden, and the family's swimming hole?

Todd hastily raised the height of the fence. Cable news ran some stories. Maybe it would help the book.

National news reporters with television cameras rolling showed up unannounced. Unshaven and overweight, Dad answered the door and spoke through a dark screen door. He looked less than sympathetic. In an earlier, more celebrated phase of his life and career, a version of Dad popping up next door to a loathsome subject of his book would be fun, if not funny. He'd push that screen door open and engage the reporter calmly and with insight and dry humor. He'd do his best Larry David and win the argument and the day. We'd all cheer him on, or at least not turn away. But that version of Dad, to those of us who knew him best, was gone.

He was deemed creepy and his behavior stalker-ish. He was losing a public relations battle with the wildly unpopular Palin. He returned to Pelham after five months, to Nina and their bleak financial situation, the new house verging on foreclosure.

Despite the otherwise glum circumstances, and possibly as her condition for taking him back, Dad and Nina renewed their vows. We were all invited to attend the backyard ceremony in Pelham.

The program for the ceremony was emblazoned with the title of the Emmylou Harris song: Calling My Children Home.

For a renewal of marital vows, the emphasis on his children was odd.

After multiple suicide attempts and threats and two arrests and losing their house and all their money and multiple affairs and one common-law marriage with another woman in California and a cruise around the world and half a year in the Sarah Palin cesspool and almost losing Mason and watching Gavin careen into addiction and valiantly fight for sobriety, and burning every professional bridge available, Dad and Nina renewed their vows. There was more to their story than the worst. And they needed each other's social security income.

They'd invited family and a handful of friends to the ceremony held under a big white tent in the backyard of their house. His grandchildren were healthy and beautiful and ran and played and the pictures on my phone told the most important story: the children were happy.

The joy found was not in the odd ceremony but everything surrounding it, namely the grandchildren. Jayson's French cousins, teenage Sebastien and preteen Cecilia and newly adopted nine-year-old Samuel from Ethiopia, and teenage Dylan and Lauren and eight-year-old Carly from Media, Pennsylvania.

Five-year-old Jayson's white button-down shirt and shorts were wrinkled as he bravely held a little toad in the palm of his hand and eyed his older, taller cousins, who posed with bubble gum cigarettes. It was an idyllic scene—my sisters and I reveling in the happiness of our children.

Then it started. We were all called forward to join Dad and Nina. The twenty or so guests looked on. It was humid and warm and he was sweating, beaming and standing tall, but heavier than he should have been. His five adult children, even Mason, who was thankfully healthy enough to travel, plus his seven grandchildren and Nina. We'd traveled from France and Washington, DC, and Philadelphia to stand with him, still bewildered from all that came before.

We were a long, uneven row of next generations. Dad and Nina in the middle.

The song was played.

No one knew what to do, so we just stood, arms draped over the shoulder of the next, the children giggling as the long track played. It was awkward. It was hard then and even now to process what exactly he was taking from that moment. All of us lined up with our own children and him, as though we were the children he'd raised, the heirs to his example. He'd put thought and care into it, with that song selection and theme, calling his children home. He'd have agreed, sure, he fucked it up in so many ways, so many times. But weren't we a beautiful bunch? Kind, empathetic people with glorious children who knew they were loved?

Can't he celebrate that, even for a day? It was more than he had any right to expect given his start on cold and lonely Green Acres Court in Rye, New York. An array of loving offspring in his lush backyard at the age of sixty-eight.

And then it was over. It would be the last time we were all together.

That fall, somehow, upon publication of *The Rogue*, he lost the public relations battle with the otherwise disgraced half-term governor. There were salacious, gossipy stories in the book. The book felt sloppy and rushed. And Palin wasn't running for president after all, so no one cared about her or the book or even my father much anymore. His publisher didn't want him for another book.

For me, it was another blissful spring afternoon in upper northwest Washington, DC. I sat under a blooming dogwood on the playground at Horace Mann Elementary. I was cooling off from half an hour in goal, fending off incoming blasts from Jayson and his second-grade classmates and friends. The ice cream truck arrived, and I traded Jayson five dollars for some shade. I snapped a couple pictures first: Jayson at the window of the truck, holding the soft ice cream cone in one hand, offering his money with the other. I edited and cropped and zoomed, then tweaked the coloring, saturated, vintage, like the 1970s, and felt flush, *wow, look at him, my son*, and I shared it with Jeanine. "Our guy," I wrote. I did this a lot, likely too much. Dopamine hits, one after another.

For Dad, he was casting about for ideas when a publisher pitched the idea of him heading out to Arizona to write about the fast-spreading wildfire of right-wing populism and what it portended for the country. He had no other income at the time, but did some math and couldn't make a hypothetical $600,000 contract make sense. So many costs. Payout structures and agent fees and taxes made it impossible, he decided.

But there were hard truths: he was old and his hip and back and knees all made walking without pain impossible. He was heavier, too, and there were wild thyroid numbers coming back from his blood work.

He was tired. He'd been through a hell largely of his own making and had little energy left to push back on the harsh assessment from a recently fired agent: no one wanted him anymore.

I felt compelled to remind him: Doesn't a publisher want you to go to Arizona and write a book for them? Clearly, your last agent was wrong. His response, if not literally then symbolically, was a deep, acquiescent sigh. It was his professional version of the waiting area in the Hospital of the Good Samaritan, Bobby Kennedy's press secretary to Kennedy's advance man, calling it in terms so stark and final: "It's over."

He waved a white flag. He was in his big leather chair in the modest house he and Nina were clinging to and that alone required more than he had.

He sat outside alone on a plastic chair smoking cigarettes. There was a small kitchen-adjacent deck and he'd head out there a few times a day. He'd smoked briefly in his twenties and resumed in his seventies. He was awake at midnight and two a.m. in the kitchen eating leftover meatball subs. His appetites and cravings and addictions still thrived. The brain chemistry wreaking havoc.

All of this was reported to me by Gavin, who was living at home again. I wanted the updates. I craved slivers of light, unexpected flourishes of optimism and planning. I needed Dad to stay in the fight, if only because the alternative was so bleak. He wasn't retiring or determining to spend time with his grandchildren like Mom had.

The center of her life was her grandchildren, from screensavers to keychain photos to framed pictures and endless hours driving one grandchild to the mall or lunch or watching the other skateboard or play lacrosse or basketball or cooking with the other. Dad was resigned to writing what was local, easiest, the least taxing on his body. And his fuzzy math convinced him it was financially prudent not to pursue a $600,000 book deal. He chose not another shot of literary redemption, not family, but simply, existence. Watching and reading about soccer for hours a day, eating and drinking too much.

The boutique literary agency Gavin had started was struggling. He'd found a stable full-time job with Verizon Wireless and was engaged to a young woman who shared his appetite for Dunkin' Donuts iced lattes and Diet Pepsi and his sense of humor and kind disposition and sobriety.

He had his father's blood and too many years bearing witness to addiction. He walked himself into church basements and then with her and once with Dad, that time when they both could have introduced themselves and only Gavin did.

The thing about Dad's cancer was the way it snuck up on him, then took over all at once. There were signs ignored or rationalized away through internet research. Abnormally high PSA did *not* necessitate a biopsy, he insisted. It's normal for men his age. And who wants to go through a prostate biopsy? And the months passed until finally, a year later, he couldn't take a piss.

The biopsy was no longer advised, but required.

A Gleason score indicates how much cancer is in the prostate. They test a few areas and the more hits, the higher the score. A year after the high PSA numbers he brushed off, his Gleason score came back the highest.

The cancer was in every part of his prostate. It likely took a year to spread that much. Surgery would have been an option a year or even six months prior, and with it almost likely remission. Now it was too late.

He started on radiation and hormone injections that chemically castrated him and failed to stop the spread. And his debtors circled. The house was being foreclosed on. There was nowhere else to turn. Roger Ailes sent a juicer and money. It bought time, kept them in the house, but it wasn't enough to last.

It was February. The margin, he said, was thin. He'd been through three rounds of hormone treatment at Dana-Farber, but his PSA was still detectable.

He found a specialist at the Mayo Clinic who told him to fly out for a PET scan and new treatment protocol depending on the results. He wrote an email to all five children, Nina, and my mother, explaining his health and financial situation.

He was fighting for $8,500 owed to him by an online publisher called Byliner. He'd written a *Boston* magazine piece about a local murder trial for $7,500. He'd pitched a magazine piece to *Vanity Fair* and *GQ* and *New York* magazine about William Styron's son, Tom Styron, a Yale psychiatry professor who suffered two suicidal depressions requiring hospitalizations for which he'd blamed his father.

William Styron was a known alcoholic depressive. Tom told Dad stories about his childhood spent witnessing insane rampages in his home by John Belushi and Dan Aykroyd that were horrifying rather than humorous.

Tom was living with Andrew Cuomo when Cuomo was married to Mary Kerry Kennedy and Tom tried to jump off the roof of Cuomo's Beekman Place apartment. The Styrons made the McGinnisses seem Norman Rockwell–esque by comparison, Dad wrote.

"Tom Styron," he told me, "had it worse than you could imagine. Bill's dreadful behavior as husband and father. You think you had it bad? At my worst, I was a better father than William Styron at his best," he insisted. I tacitly agreed. It was easier at that point. He was objectively right and what was the point of exploring it? Things sucked for the child of another famous writer. Depression and addiction were beasts. I could have had it so much worse. I'd hold on to that for later, when Jayson needed to hear it and even when he didn't.

But the story idea, a compelling one, was a nonstarter. *Vanity Fair* turned him down. So did the others.

Dad asked me rhetorically if I thought it "felt good living on money borrowed from Roger Ailes."

Terror is what he described feeling each day knowing the cancer would worsen past the point of no return. "I'm seventy," he said. "I'm overweight with a history of melanoma, borderline high blood pressure and blood sugar, and thus not an optimal case for long-term survival."

I tried to spin it. "Time. Do all you can to be healthy and buy time because treatment and remission are possible."

"I'm busting what's left of my balls," he said.

"I know," I said.

"I've been going all out with book and magazine ideas. But magazines are dead and publishing is dying."

I didn't bring up Arizona.

"My former agent said to me: 'Face it, Joe, nobody wants you anymore,'" he told me again. "I'm going to die trying to prove him wrong."

I asked him rhetorically—did my sisters and I want to be near him or somewhere else when we were kids?

I asked him if we'd wanted more of him or less.

I don't know if pointing this out helped or hurt. But I need to say it, to let him know, because I knew time was short.

I left out the rest. He didn't need to hear again the reasons why I didn't drive nine hours with Jeanine and Jayson to visit more. I didn't need to tell him that Gavin and Mason and Cynthia and Sarah all felt the same.

Cynthia told me, not long after he was gone, that she kept asking herself questions like: Why didn't she have him come over here to visit more often? They could have paid for a ticket like they'd done for Mom in the past. She searched for answers and remembered: Well, he wasn't much fun to be around, and his drinking made her so uncomfortable, so maybe she just couldn't have that kind of intimacy with him.

Then she said: Maybe she should have made the sacrifice and invited him to come and just dealt with the awkwardness of embarrassment or whatever he made her feel when he wasn't in good shape.

When she started to feel guilty about not having made more of an effort, she looked back on the whole picture, the whole story of his life, and ours, and put things into perspective and realized that everybody had limits. How much emotional upheaval could we withstand?

From our earliest childhood until the moment he died we'd all had to "ride the roller coaster of his existence."

There was no heroic transformation or moment of clarity for him. There was no drawing closer to one another, something foundational we could return to. He ended the way he'd lived, restless and agitating, if not flailing, against the currents until there was nothing, not a breath left. He broke his children's hearts. And he gave what he could, likely more than he'd thought possible.

When he was still here, still fighting, I remained in Washington, DC, offering him empty reassurances. I told him that he'd get another book deal sooner than later. I reminded him he was going to get the best medical care in the world. And that nothing mattered more than that. I'd communicated all of this on my smartphone from the comfort of Jayson's bottom bunk while Senegalese lullabies played softly, and Jayson dreamed his little boy dreams.

TWENTY-TWO

2013

AFTER

He called from the Mayo Clinic in Minnesota. He'd flown there for the PET scan months earlier. A new more aggressive treatment regimen was ordered. He was out there for the duration. If it went well, if he achieved remission, he'd ring a big gold bell.

He told me about another writer, a couple years older than me, stricken with terminal cancer. He had a wife and two children. He was going to die soon.

"Those children won't have a father," he said, choked up, started sobbing. I'd never heard him cry. I didn't know what to say. I just stared out the window of the small spare bedroom I used for an office overlooking a narrow slate patio, the basketball hoop we bought for Jayson's birthday. He was dribbling a ball and narrating as he shot on the low rim. "The Warriors are down by two and Curry dribbles and he shoots! And he gets the rebound and shoots! And shoots again and the Warriors are tied with Chicago and Rose has the ball . . . "

I watched and listened to Jayson while my father sobbed. I closed my eyes and the sounds synched, Dad's ominous tears and the lightness of Jayson's little voice meeting somewhere in the middle of me. And the balance felt off, they shouldn't be getting equal footing. I opened my eyes and knew that Dad's tears were fear and sadness and so much else that came before and couldn't be changed. Jayson's voice was everything, pure and hopeful and a remedy for so much of my Dad-induced sorrow.

He explained his prognosis. It was ominous. I tried to offer something encouraging.

"You just have to hold on. Keep fighting."

"Cisplatin is the truly bad stuff. It's napalm."

"Buy time. Eat right. No more cigarettes. No more drinking."

"It destroys everything. Appetite. Muscle. Energy. I'll be the walking dead."

"Buy time. Get through it and there will be something to help. It's all happening so fast these days with the, you know, there's . . . " And I couldn't find the words, lost them, or they were never there. This wasn't the place or time for words. That time had passed.

"Everything really is blowing away," he said. The call ended. Jayson kept playing. I pointed the lens of my smartphone camera down, in his direction and pressed record.

A year before his death, he shared his version of exactly how he'd lost his fortune.

He'd passed up $1.7 million to write the O. J. Simpson book. Maybe he was chasing losses, trying to win it back. But there was huge money to be made that had nothing to do with writing. It was the nineties, and the market was booming. And he craved the action.

On money management, he claimed he needed Gamblers Anonymous more than he ever needed AA. As he grew more addicted to benzodiazepines in the late nineties and through 2001, he was in his "maximum earning years."

His need for daily action, the buying and selling of stocks, got worse. But the dot-com bubble burst and the market collapsed.

He claimed that even in an "advanced state of deterioration," he recognized he had to do something responsible with his remaining money. He removed it from his personal trading account and gave it all, every dollar, to a man who he deemed "the most responsible money manager I could find": Robert Markman of Minneapolis, Minnesota. He would, my father said, invest only in no-load mutual funds.

What could be more prudent? He asked. He said *Barron's* profiled Markman in a way that made him seem like Fort Knox and the Bank of England. He said: "No more craziness. I've lost enough. Markman will protect what's left."

A million dollars. That was what remained after the years of self-described drug-fueled "craziness."

Yet sometime in that period Markman sent Dad what he called "some boring form" and asked him to sign it and he did.

It was authorization for Markman to no longer invest only in no-load mutual funds, but to "diversify into selected common stocks with the goal of capital appreciation."

In the end though, Markman was a fraud. He was a criminal. He'd started his own mutual fund so smaller investors could take advantage of his supposed genius. When the market crashed in 2001, of the more than 1,200 listed mutual funds, Markman's was the worst performer, losing 98 percent of its value.

"Zonked out on benzos, I let it all slide by," he told me.

He let it all slide by.

A story in *The Minneapolis Star Tribune* referred to Markman's fund as a "Ponzi scheme." According to the newspaper, the fund involved special "house accounts" in which Markman promised a clique of favored investors annual returns of at least 10 percent. When the tech bubble burst, however, Markman's investments—heavily concentrated in technology and internet-related investments—crashed hard.

The man from Minnesota to whom Dad signed over the last million dollars of his fortune, his financial legacy, shot himself in the head.

• • •

He acknowledged: when he finally weaned himself off the benzos and moved to Aliso Viejo and started teaching, his "last million dollars" was down to $100,000.

And in the decade since? That hundred thousand eroded due to what he called "rational and reasonable" living expenses and his failure to earn enough money as a writer.

An idea was floated by his old publisher friend David Rosenthal. Dad had been pitching a memoir, but Rosenthal was concerned Dad wouldn't be truthful enough about himself and would be too defensive.

"What if you wrote a memoir with your son?" he asked.

Rosenthal liked my writing. And he speculated that my involvement would help keep Dad honest by challenging him where he might be too charitable to himself or inappropriately angry at others.

Dad never mentioned it to me at the time. After his death, Gavin shared the email exchange between Dad and Rosenthal. I'd have likely said no. He was sick and broke and never more vulnerable. I was too exhausted, too angry. How much truth could I have told? How much could he have withstood?

My life was unfolding so beautifully with Jayson and Jeanine. Dad's unwinding had been taxing enough. The spillover from immersing myself with him in a story about him, and us, would have been abundant and toxic in ways I couldn't imagine.

TWENTY-THREE

2013

AFTER

The polar vortex dipped and wouldn't budge. Arctic air flooded the region. Wind chills in the teens. Punishing gusts ripped the last of the leaves, brown and dry, from skeletal oaks that lined the streets of suburban Philadelphia where Sarah lived. Winter had arrived on Thanksgiving like an uppercut to the jaw and too soon for anyone's liking.

Sarah hosted the holiday gathering with her trademark reluctant generosity. It was the last time I saw my father alive.

He and Nina and Gavin were staying at the Philadelphia Airport Hilton. Sarah's home was a four-story historic house, a bronzed plaque affixed to the exterior wall adjacent to the front door with the year of its construction. The interior was all character and Wayfair charm with Martha Stewart touches. It was cozy and warm and I admired it. My father's books, and mine, were stacked neatly on the television console shelf under the flat screen. For all of the hurt he caused her and the resentment she felt, she remained proud of him. I didn't know how many of them she'd read over the years. Likely more than me.

There was football on that no one was really watching. There were plates of cheese and crackers and Sarah made sure everyone had anything they needed and if they didn't offered to send Kevin to Wawa to get it.

Conversations bounced around with no direction. Dad's new local Northampton County courthouse story and Gavin and his girlfriend and his work and Sarah's school.

Time was short. We all felt it, despite some recent good medical news for Dad.

A small window of hope had appeared, a mirage in the end. He'd gotten more tests and better numbers than expected. Not quite remission but close. What no one knew that night: the unexplained and persistent itchiness that no amount of backscratching could relieve was the cancer. It was in his bones, his spine, a billion rogue cells bent on destruction gnawing away at his third and fourth vertebrae. He didn't know any of this that night. None of us did.

He looked like himself, white hair, red faced, too large in the middle, an extra thirty pounds he'd never lose. He sounded like himself, commanding the warm dining room with something about the story he was working on.

I held on to an image of him: emerging from the bathroom just off Sarah's den and finding six-year-old Jayson and his mother and even me dancing to something with a heavy beat and pausing to take in the scene, a smile forming, and his face flush and his body moving, trying to catch the beat himself.

The moment was fleeting. The song ended. He left the room. His dance done. I stayed behind with Jayson and Jeanine as a new song began.

On his way out of Sarah's house at the end of the night, when no one was looking, he slipped a bottle of aged Caribbean rum inside his winter coat. In the end, he couldn't help himself.

The email I received from him arrived two months before he died. His drinking and the cancer drugs he was on wreaked havoc on his mind.

He asked me for money, thought maybe he'd loaned me a few thousand a couple of years back. I never responded, and it never came up again. The chemo wasn't working. The disease was winning. There was no more time.

The last conversation we had lasted maybe five minutes. He did most of the talking, shouting his congratulations ("Holy shit! Holy shit!") after I shared the news that my next novel would be published. He was home, filled with toxins and tumors, fear and waves of pain, bald and tired. He warned me seventeen years prior not to write, to find a different line of work, a career that would fulfill me, bring satisfaction in some other way. Then, in the last email he ever sent, days before he was gone, he wrote:

Joe—

I've been thinking about and continuing to feel total joy.
    Bravo, son. I am so proud of you, but most of all so very happy for you and for this vindication of your talent—which, no doubt, you had more doubts about than anyone else did.

I love you,
Dad

He was dying. And for most of the time that he was, I wasn't by his side. I remained where I wanted to be, with my son.

TWENTY-FOUR

2023

AFTER

We stood on the court, his shots misfiring, me chasing down long rebounds on creaky knees, annoyance brewing. Where was the focus? The drive? The maturity to not waste shots and time? We were only there so he could make some shots to build rhythm and confidence before his game later that day. That's how the best players did it.

And he was fucking around, missing more than he was making. And I was verging on relapsing. I remained, charitably, a work in progress.

Not enough arc on the shot. Hold the follow-through. Five in a row. These are just to build confidence, lock in your mechanics. "Jesus, Jayson. Focus."

He shook his head. He feigned a smile, as if to say, "You dick. Shut the fuck up. Such an asshole."

"Watch your mouth."

"I fucking hate you."

I called him over. We faced one another.

He stood before me a little more than arm's reach, but so much farther. Too far. He'd recently turned fifteen and was stronger than ever, muscles forming and there was hair on his legs and a trace of it on his chin.

The tears in his eyes were all my doing. That's when he told me how much damage I'd done. It was so much worse than I'd thought.

"I was missing because I hate having you here." His voice rose. "You make everything worse. I can't stand you."

"It's my fault. Right? I'm the reason you can't focus. I was watching from the other side of the gym when you didn't even know I was here and you were missing."

"I've given up on having a relationship with you," he said and started drifting off the court, unsure steps toward the baseline where his bag lay. "You're just, like, a coach or some authority figure." He stopped. "But you're not a father."

"Jayson."

"You're just an asshole."

His chin quivered. He brought a shaky hand up to shield his face from others in the gym who might see the tears forming. He started to cry. Right there. Sitting in the gym at Bethesda Sport & Health on a Saturday morning before his afternoon game. I did that to him.

The moment unfolded like a Volvo hurtling down a dark, icy mountain pass toward a sharp bend, Jayson in the passenger's seat and my foot on the accelerator.

I wanted to grab him and hold him. I wanted to stop time, go back, redo it all from the very first day of basketball practice in sixth grade.

What would I do differently? I'd watch him struggle and hug him after and not say a word about it until he brought it up, if he even did. I'd tell him he was wonderful and he'd be great and it would get easier and if it ever stopped making him happy then he could stop, find something else that was more fun, better suited for him. And if he stuck with it and wanted my help, I'd do everything I could without condition because I was his father and loved him and always would.

"I have PTSD from you," he told me, face flushed, hands trembling. "That tryout and when you exploded and hit me," he managed. This child was so strong, I thought. He was finding words for the tears. He was speaking the truth to me, his big and powerful father. The back upon which he'd leapt every day after school for the walk to the car.

"I didn't hit you," I said.

"In the face," he said.

"That was my index finger," I offered lamely.

Even then, in that moment, I recalled leaving him at the very gym we were sitting in after he'd asked me to take him and help him only to find that he brought knockoff basketball sneakers (which are not made for real playing) that he hadn't tied tightly and were half a size too big and the earbuds were in his ears even though I told him not to wear them because they occasionally fell out and even when they didn't they were a distraction.

And his reaction to my pointing these things out and rebounding and chasing down too many errant shots and witnessing his overall poor focus and effort had me reeling and calling him "country club" and getting so pissed off that he wasn't more mature, hungrier, driven, that instead of continuing to rebound and pass and coach him, I simply left him there.

I told Jeanine she had to pick him up because I refused to do one more goddamn thing for the entitled soft little brat who had his expensive shoes and phone and earbuds and gym membership and should be dropped off on a public court in PG County or Southeast DC and figure out what toughness was, goddamn it.

I felt the same, even in that moment of emotional crisis for him. It wasn't the validity of those thoughts; it was my management of them. That was the struggle I never engaged.

My apology to him that day sounded weak and inadequate. I was never more alarmed or shaken or clueless about what to do. I wanted his tears to stop. I wanted to hold him and hug him as tightly as my father hugged me every time he said goodbye. I rested my hand on his leg just below the knee.

I thought about the last couple of years and felt queasy when I considered how hard I'd been on him.

I tried to explain myself to him.

But it was all about him and not enough about me.

My son was teetering, then reeling, and I'd pushed him, two hands in the middle of his back, hard. He was careening down a steep hill and I was running alongside telling him why.

"I'm just so profoundly sorry, Jayson," I told him. I was shaken. How had I let it happen? And not just once, but again and again?

"I'll be better. I'll do better. Not later, but now. You don't deserve anything less than my best. I've been demanding that of you and haven't come close to doing it myself. The most important thing in my life—" My voice caught.

Words in that moment were meaningless. I had to do differently and so much better.

The coach from the high school at the top of Jayson's list held a weekend basketball clinic. Jayson showed up early. First one there. Got shots up. Impressed the whole day. Coach reached out and told him, "I'm vouching for you." That was in January. His grades and recommendations and a fine interview were in place. The news came in March.

"Congratulations!" the email began.

It was summer. "He's a freshman!" the assistant coach called out to the varsity basketball players on the floor with Jayson. A scrimmage at the end of workouts at the high school he'd attend in the fall. Jayson was making upperclassmen look foolish.

"I can't believe we're going to have you for four years!" The coach conveyed his enthusiasm for Jayson's talents, leadership, and confidence on the court. "We want to build this program around you," he was told.

He was there, in that moment, because of me. In the same way that talking to reporters in my mother's living room about all the points I was scoring in high school had so much to do with my father, his absence and all the pain it caused. But pain as fuel wasn't healthy. It wasn't sustainable and wouldn't end well.

TWENTY-FIVE

2014

AFTER

Sedation was a monumental struggle, the doctor said. Dad's tolerance for the drugs they relied on to induce sleep was so high that he required multiple doses to break through.

His hands were swollen and the mask covered his bloated face. It was the fluids. He was retaining so much fluid. He was bald, too. I'd never glimpsed him without hair, only the bald spot we'd tease him about as children.

It broke me seeing him like that. That wasn't him. That wasn't our father. That was a two-hundred-pound body that breathed only because a machine filled its lungs with oxygen. It inhaled, tick tick, then exhaled.

The cycle repeated. How many breaths left before it stopped? How much time until the body expired? My father was gone but that body remained and Nina, Gavin, Sarah, and I gathered around it, gently massaging its soft, swollen hands and lightly combing the thinnest wisp of white hair that had grown back when chemo was paused after the final scans told us what we all feared.

His masked head made these slow, tortured twisting movements. Maybe he saw us. Maybe he felt my hand wrapped around his. I like to think so.

The doctor, because I'd insisted, showed me the image from the last scan. All the white in his lungs? That was infection. There was no clearing it.

"But the chemo, if we could get his lungs clear." I stopped and my throat caught and the tears came and I turned away from the doctor and Nina and Sarah and Gavin and even my father and moved to the large window and stared out at the bricks and concrete and wires and dirty snow of Worcester and the few stray flurries that didn't so much fall as drift and swirl in frigid wind that no one wanted.

There was a smudge on the window where someone's forehead had been, pressed, or resting against the cold dirty glass, overcome, exhausted, hopeless, unable to stand themselves up anymore, broken inside because the person in the bed was gone and never coming back. It was over. Done. How? How can that possibly be? Gone. And once again it was me resting my forehead against the cold glass in that dreary downtown hospital, the room without a door, only a curtain.

Don't watch your father die. Then again, maybe you should. I don't know. What do I know? I know that when they remove the tubes and machines that keep him alive, they tell you that it could be hours or a day or minutes. They tell you he might gasp or choke, but he won't feel pain, he won't be aware. My father was surrounded by love, by our hands on him, our faces at his, our voices in his ear, hushed, trying. The sounds were brutal, uneven, as the last of his life left him. He was unnaturally gray, his whole body. His mouth was agape and no one knew what to do, so someone pulled the sheet over his face, then decided against it. I found the corner of the room and fell back against the wall. I wanted to put my fists through the wall, to shatter the dirty windows, to tell every man I saw for days and weeks to come that he was a fucking loser because he was not my father, not as intelligent or knowing or insightful or funny or warm and kind or tenacious and resilient and self-deprecating and approachable and respectful and fearless and no one could be, no one comes close or ever would. All of those emotions spun inside me then and for years after.

In the hospital lounge an hour or so later someone mentioned food. A brief death announcement had been written by his attorney and Nina. They sent it out the night before. There was a television bolted to the wall in the lounge and Sarah pointed to it.

Dad's face and name filled the screen. Author Joe McGinniss, dead at seventy-one. A few more silent clips flashed by, book cover images appeared and vanished. And then blackness and then a commercial. Fourteen seconds. And he was gone.

At the distant edge of his backyard was a path shrouded by tall thick trees. Jayson, who was six at the time, walked with me along it. The ground was soft beneath us as we walked in silence. Moss-covered stones formed what was left of a wall along the path. Together, we stepped over thick, knotty roots bulging up through the earth until we reached a small cemetery. The names and years were mostly faded on the headstones that remained, some leaning into one another or fallen over completely. On the edge nearest the border was the stone Nina told me to look for. Jayson followed me to it, watching me open the small container. I lifted a patch of green moss and spread the ashes on the soil. I told my father I loved him. My son said, "I love you, Grandpa Joe." The tears that fell down his soft brown cheeks surprised me for some reason. My father adored that child. Children know when they're loved.

"*A hell of a father.*" Nina wrote that about him after his death. It was a social media post. There were beautiful photographs from the seventies and eighties in black-and-white and color of him holding us close. The words, though, left me cold and still do.

But so what? Isn't that between them, Nina and Gavin and Mason and even my sisters, too? The hell Dad endured and the hell he put us through and what now for me? What do I do with that?

I don't know. When I'm not feeling generous or forgiving, when resentment comes too easily, anger too plentiful, I'm learning to return to moments of light and hover there. The image of Jayson wiping tears from his soft cheeks because of something he felt from my father. The ephemeral moments they were together made my son feel loved. Dad did that.

TWENTY-SIX

2023

AFTER

Dad's old house in Pelham was home to Nina and her sister. I haven't been up there in nine years, since my father died, since Jayson and I covered his grandfather's ashes with green moss and said goodbye.

I want to see Gavin and meet his new wife and of course, Stella Rose, their odds-defying baby girl. There was nothing easy about her conception and arrival, but she's a wonder now. Gavin wants to buy the house and convert the basement into an apartment where Nina and her sister will reside, to be looked after and looking after. Their collective social security will allow the four of them to keep the house.

Dad suffered in the ways an addict did, moment by moment. Escape came immersed in ninety-plus minutes of freedom, joyous and unsullied by emotional baggage. Grilling steaks and pouring another gin and talking about the match or his communication with Bruce Springsteen's former assistant who was maybe possibly going to convince Bruce to let Dad write about him. Or hiking Mt. Shasta or a quick trip to the coast of Maine or Bald Head Island and back to Italy for a match in Milan.

But always the demons, the darkness of his unknowable past and the chemically corrupted brain circuitry of his present. Even at rest, sleeping as deeply as he could, his screaming told the story. Gavin and Nina startled awake by plaintive wails, Dad at war with himself until the very end.

On the smooth stone that lies where his ashes are spread, Nina wrote one word, a directive maybe, a choice we all have to make in the end, where should our energy go: "Love."

"What does change look like? Words aren't enough." That's what Jeanine told me more than once.

When I think of my teenage son, it starts like this: *Clean your room. Do your homework. Study for the quiz. Ice your wrist and take your Advil. Put down the phone! Don't leave campus for lunch for any reason. Work harder. Pay attention. Talk to your teachers. Eat less crap. Take shorter showers. Use soap when you do. Go to bed on time.*

But our relationship is in salvage mode. Repair and rebuild. He told me directly, through tears that I caused, what he needed.

I stood in Jayson's bedroom in our new house, just over the DC line in Bethesda. We owned it, no more renting. Stability and permanence. That was healthier. My father rented and moved, then rented and moved again and then again and then bought and sold and bought and sold and bought again and barely hung on to the last modest house in the end.

Jayson was eight blocks from his new high school. He had friends in a group chat on his phone. The basketball team had a group chat, too. Socialization was important for him. So the phone, then, seemed essential.

The isolation and loneliness of the pandemic had taken their emotional toll on teenagers. A basketball teammate and friend of Jayson's was so overcome with social anxiety he couldn't attend school in person anymore. Quit basketball altogether. Another sibling of a friend attempted suicide. How many other of his friends and classmates and peers endured their own private struggles? Jayson was no exception.

Jamie Raskin, who Dad met in the greenroom before an appearance on *Larry King Live* in the early 1990s, was now our congressman. I bought his book, a harrowing account of his own son who committed suicide.

There were signs and struggles, depression and psychiatrists and prescriptions and brilliance and empathy and laughter and high achievement and girlfriends and friend groups and warmth and joy and love and dogs and every reason to live. And at twenty-six he decided he couldn't. The illness won, his son wrote in a last note, his last words. Nowhere in the story does Raskin describe berating his son, raising his voice, screaming, throwing bottles of water, traumatizing his child. Because he didn't.

From the first ethereal nights in Sibley with Jeanine and snugly swaddled Jayson and his tiny fingers and perfect vitals and impossibly smooth cheeks my presence and engagement needed no prompting or reminding or negotiating. He was the story, and I was following it wherever it led. From an orphan to my lonely, restive father to me: the paternal lineage was precarious at best.

I promised the worst was behind us. He's receptive, though guarded.

I caught a side-eye grin from him. His narrowed brown eyes and head turned just enough in my direction at the punch line of a comedy the three of us were watching. And the glance back over his shoulder every morning that I dropped him off at his new high school. That hint of a smile and fingers pointing at me. A version of what he'd done since elementary school.

He needed me to know we were still connected despite the hell I'd put him through. An opportunity existed that my father had with all his children, but for reasons chemical and otherwise, he never seized. I could and had to.

In the new house Jayson did his homework at the dining room table. There was a lot. The bar was high at his new high school and with us. An entire kitchen wall was converted into a monthly calendar of assignments and due dates and practice and game times all written in colored chalk.

He was a teenager and needed reminders. So many reminders. We asked him what his plan was for the night. We made suggestions, offered help. We're a team, we said again.

I watched my tone. I bit my tongue.

I reminded him that he was a work in progress. I had him say it out loud and he did. I wrote it in black Sharpie on an index card. I am a work in progress.

"*I'm* a work in progress," I acknowledged.

"We all are, hopefully," he said.

Dad asked me for empathy, and I couldn't give it. I was asking Jayson for another chance, and he was trying. More progress, I told myself.

He came home from a varsity pre-season game in October. Was he happy with the way he played? Was he aggressive? Did he warm up the right way? Did he have fun? Did he play free, play with joy? Did he message his coach, ask him what, if anything, he could try to do better next game?

I didn't ask any of those questions. Basketball was his thing. Only if invited would I attend.

I reminded myself: he'd get out of it what he put in. And I exhaled. A lot. Deep breathing helped. If he wanted help with something basketball-related, he'd ask.

That's what I told him. I was always there and if he wanted suggestions or ideas or wanted to share anything I was always available. I had to earn his trust again.

He stood in the kitchen. He was hyped.

He talked a blue streak about the basketball he played that day. He talked me through the details of behind the back dribbles and shot fake hesis and step-back threes he hit in their team scrimmage.

Absent from his account, like always, was anything negative. He curated the highlights for me. He should have tested me. Told me he struggled or sucked that day. I'd have surprised him, maybe: "Work in progress. Tomorrow's another day."

We weren't there. Though I was closer than I had been.

I sat on the stool at the kitchen counter and let his words wash over me. He wanted sneakers for the season. I found them online and bought them for him. "You deserve them."

He hugged me and said thank you. He showed me sketches he drew, graffiti-inspired caricatures and words. He filled pages of his daily planner with them. "They're really good," I told him. "See what you do when you don't have the phone as much?" I thought, but didn't say. I bought him a sketch pad and color and charcoal pencil set instead. We'd carve out time in the summer.

"Um, this is your planner, though. So where are you going to write your assignments?" I asked.

"Oops." An embarrassed half smile.

"Work in progress. Maybe use the pad from now on?"

All I have in life is what I want to do. Dad's words stay with me. The wanting makes all the difference, right? Do you want to be with and around and immersed in the wonder that is your child? Responsibility is a reminder: this is worth it, this comes first. Jayson comes first. I want to do better for him. And when wanting isn't enough, because of traits I've both inherited and cultivated, because of my own fallibilities, I try to push myself to do better and wonder if it's enough.

Quietude and calm. That's what I wanted for him. In the aftermath of so many storms. He could find a vocation that suited and challenged him. One that brought him satisfaction. He was occasionally and slightly obsessive compulsive like his father. He was artistic. He had introvert tendencies but was charming, magnetic, and well liked.

I saw a story about a young local man who'd spent a decade or more working a stable job for the federal government after graduating from a liberal arts college. He'd always had an interest in woodworking though, something he watched his father do growing up in the Hudson Valley.

The young man returned to it and over time became so enthralled that he made it his profession. He worked mostly alone in a converted backyard shed. He spent time with each piece he created when he finished before delivering or sending it out. "The wood was alive," he said. And he liked to check in on pieces, to see how they were utilized in their new homes. He received letters from customers who thanked him again for his craftsmanship and care. He seemed fulfilled and at peace.

I shared the video with Jayson on the way home from the gym. Jayson was sure I was showing him another off-season training or "four-finishes-every undersized-guard-must-have" clip.

I told him I remembered how meticulous he was with his things, the order and balance he instinctively imposed on toys and stuffed animals and now sneakers—so many sneakers.

"You'd be good at this. Would you ever want to try it? The guy offers classes."

"Like Jesse's box," he said, referencing the *Breaking Bad* character who obsessively worked on one perfect handcrafted wooden box for his high school woodshop class. Then traded it for some meth.

"You have the talent. You could sketch and create and craft anything."

"Yeah," he said. "That's pretty cool."

Maybe we'd return to it. Maybe he'd circle back later, in a year or five. A small seed planted, I told myself.

The Geico parking lot was empty. It was a gorgeous Sunday afternoon in April and Jayson was behind the wheel of our aging Volvo. He adjusted the seat and mirror and pressed down on the brake pedal and shifted into drive.

He gripped the steering wheel with both hands as he eased his foot off the brake. The car started to drift forward.

"You can accelerate a little," I told him. He pressed too hard. The car jolted forward.

"Woah," he said. "Sorry."

I laughed. "No worries," I said. "It takes some getting used to."

He drove the length of the parking lot and back, over and over, growing more comfortable each time. I had my arm out the open window, watching some dogs play in the grass and another parent with her daughter behind the wheel of their SUV. The mother had orange cones with her to help her daughter learn to parallel park. I recalled a *Brady Bunch* episode, a driving contest between Marsha and Greg. The one who traversed a series of serpentine turns and stopped closest to the orange cone, and egg perched atop it, would win. The slightest nudge of the cone and splat went the egg.

Our egg was almost sixteen and at the wheel. But he was less fragile than he'd been. Knocked around and landed hard more than a few times. It would happen again. Girlfriends would break his heart. Friends would disappoint. Teachers and coaches would be unfair or too harsh or just dull. Injuries would occur, as they had. He would crack and bruise, mend and persevere. My commitment was simple enough: Do no more harm. Then rebuild.

Primal and immature and unresolved, my anger was too frequently too close to the surface. Helplessness was a trigger. Witnessing my son struggle. Watching my father destroy himself. Watching him drive away.

"So, Dad," I said at some point after his diagnosis, "you knew your PSA was elevated beyond a point of concern for how long? A year? And during that year the cancer spread and became inoperable. Because you read online that even significantly elevated PSA didn't necessitate a biopsy. So you did nothing. For a year. Until you could barely pee, the tumor so big."

Who lived like that? A prostate biopsy certainly wasn't any fun, but it would have found the highly treatable early-stage malignancy. Surgery and recovery and another bullet dodged. Life to be lived. Grandchildren to watch grow. Another book to write. Instead, he was fucked.

Everyone wasn't a puppy pissing on the rug, making me the idiot for scolding it. It doesn't know any better, Gavin would say. Our father was the puppy. We were the idiots scolding him. He found some peace with my father's legacy that eluded me. I wasn't there and may never be.

You can't live someone's life for them. The counsel from Cynthia and Nina and psychiatric experts I'd absorbed during the father's decline came to mind. But what if that person is your child, their well-being your primary responsibility? What if that child struggled in ways you felt powerless to change? You just had to sit there and take it?

There had to be a way forward, a step to take, that would do for my son what I could never do for my father.

Jeanine was massaging Jayson's scalp and detangling his curly Afro, grown overly long like the kids wore it. She was mothering and nurturing our egg. She was making things better, tending to unseen wounds I'd inflicted.

Even when she'd reminded him, sternly at times, that as a Black boy in America he couldn't afford to coast, to take it easy, to not care. There was no generational wealth, no trust fund. We were it. Caring and working hard weren't optional. She delivered the message, though, in a manner best suited for our sensitive son.

On a white index card, I sketched a tree with three thick roots. Academics in the middle, basketball and extracurriculars/social to the left and right. They converged into a solid trunk and blossomed into a full tree with myriad branches.

If he poured everything into any one section he risked overloading that branch and if it broke? Then what? He could load up on academics and round it out with lighter basketball, but he'd have to adjust his goals of playing for money someday, Division I or even Division III. He could play other sports, write for the student newspaper, do robotics and programming and Model UN and Black Student Union and volunteer work or get a job. Take full advantage of all that his school had to offer. Combined with meeting or exceeding his academic potential, he'd likely have all sorts of options and grow and enjoy so much of the high school experience. Or he could keep the academic standards, pick an extracurricular or two, and lean into the basketball. He was already a varsity starter going into sophomore year. He was the second leading scorer on the team in their summer league. He had every reason to believe he could use basketball to help him get into any college he wanted to attend. And gain an unparalleled level of self-confidence.

There were limitless options. He had all the power to choose and our unconditional support once he did. And he could always change his mind. Except for academics. That was nonnegotiable.

Not included in the rendering were the soil and sun and rain and storms, the external elements that could prove determinative. I wasn't the god of this world, but I was a contributor, a weathermaker. It was a role I'd asked for and earned. There was power in it, though diminishing daily.

There was a moment when Cynthia and Sarah and I tuned our father out, stopped reading his emails, stopped visiting, stopped wanting to spend more time together. That was the worst. We weren't there yet, but easily could be.

Jayson was inside, getting spot minutes on a team with a full roster that he joined late because the coach made room for him. He wanted to be on a strong AAU roster for the spring and summer, wanted to play more games. He'd missed the tryout because of thumb surgery.

Jeanine was out of town. It was just him and me. Father and son and basketball. A recipe for disaster.

A mega-sport complex with a dozen soccer pitches and indoor arenas. I sat outside next to a soccer pitch, watching boys his age play in front of their parents, some of them yelling out instructions and encouragement. It's so easy for me to observe in others: chill the fuck out, smile, enjoy the moment. That's your kid out there doing the best they can.

I watched the children of strangers play soccer while my own son was inside playing basketball.

He'd considered not coming. He was on the couch doing geometry homework, prepping for final exams. Spending five hours at a tournament, an hour's drive from home for five minutes of playing time, hardly seemed worthwhile.

That's what I said and meant it. He considered it. Absent between us: any tension at all.

I asked him what he could take from it if he went. Anything to make it worth going? It was okay to be greedy. Could he work on his pregame persona? Could he be active on the bench, talking up teammates, and work to maximize his impact when he was on the court?

"I suppose. Yeah," he said.

"I wouldn't go," I told him. "If I were you. With finals and knowing how little time you'll get and for two games and it's a long day."

He'd faced challenges like any teenager. He took academic hits and worked his way back. A biology grade that raised red flags in the first semester had become an A-. The girlfriend and sense of calm he felt walking the hallways between class was earned. The social anxiety he felt so acutely at school was easing, if slightly. None of it came easy.

I told him again: remind yourself more often just how hard you work, how much you've accomplished and matured. Give yourself a pat on the back more often. And if he didn't, we would. I would.

There was a path for Jayson and me. Everything I said could be in the form of a question now. It landed better. Less command and more suggestion:

"Three hundred makes before tonight's game" became "Are you going to shoot before the game?"

"You need to get at least a couple hours of biology done" became "What's your plan for bio tonight?"

"Do you have goals for this summer basketball-wise? For next season?"

"What's your plan for meeting them?"

"Do you want any suggestions for the game today?"

I'd done this instinctively for some reason around the subject of his girlfriend. "How are things with Sasha? Any plans this weekend?"

But school and hoops had devolved into orders and commands. I received no such commands from my father. Not one that I can recall other than rake three hundred dollars' worth of leaves to pay off the seventh-grade phone bill and don't quit the middle school basketball team. And treat Jeanine right, hold on to that woman.

He wanted a tattoo that read: *Creator of My Reality*. He'd been to the bottom and fought his way back up. He was, he said, creating his reality. I put him there, I think. I did that. But that was then. What now? Now was the point.

He had his ninth-grade girlfriend and some heartbreak, he cried and ached and slowly recovered. I reminded him just how resilient he was. How much of a fool I was at his age. Asking girls who broke up with me if they really meant it when they said: "We can still be friends."

He didn't hide his pain from me. I considered that progress. Trust was being restored, I told myself.

His starting point guard spot was earned, but in a program with a losing culture led by less than competent coaches. There was another school with a better basketball culture and similar academic reputation that wanted him to transfer. The coach called around and word came back from AAU coaches: Jayson was a special player who was worth pursuing.

He lit up when I told him this. He had earned it and the opportunity was his. He could stay where he was or try a different path.

We sat in my small office. His mother and me and Jayson sitting on our dog's bed. We told him that whatever he wanted we would support. He was sixteen. He'd worked so hard in ninth grade, matured so much. He made a name for himself in the basketball community, showing up, playing hard, doing special things. He could try to build a culture where he was or join a culture somewhere new.

Jayson was here and still reachable, not lost to me. I was needed and needy. I missed him wanting time with me instead of being alone or with his girlfriend. I wanted to hop on a train with him, head west together. I knew better. Maybe he'd remember it as I did. That would be enough.

He got up shots in the gym of his new high school where he'd be starting in the fall. Just him and me. He started in close, like I'd taught him. I stood under the basket. He made a shot and I caught it as it fell through the net and tossed it to him. He made a few more. We didn't speak. When he missed, I chased it down, passed it to him. He made some more, moving farther and farther back, swishing shot after shot. Kids drifted in for a summer league game. Jayson continued to shoot. He didn't care who was watching, a coach he knew, some players he recognized. He was sixteen and had been through some things. He'd made big decisions and set goals and struggled and persevered and shifted priorities accordingly. He was creating his reality. And I was rebounding his shots, make or miss, for the first time in a long time. And he was letting me.

EPILOGUE

The train was boarding. We stood in line for some soft pretzels and a drink. He was sixteen and always hungry. His backpack slung over his shoulders. The shorts and designer T-shirt and pristine Jordans on his feet and thin white gold necklace gave him the look he strived for: clean and cool. Or as the kids say—he put that ON. He pulled at the ends of his curls until they were just right, took the food as I paid for it.

It was summer vacation and he was heading to my mother's apartment in Swarthmore, walking distance from the college campus where he would volunteer with the Chester Children's Chorus.

Arrive early each morning and stay late and ask at the end of every day if there's anything else they needed before he left. And keep his phone turned off and out of sight unless he needed it. And have fun. These were my directives, delivered with more care than before.

He was off to learn responsibility and mature and to enjoy some breathing room from his parents. We didn't give him much choice, but neither did he resist.

I messaged my mother the first morning to make sure he was awake. He was. When the two weeks of volunteering concluded, he'd earned high praise from the program director and an invitation to return the following summer. And he wanted to, for a little longer if possible, he'd said. I was pleased, but not surprised.

What if I'd been easier on him? I could have said: be a good person and do your best with everything that matters. No matter what the outcome of any game or test I'm not going to love you any less.

If he wanted to do better, we'd figure out how. If he didn't want to do better, we'd figure out why.

Some B's and C's instead of A's? Would that have been the end of the world? I struggled in middle school, cut some corners throughout high school (a C in physics senior year comes to mind). My father struggled more than I ever had.

He could attend the local public high school. It was huge, but free. From there? As an in-state resident, the University of Maryland would be a lock. There was an easier path that required less pushing and pressure from me, meeting less resistance from him. I could be more friend than parent. It would be a challenge, but I could give him exactly what he wants.

Maybe he'd smoke some weed, even a lot. And maybe he'd drive across country with a friend after his eighteenth birthday like Gavin had. Or maybe he'd spend a summer in high school living with a Mexican family in Monterrey instead of training for his senior basketball season like I did. And maybe after all of that he'd still find himself in a good place: healthy and with interests and options and enough maturity to make them count.

Could I possibly be okay with that? Or would I be so visibly disappointed that he hadn't pushed himself harder, gotten more out of himself, that he'd avoid me? Because I'd made sure that time with me was a struggle, a chore? And eventually he'd message and call only Jeanine. And visit when I wasn't around. Because his father was a prick who made him feel shitty about himself. That's where I was heading. What a waste.

• • •

And what did we need? My mother, sisters, and I needed my father from the start. But at his core, he needed something else, something we couldn't or didn't provide. So he left.

He might tell you, in his own defense, his father was never much fun to be around, not just in the end, but always. He collected stamps, for God's sake. Where Dad's big heart and appetite and lust for life and new experiences and warmth and laughter came from, he didn't know. Certainly not home. But he ran with it. And it sure beat the alternative.

He never said it but it's true: he gave us more than he'd received. That was something. Maybe that's where grace resides.

Days after his return from Swarthmore, Jayson was talking basketball. He was trying to fix something with his shot, elevate more on the release.

We were in the kitchen, Jayson shirtless, lean and more muscular, the pay-off from four days a week of voluntary workouts with his new high school team. A single white earbud in one ear. Jeanine was cooking salmon and pasta and spinach salad. I set out plates and silverware on the kitchen island.

"Do you think you could help me with it?" he asked me. "Rebound for me. And like, help hold me accountable, make sure I'm doing it right?"

The signal from him was clear. The ask, in almost any other context, no big deal. In this house though, the ask was monumental. An opening. A rare opportunity for a father to redeem.

I hesitated, continued pouring drinks for everyone and said, glancing at him: "Always."

Repair what I broke, if there was still time.

Jayson had told me he loved but didn't like me. He'd told his mother my apologies didn't mean anything anymore; they were just words.

I was both exhausted and exhausting. Determined to do better but pissed off, not at him or Jeanine, but myself for letting it get as bad as it did. I drove that. I did that. I left the indelible imprint, the formative scar on his psyche. That emotional limp he'd walk with for the rest of his life. I did that.

I recall Cynthia's words after Dad's death. That he wasn't much fun to be around, especially when he drank. And the roller coaster we rode as his children. "It's a miracle we are as stable as we are and that we've made beautiful, rewarding lives for ourselves," she said. And I'd taken a sledgehammer to the most beautiful part of mine. Repair and rebuild, stronger than before. That's the new goal and my son is giving me a chance I didn't deserve.

Years ago, I'd picked up a parenting book, a bestseller about raising boys coauthored by two child psychologists. It sat atop a stack of books next to my desk. I'd printed a picture of seven-year-old Jayson with his big, sweet chestnut eyes looking up at the lens of my smartphone camera in the embrace of a classmate, her gaze distant, clutching him like a child would a cherished stuffed animal. I stuck it to the cover of the book, pasted it over the image of the white teenager. But I'd never read it.

When I skimmed the pages, most of what I read didn't apply. The troubled boys and exasperated, flailing fathers who were profiled weren't instructive. They were simply doing it wrong, I'd arrogantly thought. They didn't know what I knew. That's what I told myself each time I'd skim a few pages and put it down.

Later, though, after I'd sent Jayson reeling, desperate for insights and answers, I devoured it.

"Most men are burdened by unresolved feelings about their own father, no matter how far removed they are from him by distance or death. And so the pattern of desire and disappointment is handed down from father to son, a sad inheritance."

When I drop him off at the gym or the bus stop for the forty-minute commute to his new school and he glances back over his shoulder at me, every time, he raises his hand and I do the same and our eyes meet.

I tell myself there's an opening, a way back to him, a window, and it's closing so fast, too fast.

He was a few months into his sixteenth year when he wrote something to me on a birthday card. I read it once and then again but couldn't read it a third time sitting at the dining room table with Jeanine and him looking on.

Until now, to write this. And out of context it may not seem as profound and for the sake of privacy I won't repeat it here but the essence of it was: I was the man he wanted to become. That made one of us, I thought. But I was closer than I had been.

ACKNOWLEDGMENTS

This book wouldn't exist without the vision and unwavering support from Jofie Ferrari-Adler. As well, for her editorial wisdom, thank you to Carolyn Kelly for making every page better. And thank you to everyone at Avid Reader Press for their tireless work.

Thank you to Katharine Cluverius for her brilliance and teaching me so much. To Jennifer Joel, thank you for your expert guidance.

For my family, thank you for understanding.

For Jeanine and my son, you're the reason I try to do better and always will.

ABOUT THE AUTHOR

JOE McGINNISS JR. is the author of *Carousel Court* and *The Delivery Man*. He lives in Washington, DC, with his family.

Avid Reader Press, an imprint of Simon & Schuster, is built on the idea that the most rewarding publishing has three common denominators: great books, published with intense focus, in true partnership. Thank you to the Avid Reader Press colleagues who collaborated on *Damaged People*, as well as to the hundreds of professionals in the Simon & Schuster advertising, audio, communications, design, ebook, finance, human resources, legal, marketing, operations, production, sales, supply chain, subsidiary rights, and warehouse departments whose invaluable support and expertise benefit every one of our titles.

Editorial
Jofie Ferrari-Adler, *VP and Co-Publisher*
Carolyn Kelly, *Editor*
Alexandra Silvas, *Editorial Assistant*

Jacket Design
Alison Forner, *Senior Art Director*
Clay Smith, *Senior Designer*
Sydney Newman, *Art Associate*

Marketing
Meredith Vilarello, *VP and Associate Publisher*
Caroline McGregor, *Senior Marketing Manager*
Katya Wiegmann, *Marketing and Publishing Assistant*

Production
Allison Green, *Managing Editor*
Hana Handzija, *Managing Editorial Assistant*
Jessica Chin, *Senior Manager of Copyediting*
Jonathan Evans, *Associate Director of Copyediting*
Alicia Brancato, *Production Manager*
Ruth Lee-Mui, *Interior Text Designer*
Briana Skerpan, *Desktop Compositor*
Cait Lamborne, *Ebook Developer*

Publicity
David Kass, *Senior Director of Publicity*
Eva Kerins, *Publicity Assistant*

Subsidiary Rights
Paul O'Halloran, *VP and Director of Subsidiary Rights*
Fiona Sharp, *Subsidiary Rights Coordinator*